The Tacky South

SOUTHERN LITERARY STUDIES
Scott Romine, Series Editor

The TACKY SOUTH

Edited by **KATHARINE A. BURNETT
& MONICA CAROL MILLER**

Foreword by **CHARLES REAGAN WILSON**

LOUISIANA STATE UNIVERSITY PRESS ❚❚❚ BATON ROUGE

Published by Louisiana State University Press
lsupress.org

Manufactured in the United States of America
First printing

DESIGNER: Mandy McDonald Scallan
TYPEFACE: Livory

Cover illustration: Sahroe/Shutterstock.com

Library of Congress Cataloging-in-Publication Data
Names: Burnett, Katharine A., 1983– editor. | Miller, Monica Carol, 1974–
    editor. | Wilson, Charles Reagan, writer of foreword.
Title: The tacky South / edited by Katharine A. Burnett, and Monica Carol
    Miller ; foreword by Charles Reagan Wilson.
Description: Baton Rouge : Louisiana State University Press, [2022] |
    Series: Southern literary studies | Includes bibliographical references
    and index.
Identifiers: LCCN 2021053985 (print) | LCCN 2021053986 (ebook) | ISBN
    978-0-8071-7734-1 (cloth) | ISBN 978-0-8071-7789-1 (paperback) | ISBN
    978-0-8071-7790-7 (pdf) | ISBN 978-0-8071-7791-4 (epub)
Subjects: LCSH: Tackiness—Southern States. | Southern States—In popular
    culture. | Southern States—Public opinion. | Southern
    States—Civilization. | Parton, Dolly. | Aesthetics, American.
Classification: LCC F209 .T25 2022 (print) | LCC F209 (ebook) | DDC
    306.0975—dc23/eng/20220124
LC record available at https://lccn.loc.gov/2021053985
LC ebook record available at https://lccn.loc.gov/2021053986

Contents

II. *Revolutionary Tackiness*

III. *Dolly as Common Ground*

Foreword

THE SOUTHERN TACKY HALL OF FAME

V. S. Naipaul was the most world-weary looking man I had ever seen when he visited my office at the Center for the Study of Southern Culture in 1984. He was touring the University of Mississippi campus as part of his time in the American South that led to *A Turn in the South* (1989), and that well-traveled writer looked bored. The Nobel Prize-winning author's eyes lit up, though, when he viewed a framed poster that portrayed Elvis Presley walking up to heaven. As Naipaul put it, the poster showed "a tight-trousered, full-bottomed Presley playing a guitar in the lower left-hand corner, with a staircase leading up to his mother and Graceland—the Presley house in Memphis—in the sky." Country legend Hank Williams was there to greet him. Graceland was suspended in air, with surrealistic, eerie colors of bright reds and blues, and meteors flashed by. A crown decorated the canvas as well.

Naipaul was harsh in judging it as "redneck fulfillment—socially pathetic at one level," but he also saw it as "religious art of a kind, with Christian borrowings" that included "the beatification of the central figure, with all his sexuality." Graceland seemed like a version of "the New Jerusalem in a medieval doomsday painting." Throughout his book about the South, Naipaul saw the region as a postcolonial society and related it to the West Indies where he grew up. Emancipated slaves in the British West Indies at first had few heroes, he recalled, but then they embraced such cultural figures as sportsmen, then musicians, and then politicians. "The glory of the black leader became the glory of his people," he concluded. Something of that adulation from the islands "seemed to be at the back of the Presley cult." He realized that music in the South carried much of a "people's emotional needs."

Naipaul's observations provide an appropriate preview to this book on southern tacky, a phenomenon that has been largely ignored by scholars but that offers insights into American studies and southern studies. The beginning place is history. When did this phenomenon begin? Did John Smith, the worldly adventurer, set souvenirs of his travels on his desk at Jamestown? Did Thomas Jefferson build an ingenious contraption to hold his collection of southern tacky at Monticello? Neither scenario is likely. I think of tacky artifacts as mass-produced ones that are part of popular culture—characteristic of modern times and not earlier. William Gilmore Simms was apparently the first writer to evoke the term, noting in *The Partisan* (1835) a "dirty-field-tackey." The term did not come into common usage, though, until the late nineteenth century. *Century* magazine (September 1888) referred to parts of Georgia with its "'po whites and piney-wood tackeys.'" A *Peterson* magazine (January 1884) writer identified a Virginia countryman as "a specimen of the genus 'tacky,'" and we can certainly be grateful for this unexpected biological grounding to the concept.

Material southern tacky dates back to the late nineteenth century, when admirers of Confederate leaders created an iconography of Robert E. Lee, Jefferson Davis, Stonewall Jackson, Jeb Stuart, and others, and placed their images on mass-produced prints, knives, whiskey bottles, sacks of flour, roadhouse signs, decks of cards, and innumerable other products of regional business. The southern identity a hundred years ago was a white-dominated, political-military regional self-consciousness, and the Confederate images symbolized it during the initial development of a broad popular culture in the region. In the twentieth century, the southern identity became more democratized. The redneck rebel soldier on a t-shirt seemed to interest the modern South more than the men staring down from Stone Mountain.

The images of southern tacky by the late twentieth century showed that the southern identity became tied in with popular culture more than ever. Likenesses of the heroes and celebrities of music, literature, film, and television are found on magazines, posters, postcards, buttons, pins, ties, shoestrings, and matchbox covers, to name only a few of the carriers of the iconography. Dolly Parton, Hank Williams, Jr., Richard Petty, Andy Griffith, the Dukes of Hazzard, Rhett and Scarlett—all are members of the Southern Tacky Hall of Fame.

The King of southern tacky is surely Elvis. Born into a poor Mississippi family, Presley developed an aesthetic of bright colors, opulence, and sensuality that has much in common with the fantasies of other poor, rural, white southerners. With his fabulous success, he remained true throughout his life to this ideal of taste. Graceland seems to some visitors a nightmare of the garish, but it is filled with touches of vitality and good humor. His image, moreover, adorns countless artifacts because people will buy virtually anything with Elvis on it. Ten of thousands of snapshots were made of him, fan shots, and each angle of him in his jumpsuit is a token of southern tacky.

Southern tacky lacks the moral connotations of "trashy" when used to describe a southern poor (or nonpoor) white. But it has aesthetic connotations. Again, the poor white is the starting point for understanding. An 1889 reference indicated that "tacky" in the South included "a man neglectful of personal appearance." The word is also used to describe a scruffy horse, which in the etymological imagination seems close to the image of the poor white.

The issue is not exactly aesthetics; it is taste, good taste. "Good taste" suggests standards of taste. There have indeed been national and regional standards of good taste, and the consumers of tacky symbolize exactly the opposite for the standard bearers of "high taste." As essays in this collection explore, tacky has been used to clarify normative standards of appearance and behavior for mainstream culture. Older literary imaginings of the South, for example, summon up the opposite of tacky. Greenville, Mississippi, poet William Alexander Percy was a well-educated, paternalistic, and quite civilized writer whose 1941 book *Lanterns on the Levee* revealed the continuing influence of the classical tradition on the southern planter class. He likely did not have black velvet paintings on his walls. The twelve Agrarian writers associated with Vanderbilt University who contributed to *I'll Take My Stand: The South and the Agrarian Tradition* (1930) even earlier saw popular culture—which southern tacky is a part of—as one of the evil influences besetting the industrializing South of their day. "Tacky" would have given them nightmares on their farms.

Tacky is a southern variation on a phenomenon of the modern age— kitsch. The term is a German colloquialism for rubbish, and scholars suggest it is widespread in Germany, in Italy, and in the United States in general. One finds soulmates for southern tacky when buying an Empire State Building paperweight, an Eiffel Tower peppermill, a Vatican pencil sharpener, or a Taj Mahal incense burner. Kitsch tends to be serious and even pretentious. Whereas "camp" is frivolous, kitsch takes itself seriously. Southern tacky, though, often laughs at itself without necessarily intending to be frivolous. Southerners have often had to laugh at themselves, one of the experiences even a poverty-stricken region could afford.

Have African Americans been a part of southern tacky? Observers will disagree on that point. By definition, according to the *Oxford English Dictionary*, "tacky" means southern whites, and African Americans would therefore be excluded. By my broadened definition of tacky as mass-produced popular culture items relating to the South, artifacts of Black southern life do indeed qualify. A vast array of deeply racist and offensive Sambo-Mammy tacky exists in abundance, part of the cultural demeaning of African Americans in the Jim Crow South. The stereotypical southern Black person showed up in sheet music, cartoons, calendars, postcards, postage stamps, stereoscopic slides, playing cards, popular Currier and Ives prints, and comic strips. Businesses used Sambo to sell household goods such as soaps, polishes, coffee, and jellies. Aunt Jemima sold middle-class women the makings for a quick breakfast that evoked the memory of a Black cook on the old plantation. African Americans such as Oprah Winfrey and historian Kenneth Goings became collectors of such items, with Goings seeing his collectibles as "windows to American history" and "props in the racial ideology" that helped cement racial stereotypes that lasted for over a century.

Black southerners themselves have purchased and displayed articles as well that were not demeaning but might be considered a subbranch of southern tacky. Images of Abraham Lincoln, Franklin Roosevelt, and John and Robert Kennedy, for example, long adorned homes of southern rural African Americans. Often these iconic American figures were combined with pictures of such Black heroes as Joe Louis, Jackie Robinson, B. B. King, Malcolm X, and, above all, Martin Luther King, Jr. King's image rivals that of Presley's for pervasiveness in the modern South. It is found hanging in schoolrooms and businesses and is used in newspaper advertisements in cities. It is on posters and postcards, on business cards, on the walls of residential homes, and on street signs across the South. Once pervasive, church fans—cardboard fans on a wooden stick, placed in church pews to help fight the heat before air-conditioning—conveyed biblical scenes and positive images of Black life that African American churches were glad to embrace. These were mass-produced artifacts that were not tacky at all in terms of aesthetics but did present images that reflected important features of Black life in the South.

I became a collector of southern tacky during the 1980s while working on the *Encyclopedia of Southern Culture* (1989). Perhaps it is a gene inherited from my mother who was an inveterate saver of things. My first memory of a souvenir from travel did not involve the South but rather was from her trip with a favorite aunt to southern California in the late 1950s. My family was from middle Tennessee, my father growing up on a tobacco farm north of Nashville and my mother the daughter of a small-town barber nearby. The trip to California was an adventurous one for my mother, and she brought back such tokens of her trip as a snow globe of Disneyland (which had only just opened) and a miniature, mule-driven wagon from Knott's Berry Farm. For a nine-year-old boy, they were magical and perhaps set my imagination going on the appeal of miniatures, which would be a major category of the southern tacky I would later collect.

I collect southern tacky not so much because of any artistic aspect but rather because these artifacts can be indicators of a broad symbolism related to the region. They may be souvenirs of a visit to a southern theme park, resort, historic spot, or other shrine; they may be mementos of a political campaign or a religious revival or retreat. Those I am interested in display the region's icons—the Bear Bryant Coca-Cola bottle, magnolia paintings for Mississippians and bluebonnet paintings for Texans, Confederate generals on a Stone Mountain paperweight.

The peculiarly southern quality of this variant of kitsch comes from this explicitly regional iconography and from the juxtaposition of images and concepts—an Elvis bumper sticker with the Confederate flag on it (now only a collector's piece in a museum), a painting of football coach Bear Bryant walking on water and thus evoking the Jesus of evangelical hymns. Southern tacky gathers at certain shrines—the gift shops across from Graceland on Elvis Presley Boulevard in Memphis; the country music museums and parks in Nashville; the gift shops of Gatlinburg; and anything anywhere near Myrtle Beach, South Carolina, which friends from that state proudly claim as the Capital City of southern tacky.

As the editors note, southern tacky is both a mode of external labeling and a mode of self-identification. Such southern tourism locales as mentioned above developed to appeal to outsiders coming to the South, and their souvenirs reflect often demeaning stereotypes of white southerners. The national culture often presents the South as the "other" compared to supposedly mainstream middle-class national culture, and tacky things from the region reinforce such sentiments. The southern middle class and upper classes undoubtedly feel the same way about the hillbilly, one of the most often reproduced figures in the array of southern tacky artifacts. Outhouses, corncob accessories, the plastic Horny Hillbilly—these do not inspire affection from those embracing middle-class values. But other white southerners do buy and display these items, seeing the humor in them and perhaps a past they hope they have escaped.

My Southern Tacky Collection now resides at the Mississippi Department of Archives and History in Jackson, but in 1989 the University of Mississippi Museum did the "Charles Wilson's World of Southern Tacky" exhibit, with a catalog that had a black velvety background and a pink flamingo on the cover. At least three reporters did extensive coverage of it because of the popular cultural nature of southern tacky, and it led to a *People* magazine feature called "The Strange Obsessions of an Ole Miss Professor." The national press saw the whole topic as a strange obsession indeed, but the southern reporters saw themselves and their families in the exhibit, albeit not always comfortably. Syndicated columnist Rheta Grimsley Johnson wrote of her trip through the southern countryside coming to Oxford, seeing tacky on the roadside, in a sign saying "Jesus Cares" at a service station, in a mailbox made from an old ringer-style washer with flowers planted in its tub, and in a half dozen "Granny Fannies," those "plyboard cutouts of fat women bending over in a garden." Johnson appreciated the exhibit but confessed, "I felt increasingly ill at ease looking at my past under glass." The milk glass in the exhibit had been the same one that held her mother's pins and buttons, the Florida juice glasses shaped like oranges used to be on her family's breakfast table, and the ceramic pencil holder shaped like a boot was part of her Christmas decorations.

The curator for that 1989 exhibit was Susan Hannah, whose husband, writer Barry Hannah, loved southern tacky and saw the humor in it. Susan Hannah noted that she did not see the term "southern tacky" as a malicious one, "but it is very Southern. The way southerners let it roll out of their mouths makes it a fun word." One can indeed smile at the exhibit's cow cream dispenser and pig salt-and-pepper shakers, but a troubling tension lies at the heart of southern tacky as well. Confederate flags in the exhibit evoke the defense of slavery, and a George Wallace campaign pin reminds us that racism can enter modern southern—and American—politics. The Elvis poster was in the exhibit as well, reminding us of Naipaul's ambiguous reaction to its combination of pathos and almost sacred sentiments for white southerners.

As both a scholar and a collector of southern tacky, I take heart from the attention that this volume of writings will bring to the topic, and the scholarly acumen that contributors bring to the task. Consideration of southern tacky offers a new perspective on such issues as social class, race relations, gender, and globalization that now inform the study of the South. It is a topic that lends itself to the interdisciplinary approach herein, and hopefully tacky will become incorporated into future discussions of the evolving southern cultural identity.

—*Charles Reagan Wilson*

Acknowledgments

In the fall of 2015, Monica was in New Orleans for the American Literature Association Symposium on "The City in American Literature." While in town for the conference, she and Michael Bibler went to the Ogden Museum of Southern Art, where an exhibit of Cynthia Scott's assemblage chandeliers made of plastic colanders and food containers prompted a rollicking discussion of many things silly, tacky, and weirdly southern. A smartphone Google search led us to the seed of this collection: the etymology of tacky, with its roots in the South Carolina horse farms and the so-called "tackies" who tended the horses. From a bar in the French Quarter, we texted our discovery to Katie (woefully *not* in New Orleans), and the three of us began our plans to organize a panel on the "Tacky South" for the 2016 Society for the Study of Southern Literature conference, held the following spring in Boston. Subsequently, Katie and Monica organized panels on the topic for the Modern Language Association and the American Studies Association conferences; many of the essays in this collection evolved from conference papers first presented on those panels and the vibrant discussions that ensued.

Indeed, the process of putting this collection together has been nothing but vibrant and *fun*, just like the topic itself. This is all due to the excellent work by our contributors, invaluable input from colleagues and friends who attended the panels, and the always wonderful folks at LSU Press who guided the process along the way, particularly our editor, James Long, and the Southern Literary Studies series editor, Scott Romine.

More important, this collection would not be possible without the truly wonderful collaborative relationship between the coeditors. Bringing the tacky really does make everything better.

The Tacky South

INTRODUCTION

WHAT WOULD DOLLY DO?

KATHARINE A. BURNETT AND
MONICA CAROL MILLER

*R*eese Witherspoon's Draper James clothing line, which its website describes as "steeped in Southern charm, feminine, and pretty [sic]," has its own "Dolly Shop" that includes a variety of items—from tote bags to T-shirts—emblazoned with the question, "What would Dolly do?" Ironically, Dolly's own "backwoods Barbie style" that she herself has described as a combination of Cinderella, Mother Goose, and the local hooker (quoted in Edwards 1) would never be found among the understated, suburban chic sheath dresses and gingham Keds on the Nashville-based Draper James website.

Nevertheless, this online "Dolly Shop" emerged in the fall of 2019, during a period that the editor of *Time Magazine* referred to as Dolly's "cultural moment" (Fesenthal), when Dolly Parton's popularity and fame reached new heights. Long a staple in the country music scene and a bastion of tourist attractions in her hometown of Sevierville, Tennessee, Dolly was suddenly everywhere. In November, Netflix streamed her *Heartstrings* TV series, while the saccharine Hallmark channel aired the *Christmas at Dollywood* special that December (and another, equally saccharine *Christmas on the Square* in 2020). That same fall, WNYC Studios released the wildly popular and Peabody Award-winning podcast, *Dolly Parton's America*. Even high-end housewares store

3

Williams Sonoma added a line of Dolly Parton-themed products for Christmas, which included a premade gingerbread "log cabin" priced at $129 ("Dolly Parton Pre-Built Log Cabin"). In the social media and pop culture world, Dolly had reached ultimate memeification: her face and name appeared on everything from "Saint Dolly" religious candles and "Dolly for President" T-shirts to murals blazoned across the sides of buildings in the hipper sections of Nashville.

The Dolly moment became amplified to an extreme degree throughout 2020, and her influence was not limited to her role as a pop culture icon. Parton has always had a track record of philanthropic endeavors. In 2017, her hometown of Sevierville and the surrounding areas suffered a devastating wildfire, and Parton set up a wildfire relief fund that raised more than nine million dollars (Flanagan). In 2018, her Imagination Library—a book program that distributes free books for children in select areas around the world—distributed its one hundred millionth book, which Parton dedicated to the Library of Congress. In a continuation of the Dolly moment and in the midst of a global pandemic, in spring 2020 Parton donated one million dollars to Vanderbilt Medical Center in Nashville, Tennessee, to aid in research toward a COVID-19 vaccine, a vaccine which ultimately proved to be one of the first effective versions by the end of 2020 (Paulson; Cramer). And in June 2020, in response to the protests and critiques of police brutality and racial violence surrounding the murder of George Floyd in Minneapolis, Minnesota, a petition circulated to replace the Confederate monuments dotting the state of Tennessee with monuments to Parton, citing her contributions to the state and her long history of philanthropy (France).

Throughout all of this, Dolly Parton remained what she always was (and never denied): backwoods Barbie, whose appearance "cost a lot of money to look this cheap" (quoted in Edwards 27). While she was being embraced by everyone from the poshest, most polished Draper James wearers to Generation Z-ers who heard "Jolene" for the first time on Spotify, Parton maintained a look that never seemed to alter with time (as she would point out, almost to a fault). She also maintained her connection to her place of birth, and her association with the South and Tennessee, in particular, was inextricable from her role as a cultural figure and Dolly as a moment. She was formidable, but she was always Dolly, a tacky product of east Tennessee whose borderline clownish persona was immediately recognizable and also immediately categorizable.

Dolly Parton's tackiness has given her longevity and relevance as a regionally specific cultural figure in an increasingly globalized world precisely because it allows her image to straddle multiple categories and designations while maintaining her southern roots. However, as the wide range of Dolly-themed souvenirs, memes, and scholarship demonstrates, her unprecedented ascendance in the American imagination invites extended analysis because of its uniqueness. As Tressie McMillan Cottom explains, in her 2021 consideration of "The Dolly Moment," "Dolly is a celebrity among celebrities, an icon, and a national treasure because she has cobbled together a diverse, multiracial, pansexual audience for working-class feminist songcraft and queer camp subversiveness." And yet, her identification with both southernness and tackiness remains central to her persona, even as her audience has grown well beyond those borders.

Parton's self-assumed role as a trashy, tacky ambassador makes her the perfect figurehead for everything quirky, offbeat, and fun, yet still mainstream and acceptable enough to make her way into the bourgeois world of Draper James and Williams Sonoma. The word "tacky" itself has distinctly southern origins as a way to comment on a person's style. According to the *Oxford English Dictionary*, it first emerged around 1800 as a noun to describe "a degenerate, 'weedy' horse" and then later as "a poor white of the Southern States from Virginia to Georgia" ("tacky," *OED*). Although the *OED* does not draw connections between this origin and the origins of the word as an adjective describing something that is "dowdy, shabby; in poor taste, cheap, vulgar," these definitions suggest a clear link between national stereotypes of region, race, and class and urbane (and northern urban?) notions of taste, class, and sensibility. For the purposes of this collection, tackiness, then, is primarily an aesthetic mode, which encompasses a variety of fields from visual art and performance to literature and pop culture iconography. As Jolene Hubbs astutely points out in her chapter in this collection, however, "Judgements about what—or who—is tacky mark out class boundaries that masquerade as aesthetic differences."

The chapters in this collection use the insights of what constitutes and counts as tacky to consider the ideological work done in this aesthetic mode's persistent connection with the American South.

The Dolly moment reveals that the definitions of tackiness serve a function in regional representation that reaches far beyond simple aesthetics. In its introduction to the podcast, the producers of *Dolly Parton's America* muse, "in this intensely divided moment, one of the few things everyone still seems to agree on is Dolly Parton—but why?" (Abumrad and Oliaee). The short answer: she's tacky, she's southern, and, put both together, she's invincible in mainstream cultural contexts. The longer answer, of course, is much more complicated. Unlike other country artists, for whom success has been an impetus to shed their country origins, Dolly's east Tennessee roots have been a significant part of her story and brand, which includes the tacky style that has been so central to her aesthetic, and in turn, so central to her popularity and endurance as a cultural icon. Anna Creadick also attempts to answer the "Why Dolly?" question and explains in her essay for this collection, "The arc of Dolly's career has seen her move not away from tackiness, but toward it." While it would seem that this pattern would chip away at anyone's cultural cachet, as Creadick points out, "For Parton, greater success has translated into greater freedom to mock middle-class aesthetics with her own tacky taste." Creadick's discussion of Dolly's tackiness as a conscious mocking of middle-class aesthetics raises an important question about the role of tackiness: to undercut normative standards, or to reinforce. In the case of Parton, it's both. "At a time characterized by anxiety and civic division," Creadick writes, "Dolly is a mediating force, drawing fans from across the political spectrum." Parton's very tackiness and her overt connections to the South allow her to act as both an insider and an outsider in US culture, regionally specific while embraced nationally, a unifier and disruptor—a paradoxical figure who, like other tacky representations, is both, and, and always.

The irreverence at the heart of Parton's persona—indeed, at the heart of all things tacky—is the very quality that makes her popularity so ubiquitous and so sustainable. In another essay in this collection, Michael Bibler dwells on the *fun* of tackiness: while tackiness is often seen as transgressive and subversive, or even veering into dirty or distasteful, above all it is about messiness and delighting in that messiness. "Tackiness," Bibler remarks, "exposes the seams where competing hierarchies of taste and value intersect. These seams . . . reveal a uniquely democratic aspect of tackiness that foregrounds multiplicity and difference in opposition not only to conformity but also to *any* unifying system of aesthetics." It is no wonder, then, that tackiness and queerness frequently go hand in hand, or that a discussion of tackiness often diverges into discussions of kitsch and camp (as, indeed, they do in many of the essays in this collection). If we interpret "queer" as an "umbrella [term] instead of confining identities to certain designations," as Travis Rountree does in his essay for this collection, then the fun of tacky enables modes of aesthetic representation and access to audiences that wouldn't exist otherwise. On these terms, tacky is about exposing cultural and social seams, reveling in them, but never entirely undoing them. Again taking Dolly Parton as an example (and yes, all roads lead to Dolly in this collection), the irreverent seamlessness of tacky ranges from the adoption of Parton's image in drag (as in the case of performer Trixie Mattel) to an overpriced (yet perfectly assembled) gingerbread shack, yet still allows Parton to maintain a more sincere image and shepherd a long-sustained book program dedicated to early childhood literacy.

Such considerations raise the question: is the appeal of tackiness that it reinforces the borders of respectability, making the viewer feel more secure in their own conformity? Or does it encourage participation, even vicarious participation, which acts to undermine or subvert such boundaries? In this sense, southern tackiness emulates many regionally specific paradigms. In his book on one of the more persistent cultural tropes, Anthony Szczesiul describes the function of southern hospitality "in the national imaginary, both as a form of persuasion and as a meaning-making story that has been told about the South for more than two centuries" (6). In this case, the story being told is a myth that "has been used to create and promote a sense of transregional white community, solidarity, and privilege" (7). The evocation of southern hospitality as a concept becomes a way of masking or containing the violence of the region. Similarly, southern tackiness functions as a badge of belonging, a visual or behavioral code of consciously flouting conventions of appearance or behaviors.

On the other side of the coin, tackiness encodes progressive politics as being nonthreatening to the status quo. The petition to replace Confederate monuments with statues of Dolly Parton is a perfect example: everyone can agree on Dolly, and the idea allows for critiques of racism and the memorialization of racist institutions extant in the South and the US as a whole. Yet having Dolly as the replacement sidesteps the real conversations about racism that need to be held. Why not Ida B. Wells, or any number of Black Tennesseans who contributed to the growth of the state? Dolly is one of the few things everyone can agree upon, precisely because as an outlandish, tacky figure, she suggests progressivism without being a threat to mainstream norms. Tackiness by these definitions functions as a cultural outlet or escape: like the carnivalesque, it proposes subversion or change, but within the confines of existing structures and institutions, without upending or revising them.

The parameters of tackiness in the mainstream, however, do not undermine its function as an aesthetic mode. Put another way, tackiness has *value*, despite the fact that the label is generally applied to things or people deemed valueless, culturally and economically. "Tacky" is often used as a condemnation of excess or overreaching, and judgments of tackiness can be considered accusations of laziness and failure to meet normative cultural standards of respectability and taste. In this way, tackiness polices the borders of socioeconomic class status, highlighting a lack of cultural capital (which acts as a representation of economic capital). As Nancy Isenberg explains in her historical analysis of the term "white trash," "Our class system has hinged on the evolving political rationales used to dismiss or demonize (or occasionally reclaim) those white rural outcasts seemingly incapable of becoming part of the mainstream society" (xiv). So, too, do the evolving boundaries of tackiness function in part as a marker of belonging and taste.

Things or people designated as "tacky" frequently represent attempts at authenticity, trying to perform and emulate but missing the mark. Therefore, the term encompasses mainstream or popular culture manifestations that, to put it simply, aren't quite right. As Susannah Young writes in her essay, "It doesn't feel like overreach to say that much of what we consider 'tacky' has been classified as such not only because it is financially accessible but because it has been created by or for people society neither values nor respects." Indeed, the judgment of tacky reflects important connections between socioeconomic status and economic consumption, as several of the essays in this collection highlight, as choosing to buy, wear, display, or engage in the wrong commodity or activity can reveal one's ignorance, one's lack of cultural capital. Monica Carol Miller observes, "In order to break the rules governing appropriate behavior, appearance, and decor, however, one must first understand what the rules are and when they apply. Wearing a sequined red hat to a Red Hat Society luncheon with others of your social set who are similarly dressed is an afternoon of fun. Wearing the same hat to a PTA meeting would be looked at askance." Tackiness reveals a lack of knowledge of cultural expectations and norms.

Such failures to meet the mark may also be used as evidence of lack of authenticity, in attempts to reinforce retrogressive notions of southern essentialism. As with Szczesiul's discussion of southern hospitality, in these moments tackiness is evoked to simultaneously subvert and uphold the status quo under the banner of an "authentic" self. For example, in his essay on reality TV shows like *Duck Dynasty* featuring rural white communities, Aaron Duplantier notes, "Many of these folks insist their lifestyle is grittier and more palpable. . . . . This aura stems from generations of rural whites asserting their ties to the agrarian way of life, emphasizing it over immaterial pursuits of the mind favored by some Yankee. . . . *We are more real*, they might argue. *Salt of the earth*." Yet those same "salt of the earth" individuals are multimillionaires, consciously constructing and benefiting from a lower-class, less polished, *tacky* image that belies their actual socioeconomic standing.

But to return to the value of tackiness, the concept also enables moments of true sincerity that go beyond simple subversion or mocking the status quo. As Katharine A. Burnett notes in her essay, for something or someone to be labeled as tacky requires a consciousness on the part of the creator (the tacky individual) and the audience (those perceiving the tackiness). In that moment of recognition between the two, there emerges a form of "performance and ability to read tackiness [which] becomes key to achieving a sincere form of representation that can exist outside of mainstream normative standards." As a result, tackiness occupies a multivalent and often paradoxical position in popular representations: the concept can evoke moments of sincerity, be a badge of "realness," or is the result of failure to meet normative standards.

The paradoxical function of "tacky" is never more apparent than in representations and discussions of the US South in popular culture. Bring up the idea of tackiness, and the most common associations are with predominantly lower-class communities in the South: the Appalachian region, the Ozarks, areas of Florida (just to name a few). Likewise, popular understandings of the region come from entertainment frequently coded as "tacky": Dollywood, *Duck Dynasty*, and beauty pageants (again, to give just a few examples). Like the mainstream embracing of Dolly Parton, the relationship between tackiness and the South manifests a dual process, in which tackiness is imposed on the region, while at the same time representations of the region project and celebrate their own form of tackiness. The pattern mirrors the contradictory quality in the definition of tackiness itself, in which the tackiness of the US South simultaneously becomes a mode of self-definition and a mode of external labeling and limitation. Placing "tacky" and tackiness in conversations with US southern studies more broadly allows a greater engagement with conceptions of region that are both limiting and expansive.

As several of the essays note, region is a critical aspect of narratives and judgments of tacky. Many of the examples of southern tackiness throughout this collection relate to spaces and areas at the edges of the "South" proper: Florida,[1] Louisiana, Arkansas, and, most especially, Appalachia, which is almost always mentioned in discussions of the tacky. Like tackiness itself, these spaces are paradoxical and liminal. Part of the reason they are such a fixation in discussions of tackiness is that they are geographic and cultural borderlands, the seams of the South, so to speak, which lends them to labels and evocations of tackiness. But as scholars such as Ronald D. Eller have noted, such literally marginal positions allow for important insights into the larger southern and American contexts: "Appalachia is not the 'other America' that the national stereotypes would have us believe; instead, it may be more of a bellwether of the challenges facing our larger society. . . . Popular stereotypes have tended to blame the land or the culture of Appalachia for regional disparaties, but the real uneven ground of Appalachia has been the consequence of structural inequalities based on class, race, and gender, and on political corruption, land abuse, and greed" (265). That tackiness has such strong ties to southern Appalachia especially—whether Dollywood in East Tennessee or roadside attractions such as Goats on the Roof in Tiger, Georgia—points to the complex intersections of race and class at the heart of judgments of and claims to the tacky.

Indeed, as Meredith McCarroll and many others have pointed out, "There is a deep historical investment in seeing the region as 'pure white stock' and as deeply impoverished and backward" (2). Especially in discussing the South, one must address the history of racialized slavery and racism; likewise, a discussion of tackiness by necessity engages with race and racial identity. Nancy Isenberg locates the origins of the term "white trash"—a phrase habitually linked with "tacky"—in the US South decades before the Civil War: "The sectional crisis that led to America's Civil War dramatically reconfigured the democratic language of class identity." She writes, "The lowly squatter remained the focus of attention, but . . . he was now, singularly, a creature of the slave states" (135). In the context of an antebellum society reliant on slavery for its functioning, where whiteness immediately conferred privilege, "trashiness" and "tackiness" became a way to emphasize and enforce difference along class lines. Over time, those socioeconomic differences were crystallized into inherent differences passed through generations. That increasingly regionalized figure, the "tacky" of the OED definition, became increasingly racialized: "White trash southerners were classified as a 'race' that passed on these horrific traits, eliminating any possibility of improvement or social mobility" (Isenberg 136). At its roots, tackiness is about conceptions, perceptions, and representations of racial identity and how all are historically and consistently tied to the history of slavery in the US South. Therefore, all of the essays in this collection address race in some way, and tackiness becomes the critical nexus through which we can understand race, class, and regional identity.

The Tacky South responds to a repeated pattern between the US South and the rest of the nation since before the Civil War; Dolly Parton's prominence is just the most recent and ubiquitous manifestation. The so-called "Dolly moment" is an identifiable, emerging moment in the topic, when both popular writing and academic studies are increasingly occupied with questions of taste and the associated cultural markers of socioeconomic status, race, and gender—all of which are filtered through region and the US South especially. However, as the essays in this collection demonstrate, the southern preoccupation with tacky is one that stretches back well over a century and more. Dolly's popularity is part of a tradition of American infatuation with southern tackiness, whether the tackies of Paul Laurence Dunbar's work, the sequins of Nudie suits, or a shockingly blood-red groom's cake interrupting a blush-and-bashful wedding in *Steel Magnolias*.

Mainstream cultural writing on tackiness frequently references the same historical and etymological considerations that are at the heart of this project. For instance, in his linguistic analysis of the Weird Al Yankovic hit song, "Tacky," Ben Zimmer references the *OED* definition as a way to delineate the contemporary cultural patterns evinced in Yankovic's use of the term. The popular website *The Bitter Southerner* regularly features essays and multimedia pieces on topics related to "tacky," "trash," and the nominal variations of the two words, while the Dolly moment has ensured a never-ending supply of think pieces meditating on the star's unique genius.[2] On the more academic side, significant works in southern and American studies have touched on the topic of tackiness. Matt Wray and Annalee Newitz's essay collection, *White Trash* (1996) and Wray's book *Not Quite White: White Trash and the Boundaries of Whiteness* (2006), bring in notions of taste and "trashiness," while Isenberg's *White Trash: The 400-Year Untold Story of Class in America* (2016) is foundational for understanding the history of tackiness as a concept. Likewise, chapters in Scott Romine's *The Real South* (2008) discuss southern cultural touchstones that are often associated with tackiness, as does Tara McPherson's *Reconstructing Dixie* (2003). And there is no shortage of tacky ephemera, including the "Southern Tacky Collection: 1980s–1990s" at UNC-Chapel Hill and the Southern Tacky materials that are part of the Charles Reagan Wilson Collection at the University of Mississippi.

The essays in this collection explore the myriad ways, forms, and functions of tackiness in the American South. Beginning with the *OED* entry, this collection examines the shifting definitions and acts of defining the term "tacky," from its earliest uses to how those conceptions have evolved over time through regional representations. In the collected essays, *The Tacky South* explores what those shifts reveal about US culture as a whole and the role that region plays in addressing national and global issues of culture and identity. As a matter of style and taste, tacky is hard to pin down and define, and it has certainly grown beyond its southern rural origins. Yet the specters of class, race, and region still linger in contemporary notions of what registers as tacky, particularly in the way it refers to things that are cheap, vulgar, common, unsophisticated, and shabby. In his essay "Whose South?" which is a touchstone for this collection, Charles Reagan Wilson traces the proliferation of this type of southern tackiness to the nineteenth century, when images of Robert E. Lee, Stonewall Jackson, and Jefferson Davis were printed on a variety of manufactured goods, including playing cards, whiskey bottles, and flour sacks. Building on his work, this collection considers the ways in which judgments and deployments of "tackiness" have been considered consistently integral to larger understandings of "southernness" and "southern identity."

Although this collection cannot possibly offer a full historical and cultural investigation of the links between tackiness and "the South" as a construct, we offer a set of essays that open up ways to explore those connections more fully. To address the broadest scope of the conversation, the collection is structured in three sections that approach the topic of tackiness and the South from different angles: first, tackiness as a form of failure or policing, namely, who fits and who doesn't; second, tackiness as a form of subversion; and finally, representations that overlap with both definitions and emulate the dual process inherent in the function of tackiness itself.

Part 1, "Policing Tackiness," approaches the notion of tackiness from the more commonly understood use of the term: as a way to draw boundaries between what is deemed normative or "acceptable" and what is deemed outside of proper mainstream society. The essays in this section trace the use of the term "tacky" from its original etymology, through historical applications, to its manifestations in literary and cultural representations up through the twentieth and twenty-first centuries. Jolene Hubbs begins by delineating a history of class perception through the *OED* definition and examining representations of tackies in postbellum local color fiction. Joe T. Carson takes a more literal approach to tackiness in his focus on pine tar, noting that tar is a metonym for the laboring body in the nineteenth-century South and explaining how the materiality of tacky precedes and informs the application of tacky as a metaphor for taste. Elisabeth Aiken then addresses the perennially tacky space, Appalachia, to discuss the long-standing stereotypes associated with the region and the literary attempts to revise those stereotypes. Complicating the definitions and designations of the terms, Garth Sabo investigates how tacky and trash overlap in the work of Dorothy Allison, while Catherine Egley Waggoner considers how the tacky aesthetic has functioned as a rallying point of southern identity. Centering references to the tackiness of Appalachia in Vladimir Nabokov's *Lolita* along with other literary and televisual texts, Jimmy Dean Smith argues that the "tackiness" of the Daisy Mae trope in southern and Appalachian culture has been a metaphor for the industrial exploitation of the virgin wilderness. Moving into mainstream media representations, Jill E. Anderson examines the use of stereotypes of tackiness and white southern identity in the television shows *Murder, She Wrote* and *The Golden Girls*, while Aaron Duplantier investigates the troubled relationship between the audience schadenfreude evoked by these stereotypes in reality television shows such as *Duck Dynasty* and *Here Comes Honey Boo Boo*, as well as the advertising and promotional tie-ins surrounding these shows. Such stereotypes also serve as warnings for women growing up under certain expectations of white womanhood, as Monica Carol Miller discusses in her examination of the relationship between southern motherhood and warnings of tackiness.

Part 2, "Revolutionary Tackiness," focuses on the uses of tackiness to undermine and subvert normative understandings of identity and mainstream culture. Often the subjects and topics of the essays featured here are those ostracized from mainstream discourse, in which the label of "tacky" frequently denotes "lesser-than" or "other." However, each essay in this section highlights how tackiness instead implements modes of transgression, in which the concept and utilization of tackiness allows individuals to critique and upend dominant hierarchical structures in regard to race, class, gender, and, of course, taste. Jarrod L. Hayes's essay examines the historical patterns related to race and tackiness through depictions of dress and "quadroon balls" in nineteenth-century French novels, while Katharine A. Burnett explores the role of tackiness in negotiating class and race in nineteenth-century stories featuring the South and West. Moving into another popular target for tacky stereotyping, the Ozarks, Joseph A. Farmer discusses the work of Donald Harington and its role in both upholding and undercutting regional stereotypes. Focusing on another symbol of tackiness, Marshall Needleman Armintor's essay on the red velvet cake traces the cake's history in popular culture to discuss its function as a conduit for class- and race-based definitions. Likewise, Travis Rountree takes up the work of Robert Earl Keen to address how the musician undermines and critiques normative gender standards of country music. And in Michael Bibler's essay, the B-52s revel in the seams of taste and trash through the adoption and rejection of the label "tacky" in their music and persona.

As we have suggested, tackiness as a mode of expression occupies a liminal role: it can be a mode both of demarcating boundaries and of dissolving those boundaries. As a result, the essays in part 3, "Dolly as Common Ground," treat tackiness as a method of questioning and engaging with popular cultural signifiers, playing with subjects often labeled as "tacky," and exploring their value in national and global contexts. Using Dolly Parton as an exemplar, each of the essays in this section proposes a way of seeing tackiness as a new framework for understanding identity through region, one that is not limited to a single definition. In her outline of Parton's career, Anna Creadick examines how the body—in this case, the outsized femme body—becomes a mode of cultural power, both asserting and deferring. Picking up on the power of the outlandish, Isabel Duarte-Gray uses the "Nudie suit," or the flashy suits popular with musicians in the mid-twentieth century, as a starting point to highlight the "play" in tacky and southern identification, from Parton herself to southern drag made popular by performers like Trixie Mattel. And finally, Susannah Young's essay picks up on the patterns of representation identified by Creadick and Duarte-Gray to discuss how a younger generation of musicians and performers draws from Parton and earlier manifestations of tackiness to evoke new modes of gendered expression.

By ending with discussions of the function of tackiness—its value— this collection shifts the conversation surrounding regionalism and representation. Despite the surge in interest and the wealth of material on the topic, there are few if any studies specifically devoted to a study of tackiness. This leaves the field open for a collection like *The Tacky South* that merges popular fascination with critical analysis. The *OED* definition lends the term a diversity previously underrecognized, one that opens up new avenues for inquiry. This collection aims to capture popular and academic fascination with the US South and tackiness through the merging of regional aesthetics with more comprehensive understandings of gender, race, and class constructions.

NOTES

1. See, e.g., the "Florida Man" meme, first defined on Twitter in 2013: "He is a man of a thousand tattooed faces, a slapstick outlaw, an Internet-traffic gold mine, a cruel punchline, a beloved prankster, a human tragedy and, like some other love-hate American mascots, the subject of burgeoning controversy" (Hill).

2. Jessica Wilkerson, "Living with Dolly Parton," *Longreads*, Oct. 2018. See also Edwards for a recent scholarly approach to the topic.

WORKS CITED

Abumrad, Jad, and Shima Oliaee. "About." *Dolly Parton's America*, WNYC Studios, www.wnycstudios.org/podcasts/dolly-partons-america/about. Accessed June 2020.

Cottom, Tressie McMillan. "The Dolly Moment: Why We Stan a Post-Racism Queen." *Essaying*, 24 Feb. 2021, tressie.substack.com/p/the-dolly-moment.

Cramer, Maria. "Dolly Parton Donated $1 million to Help Develop a Coronavirus Vaccine." *New York Times*, 18 Nov. 2020, www.nytimes.com/2020/11/18/world/dolly-parton-donated-1-million-to-help-develop-a-coronavirus-vaccine.html.

"Dolly Parton Dedicates Her Imagination Library's 100 Millionth Book to the

Library of Congress." Library of Congress, 2018, www.loc.gov/item/web-cast-8289/.

"Dolly Parton Pre-Built Log Cabin." *Williams-Sonoma, www.williams-sonoma.com/products/dolly-parton-pre-built-log-cabin/?pkey=cdolly-parton.* Accessed October 2019.

"*Dolly Parton's America* Podcast Wins Prestigious Peabody Award." *WBIR*, 12 June 2020, www.wbir.com/article/news/entertainment-news/dolly-partons-america-podcast-wins-prestigious-peabody-award/51-527d1616-ae31-47c0-9790-3d340c3730fa. Accessed June 2020.

"The Dolly Shop." *Draper James*, 2019, draperjames.com/collections/what-would-dolly-parton-do. Accessed 26 May 2020.

Edwards, Leigh H. *Dolly Parton, Gender, and Country Music.* Indiana UP, 2018.

Eller, Ronald D. *Uneven Ground: Appalachia Since 1945.* UP of Kentucky, 2013.

Felsenthal, Edward. "Time100 Talks: Finding Hope—Leadership During Crisis." *Time*, 28 May 2020, time.com/time100talks/#may-28-2020.

Flanagan, Andrew. "Dolly Parton Provides Fire Victims 'Shoulder To Lean On.'" *NPR*, 8 May 2017, www.npr.org/sections/therecord/2017/05/08/520140609/dolly-parton-issues-final-checks-to-those-displaced-by-smoky-mountain-wildfire.

France, Lisa Respers. "Dolly Parton Statues Instead of Confederate Monuments Is What Some Want." *CNN*, 15 June 2020, //www.cnn.com/2020/06/15/entertainment/dolly-parton-confederate-statues/index.html.

Hill, Logan. "Is It Okay to Laugh at Florida Man?" *The Washington Post Magazine*, July 15 2019.

Isenberg, Nancy. *White Trash: The 400-Year Untold History of Class in America.* Viking, 2016.

McCarroll, Meredith. *Unwhite: Appalachia, Race, and Film.* U of Georgia P, 2018.

Paulson, Dave. "Dolly Parton Says She'll Donate $1 million for Coronavirus Research at Vanderbilt." *Tennessean* [Nashville], 1 April 2020.

Szczesiul, Anthony. *The Southern Hospitality Myth: Ethics, Politics, Race, and American Memory.* U of Georgia P, 2017.

"Tacky, N. and Adj. (1)." *Oxford English Dictionary Online*, Oxford UP, www.oed.com/view/Entry/196947. Accessed 16 Mar. 2019.

Wilson, Charles Reagan. "Whose South?" *Southern Cultures*, Winter 2018, www.southerncultures.org/article/whose-south/.

Zimmer, Ben. "The Gauche Origins of the Word 'Tacky,'" *The Wall Street Journal*, 18 July 2014.

I.

Policing Tackiness

PICTURING THE TACKY

POOR WHITE SOUTHERNERS IN GILDED AGE PERIODICALS

JOLENE HUBBS

*J*udgments about what—or who—is tacky mark out class boundaries that masquerade as aesthetic differences. In his now-classic study *Distinction: A Social Critique of the Judgement of Taste*, Pierre Bourdieu observes that "in matters of taste, more than anywhere else, all determination is negation; and tastes are perhaps first and foremost distastes" (49). "Tacky" is a term that, first and foremost, registers distaste. Today, the word disparages people as gaudy or dowdy, or finds fault with their shoddy or tawdry possessions. In the closing decades of the nineteenth century, "tacky" (or sometimes "tackey") operated both as an adjective and as a noun designating "a poor white of the Southern States from Virginia to Georgia" ("Tacky," def. A.2). By using the term as a taste-critiquing adjective as well as a class-defining noun, Americans bolstered associations between poor people and poor taste—and, as I work to prove in the pages that follow, those associations persisted even after the noun form fell out of use. Literary critic Jon Cook writes that "the exercise of taste is constantly drawing and redrawing the boundaries between and within classes" (100). Exercising taste by censuring tackiness engages in this bound-ary-making work, forging and fortifying differences between poor white southerners and better-off Americans.

This essay works to make the case that classism is written into the word "tacky." To trace out how ideas about what is "dowdy, shabby; in poor taste, cheap, vulgar" came to be bound up with negative stereo-types about poor white southerners, I explore what this term signified and how it circulated in the late nineteenth century, concentrating on its appearances in the *Century Illustrated Monthly Magazine*, one of the Gilded Age's most influential and august periodicals ("Tacky," def. B). In stories and essays representing life in the South—and in the illus-trations that sometimes accompanied them—the *Century* and other magazines appealed to their middle- and upper-class subscribers by presenting tackiness (as identity and as aesthetic) as the inverse of readers' own tastefulness.

THE ORIGINS OF TACKY

Telling the story of the interlinked emergence of "tacky" as a noun and as an adjective means calling into question the *Oxford English Dictionary*'s etymology for the word's adjectival form. The *OED* traces the use of the term to mean dowdy, shabby, or in poor taste to the diary that Kate Stone, the eldest daughter in a family of Louisiana planters, kept during the Civil War. In a journal entry dated February 16, 1862, Stone describes the arrival of "a weary, bedraggled, tacky-looking set" of visi-tors at her home (89). But this manuscript's history casts doubt on this date for this word. The journal was first published in 1955 as *Brokenburn: The Journal of Kate Stone, 1861–1868*, taking its name from the cotton plan-tation inhabited by the Stones at the start of the Civil War. *Brokenburn* was based on a copy of the journal that Stone made in 1900. In his preface to the 1955 edition, literary scholar John Q. Anderson suggests that Stone copied the diary into the two ledger books that served as his source text "without evident revision" (xv). Anderson does not explain what led him to believe that Stone did not revise the work, but he could not have come to this conclusion by comparing the 1860s orig-inal to the 1900 copy, because the original manuscript was lost before Anderson began editing the document that Stone produced in 1900.

Historians who have studied *Brokenburn* point to textual evidence of revisions made around the turn of the century. In the introduc-tion she wrote for the 1995 reissue of *Brokenburn*, Drew Gilpin Faust suggests that Stone reworked her diary decades after first writing it. Faust draws attention to the text's organization—that is, the narrative's "crafted structure," including its plotted "progress toward Kate's ultimate enlightenment and mature satisfaction"—as evidence of revisions (xxxi). In her 2015 Presidential Address to the Louisiana Historical Association, Mary Farmer-Kaiser argued that Stone reworked her story at the turn of the twentieth century in an effort "to recast her history" in a way that flatteringly depicted "her own place in the changing world that surrounded her" (412). Farmer-Kaiser's analysis underscores how Stone imaginatively resituates Brokenburn out of its actual geographic location—which was somewhat inland of the Mississippi River in a zone that the crème de la crème of planter elites "identified as the 'Back Country'" (Farmer-Kaiser 400)—and into the river-hugging epicenter of northeastern Louisiana's high society.

Even more suggestive than the neighbors Stone wished to seem closer to, though, are those she worked to distance herself from. In a short section called "In Retrospect" that she penned in 1900 as a preface to her journal, Stone delineates the class divides that structured southern society in the antebellum era. After opening with a few rose-tinted remembrances of some of the plantation's inhabitants, including her family members and the African Americans they enslaved, she moves to Brokenburn's less fondly recalled inhabitants: overseers: "The men were a coarse, uncultivated class, knowing little more than to read and write; brutified by their employment, they were considered by the South but little better than the Negroes they managed. Neither they nor their families were ever invited to any of the entertainments given by the planters, except some large function, such as a wedding given at the home of the employer. If they came, they did not expect to be introduced to the guests but were expected to amuse themselves watching the crowd. They visited only among themselves" (5). "In Retrospect" reveals Stone's concerns as she reviewed—and, I join Faust and Farmer-Kaiser in believing, reworked—her decades-old journal. This passage lays bare Stone's interest in emphasizing the antebellum order's stark social divisions. Entwining classism with racism through her simultaneous denigration of overseers and enslaved people, she distances both populations from planters. Painting overseers as "coarse, uncultivated," "brutified," and socially ostracized, Stone nostalgically invokes a bygone era when nonslaveholding whites sought little more than the pleasure of "watching" wealthier white people enjoy themselves.

The Civil War reversed the direction of this socioeconomically salient sightline. In the southern literary tradition, antebellum poor whites routinely figure as members of an unseen audience staring in awe at planters; in addition to Stone's wedding watchers, we might think of young Thomas Sutpen in William Faulkner's *Absalom, Absalom!* (1936), who would "creep up among the tangled shrubbery of the lawn and lie hidden" there in order to watch a planter lounge in a hammock (184). Starting after the Civil War and reaching a crescendo in the 1880s, by contrast, current and former elites trained their eyes on poor white people. With former elites abashed at the figures they cut in their reduced circumstances and up-and-comers still working to accrue cultural capital to supplement their financial capital—and finding themselves sneered at as parvenus while they did[1]—both populations turned from performing their own tastefulness to scrutinizing poor people for signs of their tackiness.

Because Stone's original diary has been lost—and because the first extant version of the text shows signs of being a 1900 revision of an 1860s original—dating Stone's description of "weary, bedraggled, tacky-looking" travelers to 1862 (as the *OED* does) is a questionable decision (89). Setting aside this doubtful date for the adjectival form of the word clears the way for proposing that the two meanings of "tacky" emerged simultaneously and might be interrelated. In the 1880s, I want to suggest, "tacky" began to be used as a noun describing poor white southerners and as an adjective describing people who are "dowdy, shabby; in poor taste": that is, people who manifest tastes associated with poor whites ("Tacky," def. B).

E. W. KEMBLE'S TACKY TYPES

The tacky sprang to life in the pages of late-nineteenth-century American magazines, engendered by fiction writers (and a few essayists) and the illustrators whose drawings often accompanied their works. Writers and artists worked together in creating this figure. Artists read the stories they were illustrating before starting their drawings. Authors made requests about how characters would be depicted before illustrators went to work and afterwards, when, as artist E. W. Kemble explained about the process, "the drawings are sent to the author with a printed slip attached requesting the criticism of the writer upon the picture and changes are made accordingly." This collaborative enterprise spawned a poor white archetype in which identity and aesthetics intertwine. Kemble's caricatures of poor white southerners for the *Century Illustrated Monthly Magazine* bear out Pierre Bourdieu's contention that people at the bottom of the social hierarchy often "serve as a foil, a negative reference point, in relation to which all aesthetics define themselves, by successive negations" (50). The tacky, a poor person with poor taste, paraded before the *Century*'s middle- and upper-class readers as a counterpoint to their own aesthetic sensibilities.

Writer Joel Chandler Harris and illustrator E. W. Kemble worked together in 1887 to introduce readers of the *Century* to tackies living in Georgia's piney woods.[2] By the time of their collaboration, both men had published the works that would make them famous: Harris's Uncle Remus tales and Kemble's drawings for *Adventures of Huckleberry Finn*. After learning that Kemble—then a staff illustrator at the *Century*—had been assigned to illustrate "Azalia," Harris asked Richard Watson Gilder, the magazine's editor, to convey to the illustrator his suggestions for how to treat the story's three character types. Harris asked Kemble to depict the tale's "decent people" with "some refinement," to portray Black characters with "some dignity," and to avoid making "the Tackies too forlorn" (Harris, *Life and Letters* 228).

Both the protagonist and the third-person narrator of Harris's local color tale work to define the characters termed tackies. Helen, the main character, labels them "picturesque" (547). The narrator calls them an "indescribable class of people" ("Azalia" 549). References to the tackies brim with superlatives—they are, for example, depicted as "steeped in poverty of the most desolate description and living the narrowest lives possible in this great Republic" (549). Both Helen and the narrator seem startled by the appearance of Emma Jane Stucky, a tacky woman Helen meets soon after arriving in Azalia. The narrator describes Emma Jane's looks by first asserting that her "appearance showed the most abject poverty," then making note of her "dirty sun-bonnet," "frazzled and tangled" hair, "pale, unhealthy-looking face," simple dress, and "pathetic and appalling" gaze (551). The first installment of this tale, which was published serially across three issues of the *Century*, ends with Helen declaring that Emma Jane's appearance "will haunt me as long as I live" (552). Responding to her guest's comments, the proprietor of the tavern where Helen is staying frames the poor white population as a segment of the region's fauna that grows no less unsettling as it becomes more familiar: "I reckon maybe you ain't used to seein' piney-woods Tackies. Well, ma'am, you wait till you come to know 'em, and if you are in the habits of bein' ha'nted by looks, you'll be the wuss ha'nted mortal in this land" (552). Harris piques readers' interest in seeing tackies, like Emma Jane, whose looks prove so disconcerting by closing the first episode of his tale with this commentary. The next installment of the story begins by reminding readers of Emma Jane's haunting looks, because the text's opening sentence describes her as moving "as noiselessly and as swiftly as a ghost" (712). In addition, this first page presents Kemble's pen-and-ink drawing of Emma Jane (see Fig. 1).

Harris's prose and Kemble's picture establish the features that make Emma Jane dowdy and shabby—everything, that is, that makes her tacky. In Harris's tale, Emma Jane seems dowdy in comparison to Helen. Emma Jane's "appearance was uncouth and ungainly," whereas Helen was always well turned out (551). Likewise, Emma Jane's "mean" and "squalid" log cabin home (712) is a far cry from Helen's Boston abode, in which the "easy-chair," "draperies," "bric-à-brac," and other furnishings contribute to an "air of subdued luxury" (541). Kemble's illustrations establish Emma Jane's tackiness not only by contrasting her with posh, fashionable Helen but also by connecting her to other poor white women depicted as tacky. Kemble produced a number of illustrations for an 1891 *Century* essay about textile mill workers in Georgia. In preparation for illustrating this article, Kemble visited mill villages in Augusta, Macon, and Sparta, and in a letter to the editor of the *Atlanta Constitution* written after his drawings appeared in the *Century*, he insisted that the portraits were based on sketches of and notes about the workers he observed in Georgia. But the similarities between his 1891 Georgia cracker (see Fig. 2) and his 1887 Georgia tacky

FIG. 1. Kemble's drawing of Emma Jane Stucky, a Georgia tacky. From Joel Chandler Harris, "Azalia," *Century Illustrated Monthly Magazine*, Sept. 1887, p. 712.

suggest that Kemble wasn't seeing these mill workers with fresh eyes so much as he was reading them according to emerging types that influenced him and that he, in turn, influenced by systematizing and disseminating them through his prodigious artistic output.

Clare de Graffenried, the author of the 1891 essay in which this image appears, has a lot to say about the bad taste on display among the South's poor white women. Declaring that "an unsuitable or grotesque fashion rules the hour," de Graffenried enumerates the fashion faux pas of Georgia's poor white population (490). Some mill women are tacky in the sense of dowdy, donning "that homeliest head-gear, the slat sun-bonnet" and a "style of dress [that] has not altered a seam in thirty years" (489). Other sartorial sins accrue to those who are tacky

FIG. 2. Kemble's drawing of a Georgia cracker. From Clare de Graffenried, "The Georgia Cracker in the Cotton Mills," *Century Illustrated Monthly Magazine*, Feb. 1891, p. 489.

in the sense of cheap or vulgar. De Graffenried takes issue with inexpensive materials, including "cheap worsted goods" and "cheap lace" (489), as well as with garments that are "ill-made, ill-fitting, of cheap texture, and loaded with tawdry trimmings" (490).

De Graffenried's commentary intertwines poor white women's identities and aesthetics. She pours scorn on mill workers' garish apparel while also imputing it to a congenital defect, explaining that their "inborn taste for color breaks out in flaring ribbons, variegated handkerchiefs, and startling vivid raiment visible miles away" (489–90). Contrasting poor white southerners' innate gaudiness with other laboring populations' more refined tastes, de Graffenried writes that "lacking in the crude, impulsive cracker nature is that sense of proportion, that fine instinct for harmony, which dominates the European peasant dress" (490). By reading color choices as class markers and ascribing such preferences to "nature," "instinct," and "inborn taste," de Graffen-ried writes class not simply onto the surface of the poor white body but into its sinews. Readers of the *Century*—"men and women of culture and wealth" (Landers 88)—were neither drawn by Kemble's pen nor described in de Graffenried's prose. This readership could shore up its social status by buying into such depictions because, as sociologist Bever-ley Skeggs explains, "attributing negative value to the working-class is a mechanism for attributing value to the middle-class self (such as making oneself tasteful through judging others to be tasteless)" (118).

By critically appraising the tacky from head to toe—from the top of her "dirty sun-bonnet" (Harris, "Azalia" 551) to the bottoms of her "satin shoes for the dusty highways" (de Graffenried 490)—better-off observers endeavor to represent poor whites' poor taste as the antith-esis of their own tastefulness. To maintain less prosperous people as a negative standard in contrast to which affluent people might define their own good taste, the valences of aesthetic choices and consumer preferences must be flexible. For instance, de Graffenried's essay pres-ents all poor white women as unfashionable even though different generations dress differently. Older women's costumes are decades out of date, "plain," and "spare" (de Graffenried 489). Younger women try too hard to stay au courant, spending between twenty and one hundred dollars each year (when de Graffenried calculates that mill workers' clothing needs could be met for just six dollars per annum) to festoon themselves with "trumpery, pinchbeck jewelry, cotton lace, coarse high-tinted flowers," and other flashy embellishments (490). By spotlighting her brightly colored frills and cheap baubles, de Graffen-ried depicts the poor white woman as a "negative reference point," as Bourdieu phrases it (50), in contrast to which the *Century* reader could define her own refined tastes.

"UNSLING YOUR KODAK": PHOTOGRAPHY AND TASTE

Across the 1890s, changes in the magazine market and advances in image reproduction technologies were among the forces reshaping the literary landscape. In the late 1880s, the *Century* had an average monthly circulation of over 200,000. By the late 1890s, circulation had dwindled to around 150,000 (Mott 475). Competition from less expensive illustrated magazines like *McClure's* and *Munsey's* played a part in this sales dip. Writing in 1895, the manager of the *Century's* art department, W. Lewis Fraser, criticized these newcomers—*McClure's* was founded in 1893, *Munsey's* in 1889—by linking low cover prices with low-quality illustrations. Fraser explained that while the publishers of the "numberless cheap illustrated periodicals" flooding the market were embracing half-tone photoengraving, their foremost concern at the *Century* was "getting as near as possible to the original," regardless of cost (479). Fraser was thinking about the fidelity with which various printing methods reproduced original works of art, but his observation also speaks to what the new pictorial options meant for the practice of illustrating works of fiction. Getting as near as possible to a fiction writer's portrayal of a character might well mean using a drawing, not a photograph, to depict that figure. The drawing and the story, each self-evidently the product of an artist's pen, work together to uphold the "willing suspension of disbelief" upon which imaginative works depend (Coleridge 6). By contrast, a photograph is, in the words of Roland Barthes, "the absolute Particular, . . . the Occasion, the Encounter, the Real, in its indefatigable expression" (4). Such inexorable realness—whether distractingly different from the writer's representation or uncannily similar to it—has the power to undercut fiction's verisimilitude.

In 1896, *The Peterson Magazine of Illustrated Literature* published a story that demonstrates how closely interwoven the adjectival and nominal meanings of "tacky" were by the end of the Gilded Age. *Peterson*, a women's magazine that enjoyed a half-century run (1842–1898), both showcases and discusses visual culture. The January 1896 installment of the magazine includes articles about etching, painting, and other fine arts and abounds with images: a total of eighty-seven illustrations appear across the issue's 112 pages. But May Lou Zoll's short story "Susanna" is not illustrated. "Susanna" engages with the emerging practice of amateur photography by arming one of the story's central characters with a Kodak camera.[3] Yet the story's shutterbug refuses to take the picture his fiancée exhorts him to capture: a snapshot of a poor white girl who is identified as a tacky.

At the start of "Susanna," Frank Jasper and his fiancée stop during a bike ride along Tidewater Virginia's back roads to speak to a poor white girl. Frank, who "was an artist," declared the girl "a caryatid in rags!" (Zoll 84). The image is apt; like a sculpted female figure taking the place of a column or a pillar to provide architectural support, Susanna upholds the bourgeoisie by buttressing its members' perceptions of themselves. Miss Bateler, Frank's fiancée, reacts to his "enthusiastic" response to Susanna by pouring cold water on it (84). Whereas Frank characterizes Susanna as an archeological treasure from the classical world, Miss Bateler recasts the girl as a zoologist's specimen, identifying her as "a native of the Virginia wilds, a specimen of the genus 'tacky'" (84).

The pair's divergent responses represent what Allan Sekula has described as "the honorific and repressive poles of portrait practice" (7). Bateler frames Susanna as an oddity whose photograph would help round out Frank's archive: "Unsling your kodak; this scene will make a valuable addition to your collection" (Zoll 84). Knowing that Susanna's beauty is what caught Frank's eye, Bateler tries to "disillusion" him about the girl's charms by underscoring her class status (84). When Frank asks Bateler to define the word tacky, she replies, "I cannot better explain its meaning than by saying that the girl . . . is its personification" (85). Bateler uses Frank's camera to mediate his relation to Susanna. Defined as a personification rather than a person, Susanna appears through the viewfinder as a body that serves "to establish and delimit the terrain of the *other*, to define both the *generalized look*—the typology—and the *contingent instance*" (Sekula 7).

The tale's poor white characters have poor taste, which lends credence to my contention that the two meanings of "tacky" were interconnected by the 1890s. Frank and Bateler attend a local social gathering as spectators because Bateler anticipates that "it will be fun to see" the "dreadfully 'tacky'" attendees (Zoll 85). Partygoers' outfits—"country boys in cowhide shoes, and girls with black gutta percha bracelets" and "red and purple silk handkerchiefs" (86)—fulfill Bateler's expectations by conforming to classed conventions: inexpensive materials (sturdy cowhide in place of calfskin or patent leather for the men and gutta percha rather than jet among the women) and bright colors make tackies' togs simultaneously too shabby and too showy. What do Frank and Bateler wear to the fete? The narrator does not tell us. Like other well-to-do characters in late-nineteenth-century magazine fiction, they establish their tastefulness not by making good fashion choices but by critiquing poor people's aesthetic failures. As "amused spectators," Frank and Bateler are there to see rather than to be seen (86).

Zoll's tale seems tailor-made for illustrations. For one thing, the rustic soirée Frank and Bateler attend epitomizes the stock-in-trade of local color writers and their illustrators, who often offered up quaint bucolic spectacles as foils for "the historical centrality, subjective sophistication, and full modernity of elite and aspiring urban readers" (Glazener 201). For another thing, photographs presented as Frank's Kodak-captured shots could do double duty by revealing not only characters' likenesses but also Frank's photography skills. Artwork of this sort would be in keeping with the magazine's graphics, because roughly 40 percent of the illustrations in the January 1896 issue of *Peterson* are half-tone reproductions of photographic portraits. But, in fact, neither Frank's photographs nor the magazine's realistic photoengravings would be likely to capture the tackiness Zoll describes. Cartoonists like Kemble took liberties with their subjects, emphasizing or even adding details. To depict Zoll's rural partygoers, Kemble might have combined some of his trademark sartorial signifiers of poverty—wide-brimmed hats, for instance—with exaggerated renderings of details from the story— maybe cowhide shoes with outrageously piebald patterns—to depict these Virginia tackies and his other poor white southerners as kissing cousins. But *Peterson*'s January 1896 issue includes only one cartoon.

The move toward realistic representation presented new hurdles to illustrating social class. Gutta percha jewelry might look like jet in photographs. Susanna, pointedly described as one of the "'high-looking' *low* girls," might look too similar to Bateler (Zoll 85). Even more important than these considerations, however, is the fact that illustrations are no longer essential for depicting tackiness. Interweaving poor people's identities and aesthetics positions tackiness as an inborn trait. As a "personification" of the term "tacky," as Bateler calls her, Susanna bears a stigmatized identity regardless of her attire (85).

"A GLANCE AT HIS PICTURE REVEALS HIS PRINCIPAL CHARACTERISTICS": FROM BAD TASTE TO BAD GENES

Both the figure of the tacky and the short stories that brought such poor white archetypes into parlors across the nation were on the wane by the end of the nineteenth century. The *OED* cites Zoll's story as the last instance of "tacky" being used as a noun designating poor white people in the South. Writing in the "Editor's Study" for *Harper's New Monthly Magazine* a few months after "Susanna" came out in *Peterson*, Charles Dudley Warner observed that local color fiction was no longer in demand. Identifying "'views' of scenery and of costume" as some of the stories' foremost charms, Warner emphasized local color's visual logics (961). But he also suggested that, "deceived by the striking appearance" of the genre's picturesque characters and colorful locales, readers overestimated local color's literary merits (Warner 961). The striking appearances of tackies, crackers, mountaineers, and other poor white southern types also deceived readers of *Harper's*, the *Century*, and other illustrated monthly magazines by habituating them to visual paradigms that construed class differences as "inborn" traits—de Graffenried's term (489)—that manifested themselves in outward appearances.

When middle- and upper-class white people unslung their cameras to photograph poor whites at the end of the century, some of them began looking to capture not their poor taste but their "pauper and criminal tendencies" (Blackmar 499). The year after Zoll's story appeared in *Peterson*, an article focusing on poor white Kansans came out in the *American Journal of Sociology*. In his essay, sociologist Frank W. Blackmar treats the nine photographs he includes as windows onto poor people's "laziness" (493), "stupidity" (494), "dissipation" (496), and other defects. "A glance at his picture reveals his principal characteristics," Blackmar writes of one man, demonstrating his belief that the body—in particular, the face—evinced one's intellect, work ethic, morality, and other character traits (493). As Shawn Michelle Smith explains, the nineteenth-century photographic archive gave rise to "a model of subjectivity in which exterior appearance was imagined to reflect interior essence" (4). Of course, photographs illustrating essays like Blackmar's differ in many ways from pen-and-ink drawings published alongside short stories. One important difference is that while writers and artists depicting tackies in magazines like the *Century* aimed to represent poor white people's aesthetic peculiarity, scholars like Blackmar sought to diagnose the causes of this population's "social pathology" (Blackmar 500).

But fiction writers may have helped lay the groundwork for this subsequent response to poor white people. In local color stories and in eugenic analyses, authors shore up middle- and upper-class white people's status—their tastefulness in local colorists' tales, their intelligence and uprightness in Blackmar's essay—by means of their unflattering representations of poor white people. In Zoll's story, for instance, Bateler's motivation for slighting Susanna seems to be that, as new money—one of the "bottom rails which came on top and set up the yellow god on the ruins of the old aristocracy," as the narrator describes her (Zoll 85)—she is uneasy about her own social position. A New South upstart in Tidewater Virginia, the symbolic heartland of the Old South's aristocracy, Bateler accuses Susanna of lacking "refinement" because it is precisely this trait that she and other nouveaux riches are regularly tittered at for being deficient in (85). By dilating on the brightly colored garments, shabby sunbonnets, and flashy trinkets that made tackies tacky—by the lights of elite chroniclers' aesthetics, anyway—Zoll, de Graffenried, Harris, and other Gilded Age writers presented poor white southerners as foils for the identities their readers wished to claim for themselves.

NOTES

1. In his local color collection *In Ole Virginia* (1887), for example, Thomas Nelson Page repeatedly jabs at such upwardly mobile whites, whom his characters derisively call half-strainers.

2. The *OED* identifies a letter published in the *Century* in September 1888 as the first instance of the noun form of tacky. In fact, Harris introduced the term to readers of the *Century* more than a year before. The first serial installment of "Azalia," published in August 1887, offers a detailed rendering of "piney-woods 'tackies'" (Harris 549).

3. The introduction of the handheld Kodak No. 1 in 1888 heralded the start of amateur photography. In 1895, the year before Zoll published "Susanna," Kodak brought to market a pocket camera weighing just one pound.

WORKS CITED

Barthes, Roland. *Camera Lucida: Reflections on Photography*. Hill and Wang, 1981.

Blackmar, Frank W. "The Smoky Pilgrims." *American Journal of Sociology*, vol. 2, Jan. 1897, pp. 485–500.

Bourdieu, Pierre. *Distinction: A Social Critique of the Judgement of Taste*. Routledge, 2010.

Coleridge, Samuel Taylor. *Biographia Literaria*, edited by James Engell and W. Jackson Bate. Vol. 2, Princeton UP, 1983.

Cook, Jon. "Culture, Class and Taste." *Cultural Studies and the Working Class*, edited by Sally R. Munt, Cassell, 2000, pp. 97–112.

De Graffenried, Clare. "The Georgia Cracker in the Cotton Mills." *Century Illustrated Monthly Magazine*, Feb. 1891, pp. 483–98.

Farmer-Kaiser, Mary. "Reconstructing Amanda Stone: Made and Remade by Marriage, War, and Memoir in Nineteenth-Century Louisiana." *Louisiana History: The Journal of the Louisiana Historical Association*, vol. 56, no. 4, 2015, pp. 389–413.

Faulkner, William. *Absalom, Absalom!* 1936. Reprint. Vintage, 1990.

Faust, Drew Gilpin. "Introduction." *Brokenburn: The Journal of Kate Stone, 1861–1868*, edited by John Q. Anderson, Louisiana State UP, 1995, pp. xxix–xl.

Fraser, W. Lewis. Open Letters, "A Word about the Century's Pictures." *Century Illustrated Monthly Magazine*, Jan. 1895, pp. 478–79.

Glazener, Nancy. *Reading for Realism: The History of a U.S. Literary Institution, 1850–1910*. Duke UP, 1997.

Harris, Joel Chandler. "Azalia." *Century Illustrated Monthly Magazine*, Aug.–Oct. 1887, pp. 541+.

Harris, Julia Collier. *The Life and Letters of Joel Chandler Harris*. Houghton Mifflin, 1918.

Kemble, E. W. Letter to the Editor of the *Atlanta Constitution*. 10 June 1891. Century Company records, Manuscripts and Archives Division, The New York Public Library, archives.nypl.org/mss/504#c1146810.

Landers, James. "Century." *Encyclopedia of American Journalism*, edited by Stephen L. Vaughn, Routledge, 2008, p. 88.

Mott, Frank Luther. *A History of American Magazines, 1865–1885*. Harvard UP, 1938.

Sekula, Allan. "The Body and the Archive." *October*, vol. 39, Winter 1986, pp. 3–64.

Skeggs, Beverley. *Class, Self, Culture*. Routledge, 2004.

Smith, Shawn Michelle. *American Archives: Gender, Race, and Class in Visual Culture.* Princeton UP, 1999.

Stone, Kate. *Brokenburn: The Journal of Kate Stone, 1861–1868,* edited by John Q. Anderson, Louisiana State UP, 1995.

"Tacky, *n.* and *adj.*" *Oxford English Dictionary Online,* Oxford UP, www.oed.com/viewdictionaryentry/Entry/11125.

Warner, Charles Dudley. "Editor's Study." *Harper's New Monthly Magazine,* May 1896, pp. 959–64.

Zoll, May Lou. "Susanna." *The Peterson Magazine of Illustrated Literature,* Jan. 1896, pp. 84–91.

THE TACKY STUFF OF PRODUCTION, ENTERTAINMENT, AND VIOLENCE

PINE TAR AND THE AMERICAN SOUTH

JOE T. CARSON

*T*he meanings of tacky prove to be sticky: the earliest definition of tacky appears as an adjective to describe a substance "slightly sticky or adhesive; said of gum, glue, or varnish nearly dry." Nearly one hundred years later, tacky emerges as an adjective meaning "in poor taste" or "vulgar," and then later as a noun referring to poor whites in the South. While the pages of the *OED* manage to keep these definitions of tacky neatly separated, the pages of American literature prove to be less successful in heading off the congealing process: the slightly sticky seems rather vulgar and perhaps inseparable from the characterizations and connotations of "poor whites." Tacky—as pejorative for taste and class, adjective for viscous fluids—makes particular sense when we read the material history of pine tar production in the American South.

Pine tar, a very tacky substance, precedes and informs the application of tacky as a metaphor for taste and signifier for class. An important product for the southern economy, tar found many applications, from shoring up ships to covering wounds on livestock. This essay will explore the use of pine tar in two distinct ways: tarring and feathering and the production of tar on plantations and shipyards. Reading Mark Twain's *Adventures of Huckleberry Finn* (1884), I explore how tar becomes a critical component in swindling and entertainment between poor whites. Twain literalizes the connection between tacky substances and tacky taste; Twain makes the connections between the various definitions of tacky the *OED* does not. However, beginning with Frederick Douglass's *Narrative of the Life of Frederick Douglass, an American Slave* (1845), we see a complicated material history wherein tar demarcates the line between freedom and slavery, mobility and imprisonment.[1] Douglass's labor and experience with tar explain why Twain's poor white characters use tar to dehumanize each other.

Certainly, for both Douglass and Twain, tar is a violent material, simultaneously signifying and performing violence toward marginalized, raced, and classed bodies. But reading Douglass alongside Twain places critical pressure on what it means to use tacky in relation to southerners and specifically "poor white" southerners. While the sojourners of the big river make ample use of tar—and they find tarring each other rather entertaining—Douglass articulates pine tar as a key component of the plantation economy. This explains why Twain's poor white characters readily use tar to punish and challenge the humanity of their victims: to tar is to evoke the dehumanizing effects of racialization under chattel slavery. Tacky becomes not only about tacky taste but a vulgar rearticulation of Blackness for entertainment.

The production and trade of tar was an integral part of the plantation system of slavery and the southern economy. Tar was made from burning split pine trees in large earthen kilns. Digging shallow pits up to twenty-four feet wide, according to Robert Outland, enslaved labor would place split pine in the pit and stack it up into a pyramid shape. The workers would then cover the entire wood pile with clay, leaving a small hole at the top, and light a fire from the top of the kiln. As the wood burned, tar ran out of the bottom into a gutter.

Described as the South's oldest industrial production, for early southern economies, pine tar was an essential and profitable commodity, so much so that tar and pitch weathered the 1837 economic crisis. Tar (and turpentine) production remained a constant, in stark contrast to the boom-and-bust cycle of cotton. Tar was a major export to England to maintain their naval stores as well as an important component of domestic ship production. As Outland notes, tar and pitch were produced primarily for nautical use: "to reduce decay, seamen slathered heavy applications of tar on the standing rigging that held masts in place and painted lighter coats on the running rigging used for raising and adjusting sails" (6). In addition to being used as grease, tar was applied to fence posts for preservation and to animal wounds to prevent infection. As Bryan Wagner argues, tar was important "not only to maritime commercial infrastructure but also to the international trade in cotton, sugar, and slaves." Wagner writes that "tar was used in places like North Carolina to pay debts and rent, and it was also used in the Atlantic trade networks by people like Edward Salter, a merchant in Bath who in 1734 had his brigantine packed with tar to be exchanged directly for a cargo of 'young negroes'" (56). The tacky liquid not only shored up ships but was also used in most things agricultural; enslaved labor produced tar, but tar itself seemingly procured enslaved individuals as a form of capital when necessary.

As we will see with Frederick Douglass, tar has a material and economic history involving the plantation and chattel slavery. In the US South, it is too simple to only associate tar with tacky taste or poor whites. If Twain provides the clear association between the tacky substance of tar and tacky as a metaphor for taste, then Douglass's narrative provides the critical material history of why tar functions so well as a means to dehumanize. It is not only that tar is readily available in the South but that it has particularly pernicious connotations for Black labor in the plantation system.

OF GARDENS AND SHIPYARDS

Tar functions as a critical component in *Narrative of the Life of Frederick Douglass, an American Slave* by delineating the line between freedom and enslavement. Here, tar still signals the violence of enslavement; however, tar in the plantations and shipyards does not align with conceptions of taste, or poor whites, as it does in Twain's river story. The earliest chapters recall Douglass's childhood and detail his introduction to the system of chattel slavery. Douglass's early narrative emphasizes the process of learning his status as an enslaved person and the precarity in being subject to violence. Scholars have often discussed these pivotal moments by reading the whipping scene of Aunt Hester. From Saidiya Hartman to Fred Moten, the moment of Douglass witnessing Hester's punishment, and her punishment itself, reverberates through scholarship. There is, however, another seemingly passive incident, involving pine tar and the garden, that mark Douglass's childhood education in what it meant to be a slave.

Describing his introduction to the system of slavery, Douglass writes, "It was the blood-stained gate, the entrance to the hell of slavery, through which I was about to pass" (18). As it turns out, the gate was stained not only with blood but with tar too. The plantation boasted a well-cultivated garden, apparently well-kept enough to warrant visitors from surrounding cities. Boasting "fruits of almost every description," the garden's "excellent fruit was quite a temptation to the hungry swarm of boys, as well as the older slaves" (25). After several attempts to prevent the garden from being pillaged, the planter's "last and most successful [attempt] was that of tarring his fence all around; after which, if a slave was caught with tar upon his person, it was deemed sufficient proof that he had either been into the garden or had tried to get in it. In either case, he was severely whipped by the chief gardener. This plan worked well; the slaves became as fearful of tar as of the lash. They seemed to realize the impossibility of touching tar without being defiled" (25). The plantation garden, sufficiently tarred, becomes a perverse Garden of Eden, and rather than eating from the fruit only to be cast out, it is the desire to eat fruit and subsequently be marked by tar that signals that one is an enslaved person. If the beating of Aunt Hester reveals the lack of authority Douglass has over his own body, the tarred garden exposes the garden as a plantation. In other words, Douglass's introduction to slavery depends on recasting the pastoral as not for his enjoyment but as a space that depends on his coerced labor to build. In his childhood naivete, Douglass assumed the pastoral belonged to both him and the plantation owner; the tar marks the distinction between free and enslaved, pastoral and plantation.

In Douglass's narrative, the planter weaponized the tacky substance to further separate the enslaved laborers from the products they produced. In the garden, the tar becomes a distinguishing marker between free and enslaved, and this is particularly pernicious because

the tar would have been made by enslaved persons on the plantation. As I discussed above, tar was an important product for southern
economies, and the Wye Plantation (where Douglass lived as a boy)
undoubtedly produced its own pine tar both for agricultural uses and
to maintain the sloop, a ship used to transport persons and goods.[2]

The tarred garden creates several significant associations: first,
it creates a distinction between those free to enjoy the garden and
those disallowed to enter the garden. In other words, tar distinguishes
between free and not. Second, the tar as a sticky substance marks only
Black bodies as those illegally entering. The overseers look for tar on
enslaved persons, and presumably white guests would not touch the
tar, or, if they did, it would not be cause for punishment. Third, since
Black bodies were those in charge of creating the tar and applying it,
this application creates a violent association with the production of
tar and one unique to tar. The equivalent would be if finding cotton
on one's person would be cause for violence that reifies the precarity
of the enslaved person's position. Tar becomes a material metaphor for
the autopoiesis of the plantation complex and chattel slavery—a strange
loop of Blackness, enslavement, and violence wherein each becomes
a justification for the others. The tackiness of tar highlights how the
plantation strives to rearticulate production as cause for enslavement.

Tar reappears later in Douglass's adult life and again marks the
distinction between free and enslaved. When Douglass lives in Baltimore with a new enslaver, he recalls watching the ships in the bay.
Envious of the ships' freedom and mobility, Douglass describes the
scene: "Our house stood within a few rods of the Chesapeake Bay,
whose broad bosom was ever white with sails from every quarter of
the habitable globe. Those beautiful vessels, robed in the purest white,
so delightful to the eye of the freemen, were to me so many shrouded
ghosts, to terrify and torment me with thoughts of my wretched condition" (59). While critics have rightly focused on Douglass's association
between mobility and whiteness, tar is the crucial component that
enables these ships to operate in the water. White sails may indeed
catch and harness the air, but the tar seals the ship and makes it water-
tight. Tar, then, marks the distinction between floating and water-
logged, mobile or sunk, free or dead.

Though Douglass's description focuses on the sails, Douglass also knew firsthand how the ships were constructed and sealed. Thematically, *Narrative of the Life* offers two specific ways of resistance: violence and writing. Between Douglass's fight with the "slave breaker" Covey and the focus on developing writing skills (Douglas even practices writing on the ships themselves), it is easy to overlook Douglass' skill and training in the trade of caulking. But because Douglass is familiar with these practices, it changes the way we should read his descriptions of both the ships and the tar applied to the garden fence. Shortly after his arrival in Baltimore, Douglass was allowed to hire his labor and work in the shipyards. Describing his tasks, Douglass lists the common commands shouted at him. Of the many, he lists a command specific to tar: "I say, darky, blast your eyes, why don't you heat up some pitch?" (80). And once Douglass develops a specific trade within the shipyard, he becomes a caulker—the person that applies tar to the ships. After being violently attacked at the first shipyard, Douglass worked for a different one, and he writes, "There I was immediately set to calking, and very soon learned the art of using my mallet and irons" (83). He continues, "In the course of one year from the time I left Mr. Gardner's, I was able to command the highest wages given to the most experienced calkers" (83). Before Douglass was an abolitionist and a writer, he professionally heated and applied tar in order to seal ships.

In some sense, Douglass's time working with tar also begins his education in economics; in the shipyard, he learns letters and simultaneously realizes his labor generates income, which he is not allowed to keep. When Douglass worked as a caulker in the shipyards, he was paid for his time; however, at the end of the week, Douglass had to pay his enslaver the earnings. Keying into this moment, Chad Luck argues that his loss of wages becomes a significant point in Douglass's critique of slavery. Luck writes, "But handing over the fruits of his labor, week after week, recalls the discontentment he feels when considering the slave traders' theft of African slaves. Here again he is forced to contend with an unequal exchange and with the stinging sense of entitlement denied" (170). The theft of wages earned represents, in Luck's words and from Douglass's viewpoint, a "perversion of a reciprocal economy" (170). While this is certainly correct, the focus on wages misses the perversion of production: namely, while slavery is the perversion of exchange value (in that Douglass cannot keep the value abstracted from his labor), the tarring of ships corrupts the use value—tar transforms from mere product to a poignant symbol of enslavement.

BURNING STRAY DOGS; OR, TO TROD THE BOARDS

In *The Adventures of Huckleberry Finn*, tar appears most often in the vigilante act of tarring and feathering. In true Twain fashion, tarring operates as part of a larger game of confidence between poor whites, and as much as tarring and feathering might vaguely concern some notion of justice, it is equally a point of entertainment.[3] As a staple of backwoods entertainment, and often in response to bad entertainment, tarring for Twain goes hand in hand with tacky taste. Furthermore, on the big river and its small towns, tarring highlights anxieties over and intersections between masculinity, locality, and class. As John Mayfield argues, "a rivalry for dominance, physical or otherwise, is present in every form of Southern humor, and it does not matter if the style is rough and woodsy or refined and urbane. The stakes are high: manhood itself" (xxi). To put an even finer point on Mayfield: the stakes are about white manhood. In the hinterlands of the Mississippi, tarring marks the difference.

Twain populates his backwoods Mississippi River communities not with confidence men and victims but poor whites competing to swindle each other with violent repercussions for the loser. The self-proclaimed king and duke first meet each other while escaping a mob attempting to tar and feather the duke. After swindling the town with a "little temperance revival," the duke awoke to an angry mob: he was told "the people was getherin' on the quiet with their dogs and horses, and they'd be along pretty soon and give me 'bout an hour's start, and then run me down if they could; and if they got me they'd tar and feather me and ride me on a rail" (833). Intriguingly, the townspeople not only offer the confidence man a head start but also propose a conditional punishment: namely, *if* they catch the duke, then they would tar him. As Rachel Pollock writes, "Some perpetrators appear to have viewed it as all in good fun, like pelting rotten fruit at some loser locked up in the stocks . . . whereas others approached it as a serious torture: heat the tar to boiling, hold the unfortunate offender down, pour it into the face, over the hair, open the mouth." She adds, "At pine tar's melting point of 60°C (140 F), a victim develops first-degree burns within three seconds of exposure" (136). Tarring has the potential to cross the line from entertainment to very violent within a few degrees.

While, during the late eighteenth and early nineteenth centuries, tar and feathers might be used politically, Twain's backwoods pair tar with taste rather than politics. Early American tarring practices were often associated with political principals. As Benjamin Irvin argues, revolutionary organizers utilized the practice of "tar-and-feathers" as "a means of both distinguishing friend from foe and asserting one's allegiance to the cause of liberty" (225). And by the early nineteenth century, Irvin continues, "In slaveholding areas of the country, tar-and-feathers was increasingly used against 'Negro criminals' and antislavery advocates" (225). But for Twain, there is a serendipitous relation between tar and tackiness: namely, the tackier the performance, the closer the proximity of tar.

In the competition of swindling and dodging, the tar bucket undergirds the performances the king and duke offer local towns. After a failed Shakespeare performance, the king and duke offer an even tackier routine: the Royal Nonesuch Show—fifty cents, women and children not allowed. Following the elaborate introduction to a packed house, the king enters: "a-prancing out on all fours, naked; and he was painted all over, ring-streaked-and-stripped, all sorts of colors" (854). To Huck's surprise, "The people most killed themselves laughing" and called for two encore performances (854). However, after the audience realizes that is the only act for the evening, they feel cheated. One audience member declares, "we are sold—mighty badly sold. But we don't want to be the laughing stock of this whole town. . . . What we want, is to get out of here quiet, and talk this show up, and sell the *rest* of the town. Then we'll all be in the same boat" (855). In the game of confidence, the audience has lost to the king and duke, for now. And if they are to lose, they don't want to be the only losers.

On the final night, Huck notices the audience has brought a few items along with them to the show: "I smelt sickly eggs by the barrel, and rotten cabbages, and such things; and if I know the signs of a dead cat being around, and I bet I do, there was sixty-four of them went in" (856). Escaping even before offering a performance, the king and the duke had anticipated the duped audience might be coming for revenge. The duke declares, "Greenhorns, flatheads! *I* knew the first house would keep mum and let the rest of the town get roped in; and I knew they'd lay for us the third night, and consider it was *their* turn now" (856). The duke and the king escape the communal wrath and being pelted with rotten eggs and dead cats, but the two scoundrels won't dodge the tar bucket forever.

Furthermore, it cannot be a coincidence that the response to these performances involves tarring: the threat of tarring and feathering is the materialized end of a long line of increasingly tacky performances. The king and the duke, from Twain's descriptions, fit the pejorative bill for tackiness: the king dances naked only after the audience does not care for the failed, low-brow (and inaccurate) versions of Shakespeare. Along the river, Twain couples the violent, extra-legal uses of tar and tackiness with taste and sensibility. In other words, the king and duke may very well be the progenitive figures of tacky's association with poor white taste.

But it is not only tasteless performers that fall victim to mob wrath along the river, and the use of tar products as violent entertainment keys into the problematic intersection of masculinity, locality, and what it means to be human in the backwoods South. Specifically, the townspeople spare some turpentine in order to burn alive stray dogs to pass the time. As Huck travels the river, he notices a severe dearth of entertainment in the small "one horse" towns. Aside from bartering chaw from each other, the other sole amusement involves torturing animals. Huck states, "There couldn't anything wake them up all over, and make them happy all over, like a dog-fight—unless it might be putting turpentine on a stray dog and setting fire to him" (847). Much like tar and pitch, turpentine is a product harvested predominately from pine trees and was a key component to not only naval stores but the southern economy. That the townspeople use turpentine to burn stray dogs clearly speaks to a rough sensibility, but it is significant that they choose to torture animals. The act of tarring or burning with turpentine reveals the stakes of backwoods masculinity as a category entitled to violence.

In the same town that burns dogs for fun, the townspeople call for a lynching—again, not for justice but for entertainment. The lynching, however, does not come to fruition as their intended victim rebukes the mob, and the chastisement reveals the stakes of masculinity at play in these attacks. When a local drunk, Old Man Boggs, threatens to kill Colonel Sherburn, and after the drunkard screams obscenities outside the store front, Sherburn steps out and declares: "I'm tired of this; but I'll endure it till one o'clock. Till one o'clock, mind—no longer. If you open your mouth against me only once, after that time, you can't travel so far but I will find you" (848). True to his word, when Boggs continues his threats after one o'clock, Sherburn exits the house, kills Boggs in the street, throws the pistol on the ground, and leaves. Sherburn offers the same temporal delay the poorer residents offered the duke— the offender has a certain temporal window and then will be hunted. Sherburn, being of a higher class, kills without impunity.

Shortly after Boggs's death, the townspeople call for Sherburn to be lynched, and they march to his home, "snatching down every clothes-line they come to" in order to hang him (850). (It seems with mob violence, objects at hand—clothes-lines and turpentine—serve best). But Sherburn reprimands them, shotgun in hand: "The idea of *you* lynching anybody! It's amusing. The idea of you thinking you had pluck enough to lynch a *man!* Because you're brave enough to tar and feather poor friendless cast-out women that come along here, did that make you think you had grit enough to lay your hands on a *man?*" (850–51). Tar and turpentine are fine implements for women and dogs but not enough for a "*man*," and perhaps the mob isn't brave enough to tar any woman or animal but only cast-out women and stray dogs. Gritless and defeated, the mob departs and leaves Sherburn alone, and we learn that the entertainment of tarring has specific parameters: namely, it is easiest to tar the unknown and unprotected.[4]

While Twain draws out the issue of masculinity with the scene of Colonel Sherburn, Twain exposes how tarring shapes conceptions of humanity, or otherwise, when the king and the duke finally meet their end. Regaling Tom with his adventures on the river, Huck is interrupted by a "rush of people with torches, and an awful whooping and yelling, and banging tin pans and blowing horns"—the mob that finally caught the king and the duke. Huck narrates: "as they went by I see they had the king and the duke astraddle of a rail—that is, I knowed it *was* the king and the duke, though they was all over tar and feathers, and didn't look like nothing in the world that was human—just looked like a couple of monstrous big soldier-plumes" (912). The act of being tarred and feathered, again, teases the line between human and other, human and monstrous animal. Twain renders Huck's speech in the past tense; it is significant Huck "knowed" that the bodies on the rail "*was*" the king and then duke. The act of tarring has stripped the two swindlers of their identities—their false identities of the deceased's brothers and of their false historical titles.

The effects of tar on their status as human proves profound: Huck suggests the two no longer "look like nothing in the world that was human" (912). Here, the act of tarring and feathering evokes the larger social and economic constructions of tar; namely, tar is inseparable from the history of slave labor and reification. To tar is to harness this systemic violence from the plantation, and as Twain suggests, it is this act of dehumanization, through chattel slavery and/or extralegal violence, that southern society finds its power and entertainment. Furthermore, that tarring serves as or in response to entertainment, we see Twain's text as a key moment in which tackiness as an indicator of taste and as a materiality merge on the page.

Douglass's descriptions of tar reveal the racial and economic legacies of "tacky" in the South. In Maryland plantations and shipyards, tar marks the limits between free and enslaved while the tacky applicant greases the wheel, both figuratively and literally, of the slave-plantation economy. Historically, these practical functions of tar also operated on the Mississippi River to keep steamboats and the Delta economy afloat. But Twain uses tar not to distinguish between free and enslaved but as a weapon in a game of class, confidence, and taste. It is no surprise that a product so integral to enslavement becomes a key prop in dehumanizing rubes and con men.

But Douglass's early experiences with tar also reveal the paradox of production when it comes to tar and tackiness. The tar-coated-garden weaponized pine tar against the very laborers that were forced to produce it; to touch tar (or to be associated with the products one produced, broadly speaking) was to be deserving of punishment and to be less than human. In the same way, tacky taste becomes an equally damning association; that is, to produce something tacky is to be tacky. Much like the stickiness of tar, it becomes harder and harder to disassociate tackiness once it is recognized as such. This seems as true for contemporary southern culture as it did for Twain's coterie of confidence men. Tacky is hard to scrub off.

NOTES

1. I purposely avoid Joel Chandler Harris's "The Wonderful Tar Baby Story," chiefly because Bryan Wagner already provides a brilliant political reading of the tar baby narrative and also argues "The Tar Baby" narrative exists narratologically among many different cultures inside and outside the US. While Harris's rendition may be tied to the South, the story itself proves more complicated.

2. See Elizabeth Pruitt's "Transatlantic Roots" (2017).

3. While tarring, historically and in novels, often did not end in death, there is a pernicious history of lynching in the South being a form of entertainment. See Sandy Alexandre's *The Properties of Violence* (2012), especially chapter 1.

4. A similar scene occurs in *The Adventures of Tom Sawyer*: "The villagers had a strong desire to tar-and-feather Injun Joe and ride him on a rail, for body-snatching, but so formidable was his character that nobody could be found who was willing to take the lead in the matter" (490).

WORKS CITED

Alexandre, Sandy. *The Properties of Violence: Claims to Ownership in Representations of Lynching.* U of Mississippi P, 2012.

Douglass, Frederick. *My Bondage and My Freedom.* Library of America, 1994.

———. *Narrative of the Life of Frederick Douglass, an American Slave.* Library of America, 1994.

Hartman, Saidiya. *Scenes of Subjection: Terror, Slavery, and Self-Making in Nineteenth-Century America.* Oxford UP, 1997.

Hirsh, James. "Covert Appropriations of Shakespeare: Three Case Studies." *Papers on Language and Literature: A Journal for Scholars and Critics of Language and Literature,* vol. 43, no. 1, 2007, pp. 45–67.

Irvin, Benjamin H. "Tar, Feathers, and the Enemies of American Liberties, 1768–1776." *New England Quarterly*, vol. 76, 2003.

Luck, Chad. *The Body of Property: Antebellum American Fiction and the Phenomenology of Possession.* Fordham UP, 2015.

Mayfield, John. *Counterfeit Gentlemen: Manhood and Humor in the Old South.* UP of Florida, 2009.

Moten, Fred. *In the Break: The Aesthetics of the Black Tradition.* U of Minnesota P, 2003.

Outland, Robert B. *Tapping the Pines: The Naval Stores Industry in the American South.* Louisiana State UP, 2004.

Pollock, Rachel E. "How to Tar and Feather a Thief." *Fourth Genre: Explorations in Nonfiction*, vol. 14, no. 2, 2012, pp. 133–46.

Pruitt, Elizabeth. "Transatlantic Roots: Cultural Uses of Plants at the Wye House Plantation." *Atlantic Crossings in the Wake of Frederick Douglass: Archaeology, Literature, and Spatial Culture*, edited by Mark P. Leone and Lee M. Jenkins, Brill, 2017, pp. 3–20.

Twain, Mark. *The Adventures of Huckleberry Finn.* In *The Unabraded Mark Twain*, edited by Lawrence Teacher, Running Press, 1976, pp. 747–956.

———. *The Adventures of Tom Sawyer.* In *The Unabraded Mark Twain*, edited by Lawrence Teacher, Running Press, 1976, pp. 437–586.

Wagner, Bryan. *The Tar Baby: A Global History.* Princeton UP, 2017.

TACKY MOUNTAIN COUSINS

THE RISE AND CONTINUING DEMISE OF THE APPALACHIAN STEREOTYPE IN SOUTHERN MOUNTAIN LITERATURE

ELISABETH AIKEN

*M*ention the southern Appalachian Mountains in virtually any venue, and you're bound to hear mention of someone's vacation to Gatlinburg, Tennessee. This town outside Great Smoky Mountains National Park has continually turned a profit off not only its proximity to the national park but also the well-known and widely accepted stereotype of the tacky mountaineer. The juxtaposition of Gatlinburg's crassness just past the gates of the national park embodies much of the contradiction inherent within the Appalachian region and begs the questions addressed in this essay: how and why did the southern Appalachian region, with its steep slopes and lush growth, seemingly impenetrable to the non-native traveler or writer of days past, spark exotic, non-normative myths and legends that recent years responded?

The answer to that question is rooted in the written record of the region's history and is inextricably intertwined with Appalachia's geography and natural resources. According to Ronald Lewis, "The idea of Appalachia as a homogeneous region physically, culturally, and economically isolated from mainstream America has its genesis in fiction" (22); indeed, scholars have traced the negative stereotype of the barefoot and ignorant hillbilly back to the earliest colonial writing regarding the region, and Appalachian stereotypes follow in a long line of typifying nonelite populations. Early writing about the South focuses on negative impressions of its (white settler) inhabitants while also exalting its abundance of resources. William Byrd II provides us with perhaps the most well-known example. Born in Virginia in 1674 and educated in London, Byrd ambitiously sought the governorship of Virginia; stymied, he served for decades on the Virginia Governor's Council and acted as lead Virginian in an expedition (along with a group of North Carolinians, led by Edward Moseley) to survey the boundary dividing the colonies of Virginia and North Carolina. Byrd was well-aware of the economic value of the land he was surveying, and his interest in the commodification of the land is reflected in his subsequent purchase of twenty thousand acres in the Dan River Valley of North Carolina. Byrd wrote two texts based on this expedition: one, *The History of the Dividing Line* (1728), is the document intended for publication and public consumption. In this text, Byrd describes the fertility of the land, claiming, "[S]urely there is no place in the world where the inhabitants live with less labour than in North Carolina. It approaches nearer to the description of Lubberland than any other, by the great felicity of the climate, the easiness of raising provisions, and the slothfulness of the people" (27). Byrd continues on to refer to North Carolinians as inherently lazy, content to sleep late and loiter with their pipes (27). It's not a stretch to see the seeds of detrimental stereotypes of lower-class white southerners often associated with Appalachia in Byrd's description of the following scene: "There was a poor dirty house, with hardly any thing in it but children, that wallowed about like so many pigs. It is a common case in this part of the country, that people live worse upon good land; and the more they are befriended by the soil and the climate, the less they will do for themselves" (119). Intriguingly, while these characterizations are prominent in the public *History of the Dividing Line*, they are notably absent from his second text documenting the expedition, *The Secret History of the Dividing Line*—a difference that leads scholars to question his motives. Katherine Ledford identifies the cultural role these characterizations play in "A Landscape and a People Set Apart: Narratives of Exploration and Travel in Early Appalachia," writing that Byrd's "characterization of frontier/mountain people as lazy, dirty, and socially backward was the first such focused critique. The changing economic value of the western land settlers inhabited influenced this characterization" (56). In publicly decrying the early inhabitants of North Carolina, Byrd is cementing the cultural chasm between the frontier and coastal communities, solidifying his place among the coastal elite and providing justification for capitalist ventures from which Byrd and other colonial aristocrats stood to profit.

In "Beyond Isolation and Homogeneity: Diversity and the History of Appalachia," Ronald Lewis asserts that Appalachia as a cultural construct was "born in the fertile minds of late-nineteenth-century local color writers, [and] was invented in the caricatures and atmospheric landscapes of the escapist fiction they penned to entertain the emergent urban middle class" (21); this birth can be traced directly back to Will Wallace Harney's description of the Cumberland plateau, "A Strange Land and Peculiar People." Published in October 1873 in *Lippincott's Magazine of Popular Literature and Science*, this essay looms large in Appalachian scholarship. While ostensibly a Civil War tale, Harney encases the tale in his musings about the land through which he is journeying, noting their abject poverty with examples that are reminiscent of Byrd's claims: "We passed a poor man with five little children—the eldest ten or twelve, the youngest four or five—their little stock on a small donkey, footing their way over the hills across Tennessee into Georgia. It was so pitiful to see the poor little babes-in-the-wood on that forlorn journey; and yet they were so brave, and the poor fellow cheered them and praised them, as well he might" (431). Included in Harney's essay are his observations of Kentuckians' physical form, generalizing that the "natives of this region are characterized by marked peculiarities of the anatomical frame" and explaining their speech as having "verbal and phraseological peculiarities of its own" (431). He describes several agricultural practices and beliefs ("they believe in the influence of the moon on all vegetation" and "A change of the moon forebodes a change of the weather, and no meteorological statistics can shake their confidence in the superstition"), concluding that "by shooting arrows all day, even a blind man may hit the mark sometimes" (431). Harney's tone and point of view throughout this essay remind his readers of the work begun by writers like William

Byrd over a century before: Appalachia is a place unto itself, a "strange land" enclosed within their country, full of "peculiar people"—that is, people different from (and implicitly lesser than) the readership of *Lippincott's Magazine of Popular Literature and Science*.

Two local color writers who followed in Harney's footsteps by defining "Appalachia's people in a new light, cataloging an inventory of behaviors and customs that set the people apart from what was then considered to be the American mainstream" (Williams 198) are Mary Noailles Murfree—who published works such as *In the "Stranger People's" Country* in 1891 under the nom de plume Charles Egbert Craddock and continued to publish throughout the 1890s—and her contemporary John Fox, Jr. (whose work, *A Cumberland Vendetta*, was published in 1896, followed by collections such as *Blue-Grass and Rhododendron: Outdoors in Old Kentucky* in 1901 and the novel *The Trail of the Lonesome Pine* in 1908). Mary Noailles Murfree, born in 1850 in Murfreesboro, Tennessee, was well educated, having attended finishing school in Philadelphia for three years, and after the Civil War her family lived for several years in St. Louis. As an adult, she returned to Murfreesboro and lived there until her death.

Murfree drew inspiration for her many works from her experiences at a resort in Beersheba Springs, located within the Cumberland Mountains of Tennessee, where she spent many summers during her childhood. Murfree's experiences here influenced her writing, which demonstrates her sympathy for the mountaineer in writing from the position of an outsider (D. Miller 33). According to Carvel Collins, her encounters with native Appalachians were limited to "humbler people who came to the resort to sell produce or stare at life around the Springs" (qtd. in D. Miller 32). These limited experiences inspired Murfree's successful short stories, which were first published as a collection, *In the Tennessee Mountains*, in 1884. Surprisingly, she only traveled deep into the Appalachians with her father after completing the stories that would comprise this collection; it is no surprise, then, that Murfree's position as a youthful outsider led her to romanticize Appalachia as a "strange land, while the mountaineers appeared a peculiar people, if only for their willingness to live in a wilderness" (Shapiro 20).

Nowhere is Murfree's characterization of Appalachia clearer than in the opening paragraphs of her novel, In the "Stranger People's" Country. In this excerpt, the narrator has introduced the ancient "pygmy dwellers" of Tennessee and their burial mound in the Great Smoky Mountains, explaining what "quiet neighbors" they have been:

> In fact, the nearest mountaineers start, with a dazed look, at a question concerning them, then become mysterious, with that superstitious, speculative gleam in the eye as of one who knows much of uncanny lore, but is shy to recount.
>
> "I do declar' I never war so set back in my life ez I felt whenst that thar valley man jes' upped an' axed me 'bout'n them thar Leetle Stranger People buried yander on the rise," declared Stephen Yates, one July evening, as he stood leaning on his rifle before the door of his cabin in the cove. (1)

This brief passage demonstrates several tools Murfree regularly drew from in her fiction: a passage of elegant, standard narration juxtaposed against highly stylized dialect combined with insinuations that mountaineers are lawless and unclean. Passages such as this reinforce misperceptions about Appalachia being geographically isolated and thus separate from the rest of the country. Murfree was so successful that Cratis D. Williams wrote that her work has remained unmatched by other writers since she "created the literary mountaineer and the props that go with him, her archetypes and stereotypes in character, setting and atmosphere have remained standard instruments" (qtd. in Williams 198).

No discussion of Appalachian local color writing in the late nineteenth century is complete without a discussion of John Fox, Jr. Born to a schoolmaster outside Paris, Kentucky, Fox was educated first at Transylvania University in Kentucky before transferring to and graduating from Harvard University. Though he lived and wrote as a journalist in New York City for a brief period following his graduation, he soon returned home to Kentucky and eventually moved to Big Stone Gap, Virginia. While publishing short stories and his first novel, The Kentuckians (1897), Fox became well known on the lecture circuit, offering what quickly became a popular combination of "singing, banjo playing, mimicry, and dramatic staging [that] was praised in press accounts for his entertaining, if demeaning, renditions of mountain speech and structures of feeling" (Wilson 99). His 1908 novel, *Trail of the Lonesome Pine*, was adapted for stage and film, and the play has been in production as an outdoor drama in Big Stone Gap, Virginia, annually since 1964.

Fox's writing cemented in the American consciousness stereotypes similar to those employed by Murfree. *Trail of the Lonesome Pine* is a love story between Appalachian-born June Tolliver and "furriner" and engineer, Jack Hale. June is young and naïve when she first spies Hale climbing up the mountain path. Consider this description of her as she hides above the trail to furtively observe Hale: "With a thumping heart she pushed slowly forward through the brush until her face, fox-like with cunning and screened by a blueberry bush, hung just over the edge of the cliff, and there she lay, like a crouched panther-cub, looking down. For a moment, all that was human seemed gone from her eyes, but, as she watched, all that was lost came back to them, and something more" (Fox). Fox likens June's physical qualities to those of an animal, thus aligning her with the wilderness. Indeed, in this example, June is more animal than woman; the implication is that she and fellow mountaineers are somehow inhuman and thus have a more primitive understanding of their world. This positioning also further separates June from the so-called civilized, educated, and well-mannered world of the East Coast that Jack Hale represents.

The popularity of Fox's works cannot be disputed; even contemporary scholars consider him the "most popular author of the genre" (Lewis 21). In addition to their mainstream appeal, Murfree's and Fox's writings have deeper implications that are ingrained in our collective perception of Appalachia. By highlighting what Harney referred to as "A Strange Land and a Peculiar People," both writers are credited with having "created" Appalachia through their local color writing, and Lori Robinson notes Murfree is credited with creating the "pervasive stereotype of mountain people completely outside the values of the dominant American culture" (63). Not to be outdone, Fox also contributed significantly to this "othering" of Appalachian people in the American consciousness; according to Lewis, he "perpetrated and then perpetuated the myth of Appalachian otherness to facilitate absentee corporate hegemony by marginalizing indigenous residents economically and politically. In short, for Fox (and how many others?), 'Appalachia' was a willful creation and not merely the product of literary imagination" (22).

The construct created by the writings of Harney, Murfree, Fox, and others was so widely accepted that it inspired its own artistic genre. John Alexander Williams reminds us that "Appalachia's image as a territory of cultural deviance was reiterated in dozens of popular magazine articles in the early twentieth century and by numerous two-reel 'mountain melodramas,' some filmed on location in the Blue Ridge Mountains and shown in movie theatres all over the country" (199). One might ask why this negative stereotype of Appalachian people was so universally accepted in the late nineteenth and early twentieth centuries. The answer has to do with both geography and timing. Much of Appalachia is adjacent to or considered part of the American South, a region that, as Jennifer Rae Greeson claims, "as an internal other from the start of U.S. existence, lies simultaneously inside and outside the national imaginary constructed in U.S. literature" (3). That national imaginary fluctuated greatly in the nineteenth century, and Appalachia played a significant role during the challenges of Reconstruction. Lori Robinson argues, "Through these literary texts, this white, Southern region was contained and made safe just at the moment when the larger culture wanted to distance itself from the challenges to regional and racial identity that Reconstruction had made possible" (64).

In other words, the creation and perpetuation of these Appalachian stereotypes—and the misconception of Appalachia as a remote place of Others—played into the national narrative of mainstream, homogenous cultural dominance. Appalachia was portrayed as both far away in place and in time and, in contrast, reinforced the growing identity and cultural strength of homogenous, middle-class American hegemony. The resulting Appalachian stereotypes served dual purposes at the turn of the twentieth century: helping the South assimilate back into dominant American culture after the tumultuous Reconstruction period and also providing that same American culture with a marker of progress, a waterline against which to measure success.

And so the stage is set to consider the role that more contemporary literature plays in acknowledging the damning Appalachian stereotype. Examples of contemporary writers addressing and ultimately refuting or challenging these damaging stereotypes abound. One such example comes to us from writer Ron Rash. Rash, a poet, novelist, and short story writer, acts as archivist and demonstrates the role that literature plays in preserving culture. He integrates the accepted concept that Appalachia is a consumable culture in his novel *Saints at the River* through the character of Billy Watson: "He wore a torn flannel shirt and faded overalls. A black beard draped off his chin like Spanish moss. All his costume lacked was a corncob pipe. Billy had a degree in agriculture from Clemson University, and his family owned the biggest apple orchard in the valley, but he'd decided after college that his true calling was playing Snuffy Smith to fleece tourists. He swore if he could find a cross-eyed boy who could play banjo, he'd stick that kid on the porch and increase his business 25 percent" (21). Rash is not alone in being painfully aware of the prevalent Appalachian stereotypes and their translation into a "consumable Appalachian identity": for example, Fred Chappell addresses it directly in his novel *Look Back, All the Green Valley* when Jess Kirkman decides to eat at a restaurant named Hillbilly Heaven, an establishment with a sign that depicts a "towering caricature of a mountaineer. The figure was the cliché we all recognize, with its big floppy hat, its goofy facial expression, the balloon-toed bare feet, and the corked jug marked XXX" (93). Indeed, incorporating and mocking these stereotypes is one way these writers resist the identity that has been foisted upon Appalachia and its inhabitants.

In her collection of short stories titled *F*ckface*, Leah Hampton frequently plays with the tension that results from the clashing of cultural expectations. In "Sparkle," native Tennessean Beth is stunned and hurt when, upon touring Dolly Parton's home cabin preserved at Dollywood, James (a scientist who is decidedly not Appalachian) observes her objectively and asks, "'Did you grow up in a place like that?'" Beth's visceral reaction is both physical and verbal: "Well, I mean please. My face went hot, and my stomach whomped fiercely. . . . 'No, Professor,' I said. . . . 'I had plumbing and everything.'" She then continues to play on the presumed stereotype that instigated James's question, stating, "'Heck, I even read a few books when I was a kid, when I wasn't losing teeth. . . . Even managed to gra-jee-ate college'" (176). Beth continues to deflate James's contrived assumptions by identifying his oblique reference to "Araby" from James Joyce's *Dubliners* and offers to loan him a copy. James is stunned, and stumbles over his words: "'Oh, right. Sure. Sorry. I just assumed you wouldn't . . .'" (183). However, Hampton complicates Beth's role just as readers might be tempted to pity her as a victim. Beth is complicit in perpetuating James's belief in the Appalachian stereotypes as readers learn that she had entertained him with exaggerated stories of her cousin Bigun, stories that inadvertently reinforce the perception of her cousin as a slow, bumbling, and easily angered giant. Beth chooses against revealing Bigun's given name or accurate details of either his life or his death—details that may have led James to view Beth and her family as complex, nuanced people rather than a stock of Appalachian characters. By the end of the story, Beth, who had been enamored by James, acknowledges both her shattered illusions about him and her role in creating his own illusions, sadly noting that "[all the delicate things] break if I ever try to get them in my hands" (187). In "Sparkle" and other stories in this collection, Hampton rightly identifies the damaging and static images that continue to define Appalachia on the national stage and very often delights in mocking characters that continue to entertain such stereotypes as monolithic truths—all while constructing complicated and contradicting characters who hail from the region.

Perhaps the clearest example of the impact of these stereotypes imposed on Appalachia and the resulting expectations for an easily consumable identity comes from the poetry of Jim Wayne Miller. Miller's character of the Brier features in the collection *The Mountains Have Come Closer;* the Brier is a preacher but not an ordained minister, a speaker who does not even carry a Bible in the poem "The Brier Sermon." Fellow Appalachian writer Robert Morgan claims of Miller's Brier poems that "no one has been able to better describe and enact the sense of loss, the paradoxes of identity in the mountains. The narratives, the dramas, the monologues and multiple voices have captured for all time the ironies of our place in geography and history" (5). A "brier" is someone who was raised in a rural location—such as much of Appalachia—and moves into an urban area, and Miller himself saw the Brier as an "Appalachian Everyman" ("In Quest of the Brier" 162). While the Brier himself does not fit the mountaineer stereotype long affixed to the region, his can be seen as a poetic and prophetic voice representing the region and its people; Miller affirms this, stating that "the Brier, while he is just one figure, is representative of and stands for a collective experience, the experience of a whole group of people numbering in the millions of Americans" (162).

Though the Brier is himself not barefoot and rustic, it's telling that those from outside Appalachia expect him to be. In "The Brier Losing Touch with His Traditions," the Brier was lauded for being an authentic chair maker, celebrated in newspapers for his traditional skills and tools. Upon being inundated with orders, he moved from eastern Kentucky to Cincinnati to facilitate his work, but he was quickly excoriated for using "an electric lathe and power drill" and his "orders fell off" (lines 13, 16):

> So he moved back down to east Kentucky.
> Had himself a brochure printed up
> with a picture of him using his hand lathe,
> bearded, barefoot, in faded overalls.
> Then when folks would come from the magazines,
> he'd get rid of them before suppertime
> so he could put on his shoes, his flowered sport shirt
> and double-knit pants, and open a can of beer,
> and watch the six-thirty news on tv
> out of New York and Washington.
>
> He'd have time to be himself. (lines 21–31)

In this poem, Miller's Brier is well aware of the imposition of the static Appalachian stereotype and is limited by its strict expectations. Just as many commercial ventures in Gatlinburg, Tennessee, do today, he has made the decision to continue the public performance while he must, fulfilling the demands of "mainstream" American culture that "expect[s] Appalachians to produce an enforced, constructed, consumable Appalachian identity" (Pryse 6) and then shed the persona as one would a uniform following a shift at work. The Brier highlights the constructed nature of the Appalachian stereotype, while subtly reminding readers that Appalachia and its people are removed in neither time nor space from contemporary American culture.

While the discussion of race and ethnicity in Appalachia deserves an essay of its own (and has been discussed with insight and at great length in a variety of sources), former Kentucky Poet Laureate and recipient of the 2014 NAACP Image Awards Frank X. Walker provides further resistance to the homogenous, tacky Appalachian stereotype. Creator of the term "Affrilachia" and founder of the Affrilachian Poets movement, Walker encourages wide use of the term, defining it as a "term that helps create a space for them to be seen and heard" ("Re: Affrilachian"). He argues that the "act of using it is a socio-cultural and political one that has more to do with liberation and affirming an identity rooted in the continent and all the ways it is culturally and historically present in the Appalachian region" ("Re: Affrilachian").

In Walker's first collection of poetry, *Affrilachia*, the poet frankly addresses Appalachian stereotypes and his lack of experience with known "Appalachian" skills, writing that he is ". . . inexperienced/ at cutting/ hanging/ or chewing tobacco" ("Affrilachia" lines 23–26). Despite not fitting into expected Appalachian identity, Walker firmly grounds his identity in the region:

> yet still feeling
> complete and proud to say
> that some of the bluegrass is black
> enough to know
> that being 'colored' and all
> is generally lost
> somewhere between
> the dukes of hazard
> and the beverly hillbillies
> but
> if you think
> makin' 'shin from corn

> is as hard as Kentucky coal
> imagine being
> an Affrilachian
> poet
>
> (lines 27–43)

Walker connects the challenges he faces in his work as poet and his identity as Affrilachian to common stereotypes and representative images. In doing so, he gives voice to the truth that while Appalachia is far from the white, blue-collar region of shallow stereotypes, any racial identity other than white is erased from popular representations of the region.

While contemporary writers such as Rash, Chappell, Hampton, Miller, and Walker continue to use their platform to diffuse the power of deeply embedded and tacky stereotypes, as these examples suggest, the dominant image of the Appalachian mountaineer in all its forms lies at the forefront of our perceptions of Appalachia. Fred Chappell offers us perhaps the best justification for using fiction and poetry to resist this imposed understanding of the region: "Any art form which is successful is necessarily its own justification. . . . Because what fiction emphasizes is not sequence, not chain of event, but instead the separateness of moments of time, the extreme individuality of persons and objects" (Chappell, "Six Propositions" 515).

WORKS CITED

Baker, Peter. "DirecTV Ad Full of Mountain Stereotypes." *Lexington Herald Leader*, 29 Oct. 2013, www.kentucky.com/opinion/op-ed/article44451162.html.

Byrd, William. *History of the Dividing Line in the Year 1728*. 1728. *The Westover Manuscripts. Documenting the American South*, 2001, docsouth.unc.edu/nc/byrd/byrd.html.

Chappell, Fred. *Look Back All the Green Valley*. Picador, 1999.

———. "Six Propositions about Literature and History." *New Literary* History, vol. 1, no. 3, 1970, pp. 513–22. *JSTOR*, www-jstor-org.saintleo.idm.oclc.org/stable/468269.

Fox, John, Jr. *The Trail of the Lonesome Pine.* Charles Scribner's Sons, 1908. Project Gutenberg, 2018, www.gutenberg.org/files/5122/5122-h/5122-h.htm.

Greeson, Jennifer Rae. *Our South: Geographic Fantasy and the Rise of National Literature.* Harvard UP, 2010.

Hampton, Leah. "Sparkle." *F*ckface.* Henry Holt and Company, 2020, pp. 168–87.

Harney, Will Wallace. "A Strange Land and a Peculiar People." *Lippincott's Magazine,* vol. 12, Oct. 1873, pp. 430–32. Project Gutenberg, 2004, www.gutenberg.org/files/13964/13964-h/13964-h.htm.

Hillbilly Days. Pike County [Kentucky] Tourism, 2020, hillbillydays.com. Accessed 12 July 2020.

Huggan, Graham, and Helen Tiffin. "Green Postcolonialism." *Interventions* vol. 9, no. 1, 2007, pp. 1–11.

Ledford, Katharine. "A Landscape and a People Set Apart: Narratives of Exploration and Travel in Early Appalachia." *Back Talk from Appalachia: Confronting Stereotypes,* edited by Dwight B. Billings, Gurney Norman, and Katharine Ledford, UP of Kentucky, 1999, pp. 47–66.

Lewis, Ronald L. "Beyond Isolation and Homogeneity: Diversity and the History of Appalachia." *Back Talk from Appalachia: Confronting Stereotypes,* edited by Dwight B. Billings, Gurney Norman, and Katharine Ledford, UP of Kentucky, 1999, pp. 21–43.

Miller, Danny. *Wingless Flights: Appalachian Women in Fiction.* Bowling Green State U Popular P, 1996.

Miller, Jim Wayne. "The Brier Losing Touch with His Traditions." *The Mountains Have Come Closer.* Appalachia Consortium P, 1980.

———. "In Quest of the Brier." *Every Leaf a Mirror: A Jim Wayne Miller Reader,* edited by Morris Allen Grubbs and Mary Ellen Miller, UP of Kentucky, 2014, pp. 153–74.

Morgan, Robert. "Introduction." *Every Leaf a Mirror: A Jim Wayne Miller Reader,* edited by Morris Allen Grubbs and Mary Ellen Miller, U P of Kentucky, 2014, pp. 1–9.

Murfree, Mary Noailles [Charles Egbert Craddock]. *In the "Stranger People's" Country.* 1891. Edited by Marjorie Pryse, U of Nebraska P, 2005.

Nixon, Rob. *Slow Violence and the Environmentalism of the Poor.* Harvard UP, 2011.

Plumwood, Val. "Decolonizing Relationships with Nature." *Decolonizing Nature: Strategies for Conservation in a Post-Colonial Era,* edited by W. M. Adams and Martin Mulligan, Earthscan, 2003, pp. 51–78.

Pryse, Marjorie. "Stereotype, Authenticity and the Metaphor of Appalachia as an 'Internal Colony.'" American Studies Association Conference. Baltimore, 20 Oct. 2011. Unpublished paper used with the author's permission.

Rash, Ron. *Saints at the River.* Picador, 2004.

Robinson, Lori. "Region and Race: National Identity and the Southern Past." *A Companion to the Regional Literatures of* America, edited by Charles L. Crow, Blackwell, 2003, pp. 57–73.

Shapiro, Henry D. *Appalachia on Our Mind: The Southern Mountains and Mountaineers in the American Consciousness, 1870–1920.* U of North Carolina P, 1978.

Walker, Frank X. "Affrilachia." *Affrilachia.* Old Cove P, 2000.

———. "Re: Affrilachian." Email to listserv. 20 Mar. 2018.

Williams, John Alexander. *Appalachia: A History.* U of North Carolina P, 2002.

Wilson, Darlene. "A Judicious Combination of Incident and Psychology: John Fox Jr. and the Southern Mountaineer Motif." *Back Talk from Appalachia: Confronting Stereotypes,* edited by Dwight B. Billings et al., UP of Kentucky, 1999, pp. 98–118.

WE WERE THE BAD POOR

TRASH AND THE LIMITS OF TACKINESS

GARTH SABO

*I*n 1957, a nine-year-old boy moves with his family from Nashville to El Paso but returns yearly to the town where he grew up. During these road trips, he becomes enamored of the various souvenirs and memorabilia he compiles from amusement parks and tourist attractions. The boy derives a sense of his southern identity from these mass-produced trinkets, which he would later identify as "Southern tacky."

Years earlier, near Knoxville, a mother chides her hungry children. "I can't make nothing out of these brats," she says. "Seems like they're all bound to grow up to be trash." At night, the children play a game, whispering their plans for a better future. "When we grow," the oldest son begins, and each completes the line in their own stead. "I'm gonna move to Texas." "I ain't never gonna eat tripe no more." "I'm gonna have six little babies and buy them anything they want." "Gonna treat them good." "Gonna tell them how pretty they are." "Gonna love them, love them."

These two stories, the first a story from Charles Reagan Wilson's childhood recollected in "Whose South?" and the second a passage from Dorothy Allison's "Meanest Woman Ever Left Tennessee" (28–30), written to approximate a story her family refused to tell, have more in common than a journey, whether real or imagined, between Tennessee and Texas. The appeal the tacky holds for a young boy returning home is inseparable from the condemnation the children labeled "trash" feel as they concoct their plans to flee. The difference between these two terms, I will show, is more a matter of degree than kind. The epithet "tacky" belittles the people, communities, and behaviors to which it is applied, certainly, but at the same time it reassures—or possibly threatens—the low of "tacky" with the lower still of "trash."

The fact that one of these stories is biographical while the other is a work of fiction does little to separate Wilson's interest in the tacky from Shirley Boatwright's condemnation of her children as trash in the story for which she serves as the titular figure. In the introduction to the 2002 edition of *Trash*, Allison recalls that she "originally claimed the label 'trash' in self-defense. The phrase had been applied to me and to my family in crude and hateful ways. I took it on deliberately" (xv). In the same introduction, she describes the genesis of "Meanest Woman Ever Left Tennessee" as an attempt "to work out in my own mind what it must have been like to have been my grandmother—and her mother, my great-grandma about whom I knew almost nothing, except that her children hated her" (x). Her invention of the specifics of the Boatwrights' circumstances does little to alleviate the real sting Allison herself recalls at having been condemned as trash in a way similar to the life she imagines for her grandmother.

In this essay, I want to untangle the ways that trash operates as a limit to tacky, and how trash's role as the abject outside of the cultural discourse of tackiness might offer a new vantage point from which to consider those cheap, vulgar, common, and unsophisticated things at the heart of this collection. As I do so, writing this from my home in Michigan, I am especially cognizant of Pat Conroy's admonition in *Lords of Discipline* that "It's impossible to explain to a Yankee what 'tacky' is. They simply have no word for it up north, but my God, do they ever need one" (221). Tacky is a slippery notion, but there are certainly some related terms that can help to limn its boundaries. In "Whose South?," for instance, Charles Reagan Wilson shows little perturbation slipping from "tacky" to "kitsch"; he calls one "a term out of Southern vernacular" for the other. He is not alone in this comparison. Catherine Lugg uses tacky as an adjective form of kitsch in her short book on *Kitsch: From Education to Public Policy*, and, while it may constitute an act of academic tackiness to turn to the free encyclopedia, it is worth noting that Wikipedia searches for "tacky" automatically redirect to the page for "kitsch" as well ("Kitsch").

It is important to maintain tacky and kitsch as separate, distinct concepts, especially in light of the regional specificity of the former in constructing southern identities. However, Gillo Dorfles's etymology of the German word *kitsch* as the "use of refuse taken bodily from the rubbish dump" (3) suggests that whatever the relation between kitsch and tackiness may be, they both seem to name material, behavior, and persons that are just a step removed from the dump, wasteland, and other places where trash is found. Naming this kinship between the two terms helps to explain the frequency with which questions of tackiness give way to accusations of trashiness. The prevailing opinion among various southern lifestyle and etiquette blogs seems to be that invoking tackiness insinuates that the more severe designation of "trash" is just a hair's breadth away. Writing for *Porchscene*, Deborah Fagan Carpenter reports that "tacky" is "definitely handy" for criticizing something that "might be considered in poor taste, garish, gaudy, cheap, tawdry, loud, flashy, showy, or trashy." The progression in intensity among the adjectives Carpenter chooses for her list is instructive here, with "trashy" as the final, most extreme possibility of behavior that "tacky" exists to police.

Kelly Kazek's post on the *It's a Southern Thing* blog traces the etymology of tackiness back to the Carolina Marsh Tacky horses, whose "lack of breeding" later became "a description well-to-do Southerners used to describe the poor, or anyone else they considered 'trashy.'" The epithet "tacky" reveals a mode of control predicated on creating and maintaining strict standards of inclusion, from which "trash" is simultaneously excluded and to which it proves to be essential. Alongside this historical progression from wild horses to self-deprecation to class warfare, we might pay attention to other connotations of "tacky" as well. Kelly Kazek questions "how . . . a word that refers to stickiness [can] come to mean something that is gaudy or garish," and this haptic, sensory implication of tacky ought to enter more fully into our conversation. In the broadest sense, to be tacky names an unpleasant, liminal sensation. In the original sense of the word, tacky is neither fully wet nor fully dry; in its regional inflection, tacky neither fully conforms to nor fully rejects the social code. In both cases, something tacky sticks to you, lingers where it is unwanted, makes a mess, and leaves a mark.

I would suggest that we see the sensory unpleasantness that tackiness connotes as fundamental to its relation with trash. Trash also is sticky, in that it persists materially after its erasure from the sphere of usefulness. As Dorothy Allison puts it: "Trash don't know the meaning of use. Just like you kids" (25). Accusations of trash stick to us and cause others to recoil, as Shirley Boatwright's distaste for her children makes painfully clear. Contact with waste matter has long been associated with concepts of filth and the capacity to stain, as William Viney indicates in *Waste: A Philosophy of Things* by associating "discarded things [with] notions of disorder, abjection, and disgust" (2).

The potential to stain is surely a component of the social-regulatory function that accusations of tackiness perform. In the same way that contact with something tacky makes you sticky as well, to call something tacky is to become tacky yourself. "To a true Southerner," Deborah Fagan Carpenter notes, "it's fine to think that someone's outfit is tacky, but, to openly disparage someone's outfit would be the ultimate tacky." This inability to speak in anything but the abstract without implicating oneself renders the borders of tacky behavior hazy and ill-defined. Carpenter's earlier insistence that "tacky" must be "specific to something, or someone that's—well—offensive" uses that interjection "well" to break the clarity of the line and represent the way that tackiness can be recognized and acknowledged but not named.

This suggests some degree of shared class consciousness between offenders and accusers of tackiness, which is readily apparent in Wilson's tale of discovering his family's southern culture while traveling back to the South from the Southwest with which this essay began. Wilson's anecdote is framed not as the creation of his southern identity through seashell sculptures, toothpick dispensers, or themed paperweights but rather as his discovery that, "in retrospect," he and his family "were Southern in culture." To be sure, the claim that these "mass-produced objects regarded by people with 'good taste' as being in 'poor taste' featured an explicit southern dimension worth pondering" is remarkably valuable. But even Wilson's use of scare quotes around "good taste" and "bad taste," which ostensibly show his skepticism for the validity of those distinctions, reify a sense that the discourse of tackiness operates as a negotiation between those who are doing well observing certain mores of material culture and those who, whether accidentally or intentionally, are not.

When trash is invoked, this mutual sociality is wholly absent. Questions of taste are supplanted by insinuations of moral failure. Dorothy Allison recalls hearing herself "referred to as 'that trash' in a motel corridor in the central valley in California" only "a couple years" before she penned the introduction to the new edition of *Trash* in 2002. Allison's description of the setting for this memory is telling of the alienation it engenders. The proliferation of details, inclusive of both her immediate physical surroundings and geographical location, suggests the painful clarity this experience must have, while her avoidance of definite articles and place names constructs a sort of no-place for encounters with trash to occur. On the one hand, a motel corridor is a space designated for liminality and impermanence; on the other, it is also a constrained space of heightened contact. This all serves to highlight the physical proximity of the exchange against the vast social distance created by the stranger's epithet. In this sense, "trash" is a pejorative that cuts with indifference to the wound it causes. To call something "tacky" indicates that some social behavior threatens an as-yet uncrossed limit of social connection, but "trash" treats the same limit as irrevocably crossed. As class and cultural lines are drawn, then, "tacky" reveals a power structure from the inside, whereas "trash" can offer an external view of the same structure.

For, to be sure, "tacky" reveals a mode of control predicated on creating and maintaining strict standards of inclusion, which "trash" is simultaneously excluded from and essential to. The tragedy of "Meanest Woman Ever Left Tennessee" is that Allison dramatizes this control mechanism by showing it used aspirationally. Shirley Boatwright condemns her husband and children as trash in order to shore up her belief in herself to be "one of the quality. 'The better people,' she told her daughters. 'They know their own'" (21). The timing of this insistence, which immediately follows the story's first insistence of her calling the children "devils and worms and trash" (21), makes it clear that, for Shirley, naming another trash is a key means by which she indicates, or likely seeks to attain, this realm of "better people," though her use of the third-person "they" rather than the first-person "we" adds a degree of uncertainty to her claims to quality. Shirley's instruction to "watch how it goes; you watch how people treat me down at the mill" nonetheless reiterates the act of separation between mother and children instantiated by her "trash" remark. The air of quality that she has achieved, or imagines having achieved, among her coworkers at the mill does not transfer to her children because, in this case, the relation of tacky to trash is conceptual, not genetic. Her insistence on condemning her kin as trash is a bulwark against being so named herself.

It is not surprising that Shirley Boatwright specifies the mill as a privileged site for proof of her refinement, as avoiding tackiness and trashiness is often a matter of restricting certain behaviors or tastes to the places designated for them. If, as Valerie Fraser Luesse suggests in her list of "Things Mama Says Are Tacky" for the online imprint of *Southern Living* magazine, "tacky is as tacky does," it is clear that tacky does the wrong thing in the wrong place at the wrong time. William Viney attributes such material disruptions of space and time to waste items like trash, the recognition of which requires "an acknowledgment of time's passing, its power to organize notions of wearing, decay, transience and dissolution and its power to expose that organizing function" (3). The problem of trash is always one of unwanted visibility and overexposure. Trash belongs only insofar as it is unseen and offends by being noticed.

In the original introduction to *Trash*, Dorothy Allison positions her family history as trash, outside and counter to social narratives of proper southern etiquette. She notes that her family's lives "were not on television, not in books, not even comic books," and attributes this invisibility to "the inescapable impact of being born in a condition of poverty that this society finds shameful, contemptible, and somehow oddly deserved" (vii). Allison traces the lineage of this contempt back to a notion of what we might call "properly tacky poverty," and I want to turn to a slightly longer passage from "Stubborn Girls and Mean Stories," her introduction to *Trash*, to show what's at stake in these mythologies of poor southern identities. Allison writes:

> There was a myth of the poor in this country, but it did not include us, no matter how I tried to squeeze us in. There was this concept of the "good" poor, and that fantasy had little to do with the everyday lives my family had survived. The good poor were hardworking, ragged but clean, and intrinsically honorable. We were the bad poor. We were men who drank and couldn't keep a job; women, invariably pregnant before marriage, who quickly became worn, fat, and old from working too many hours and bearing too many children; and children with runny noses, watery eyes, and the wrong attitudes. (vii)

I have been at pains to show how "tacky" gives a name to Allison's good poor, who, though lacking in social capital, still endorse the myth of poverty as honorable, if temporary. To return to the competing tales of trash and tacky with which this essay began, it is telling that so much of Wilson's recollection of his childhood encounters with southern tacky is explicitly, even self-consciously, coded in this same narrative of honorable poverty that Allison mentions being excluded from (and by). Wilson sets the scene for his boyhood anecdote by revealing that his parents "were what historians would call the 'plain folk'—not wealthy, not the stereotypical poor whites, but, in [his] father's case at least, poor in worldly goods as a child." The normative power of associating these so-called "plain folk" with their transitional experience of poverty is palpable in a passage like this. Wilson takes care to distance himself from any insinuation of family wealth, but he also triply insulates himself from association with any meaningful form of poverty as well. His family's exposure to poverty is restricted to his paternal side. Their experience with scarcity is coded as explicitly material, not moral, with his attention to the "worldly goods" they lacked. Their poverty is also notably temporary, lasting only through his father's childhood.

Unlike Dorothy Allison's family, then, who "had generations before us to teach us that nothing ever changed, and that those who did try to escape failed" (viii), the upwardly mobile Wilsons seem to have lived as model examples of the so-called "good poor." Charles Reagan Wilson's exposure to and affinity for tackiness, then, can be explained by continuity of contact between his social stratum and the higher echelons of genteel southern society he simultaneously distances himself from and genuflects towards. He even shares elements of Allison's language of socioeconomic mythology, noting that his family "could not afford the legendary 'help'" so ensconced as a signifier of proper southernness. Yet the distance he professes between himself and the self-conscious southerner, as he calls it, seems far less vast than that between himself and the "poor whites" who appear only briefly and only as stereotypes in "Whose South?" By their omission, Wilson subtly reifies a portrait of the South as containing two elements: those who belong fully, and those who can be returned to the fold by identifying the tacky tastes that divorce them from the social center. Allison's trash, the bad poor, disrupts this narrative by revealing it as "fantasy" and contrasting it with the long histories and deep roots of the lives Allison's kin survive on the outside.

Now, to be sure, it would do Charles Reagan Wilson a disservice to read "Whose South?" only in the limited sense I have laid out above. Wilson's goal is to map the contours of a collective identity he calls "twenty-first century Southerners," which must be inclusive of "the presence of peoples of a variety of cultural ways." This is a valuable goal, and his instinct to use tackiness as a means to accomplish it is smart. He recognizes the social-organizing power imbued within the concept and leverages it to suggest that tacky tastes inform identities just as much as their genteel counterparts. The present volume recognizes the truth of that very claim, and the other essays collected here do well in showing how tackiness reveals and constructs a sense of southern selfhood that is more variegated than figures of "good taste" like the belle or gentleman might imply. However, it is important to note that "tacky" is not a tool of infinite scope. There are limits to tackiness and its potential to include, which I am attempting to attribute to the historical and etymological baggage the term carries. Remaining attentive to the ways that tacky is entangled with trash should, I hope, allow us to see how even inversions of the term's traditional usage can still cut, and deeply.

That Allison relies so heavily on the contest of wills between Shirley and her daughter Mattie, Allison's grandmother, to mythologize the people too poor to be tacky is no coincidence. Reading *Trash* alongside southern etiquette condemnations of tacky behavior makes it clear that both tackiness and trashiness target women; that is, these concepts exert lopsided pressure toward the domestication of women. Carpenter makes this patently clear in her entry for *Porchscene* through the subtle way she shifts between describing the notion of "tacky" as broadly southern and noting that these "trivial rules were pretty much ingrained in the psyches of women of [her] generation." There is no doubt that accusations of tackiness can be leveraged against a wide array of actions or items, but it is equally clear that those accusations strike against women more frequently and with greater force.

Dorothy Allison indicates that this gendered element persists even when the discourse shifts from the ingroup-facing "tacky" to the outward "trash." Though all of Shirley's children are liable to be named as trash as a result of situational offenses, the path between action and condemnation seems slipperiest when trod by her daughters, especially Mattie. Shirley contests her husband Tucker's insistence that Mattie is "a good girl" by repeating, "She's trash. She's nothing but trash, and you know it" (29). Here, the binary opposition implied by pitting "good girl" against "trash" suggests that Mattie must be fully one or the other, which restricts Mattie's actions to an absurdly narrow band of often ill-defined social norms for her behavior both within and beyond the walls of the family home. For instance, the only codified examples of these lines of social transgression pertain to the domestic sphere that "Meanest Woman Ever Left Tennessee" reserves for its female characters, however reluctantly. The Boatwright family always transfers the rice and beans they rely upon from their cooking vessel to serving dishes, as "only trash served food out of a cooking pot" (29). "Tacky" and "trash" both seem to operate as modes of control against women in general, particularly as a means to subtend other manifestations of southern patriarchy.

Confounding this gendering of the targets of the tacky/trashy distinction is the fact that the source of this pressure is most often attributed to a maternal antagonist. Dorothy Allison's imagination of her great-grandmother Shirley renders this abusive power of condemnation most visible, and it stands out as well that, though she labels all her children "trash," the bulk of her ire is saved for her daughters and their perceived ability, or lack thereof, to conform to certain gender expectations. Valerie Luesse likewise attributes her crowd-sourced list of tacky behaviors to an indistinct, communal "Mama." In addition to allowing the readers of *Southern Living* to observe the prohibition against naming tackiness directly, which would risk becoming tacky themselves, by simply reporting on what "Mama" would find tacky, Luesse's list wields the Mama figure to obscure the spatial and temporal social organizing principles that trash lays bare. She notes that, though "[t]his is the modern South, and we're no longer bound by the rules and regulations set forth by our fore-Mamas," there yet remain "things that Mama still finds tacky." Here, the suggested break from "rules and regulations" signals an antihierarchical interest, but the unbroken lineage with these fore-Mamas belies that suggestion. In particular, the combination of the distant "fore" here with the intimate "Mama" paints a pattern of behavior proscription that is simultaneously familiar and foreign. Luesse's modern South may have come a long way, but the traditions of its forebears seem hardly to have been diminished by the distance.

Gender is far from the only fault line against which the tension of tacky and trashy exerts pressure. Allison acknowledges that she has been dismissed as "trash" fairly infrequently in her life. As a child, what she heard "more often" was the phrase "white trash" (xv). In their edited collection bearing this title, Matt Wray and Annalee Newitz suggest several ways that the "white trash" stereotype helps contest the invisibility of whiteness to whites. As Wray and Newitz note, "whiteness serves as a sort of invisible norm, the unraced center of a racialized world" (3). They go on to argue that this "allows us to understand how tightly intertwined racial and class identities actually are in the United States," since "white trash" is "racialized (i.e., different from 'black trash' or 'Indian trash') and classed (trash is social waste and detritus)" (4).

I, of course, agree with Wray and Newitz's mission of rendering whiteness visible as a social construct, but Allison complicates their approach. *Trash* begins with her memory of hearing "white trash" as an adult and seeing "all too clearly the look that would cross the face of any Black woman in the room when that particular term was spoken" (xv). Allison's description of "the look" suggests that Wray and Newitz are mistaken when they contrast "white trash" with its "black" or "Indian" equivalents, because these latter racializations only exist in the abstract. Allison recognizes that "white trash" polices racial identities by positioning whiteness as an extraordinary factor in an accusation of trash. She realizes, "like a splash of cold water" (xv), that the hatefulness of the epithet derives from its presumption that trash is always already not white.

These specters of race persist as trashy gives way to tacky in the repertoire of power negotiation tactics. Equations of tackiness with trash are often accompanied by a persistent racial dynamic as well. While celebrating "tacky" as "an irreplaceable, multi-use, charming, Southern word," Deborah Fagan Carpenter notes its origin as "a description that aristocratic Southerners used to refer to 'poor whites.'" Ben Zimmer notes that "tacky" began as a self-deprecating term for "poor white Southerners who were identified with their equine counterparts" before it eventually "made the move from noun to adjective." Tacky ceased to be self-deprecating and instead is a means to describe *other* people "who are somehow untidy, fashionable or uncouth." Tacky and trash both get caught in the orbit of rules of etiquette that have, at their bottom, race in mind when determining taste. One thing that Valerie Fraser Luesse implies but leaves unsaid is that Mama's insistence that white shoes after Labor Day are tacky is intimately entangled with power structures that presume non-white skin to be trash. Tacky and trashy, then, are mobilized in tandem, with "tacky" governing the behavior of cultural outliers and bringing them back to the fold and "trash" working to disavow the humanity of those who have been systematically rendered illegible and invisible.

There is something to be said, then, in Dorothy Allison's decision to align herself with this second group throughout *Trash* and indeed throughout her canon. She has recognized, as we all might, the value of an extreme act of self-alienation from a social order that is predicated on her own erasure. She turns to trash to wield its power as the abject outside. Aleida Assmann writes of the political power that dumps and their contents can wield, acting as "a subversive counter-memory that cannot be controlled by the institutions of political power" and through which "authors and artists have created various forms of cultural counter-memory, their refuge for the forgotten and rejected" (81). Allison makes it clear that this is the power she wields in her text.

In recognition of this, this essay ends as it began, with Allison alongside Wilson and questions of trash and the tacky in our minds. Wilson draws "Whose South?" to its conclusion with a call to "shoulder [the] burdens, embrace [the] complexities, appreciate [the] diversities, revel in [the] joyful noises and delightful flavors, and build on [the] history" of the South in a way that allows more people into the fold as southerners. Tackiness is one way, among many, he offers to pursue this goal, and, as this collection will attest, it is a suggestion worth heeding. As we do so, deploying "tacky" in new ways and with an eye to critique the positions of privilege from which it has traditionally emerged, toward this end, however, we ought to ask the same question Dorothy Allison answers by naming her collection *Trash*. Doing so, she writes, is meant "to raise the issue of who the term glorifies as well as who it disdains" (xvi). Let us be sure that the new ways of glorifying tacky tastes, tacky behaviors, and tacky people do not disdain the marginalized, invisible people who have always fallen just outside the limits we draw for the term.

WORKS CITED

Allison, Dorothy. *Trash*. Penguin, 2002.

Carpenter, Deborah Fagan. "Tacky! Tacky! Tacky!" *Porchscene: Exploring Southern Culture*, 21 Mar. 2018, porchscene.com/2018/03/21/tacky-tacky-tacky/.

Conroy, Pat. *Lords of Discipline*. Houghton Mifflin, 1980.

Kazek, Kelly. "How the Word 'Tacky' Originated in the South and How to Use It Properly." *It's a Southern Thing*, southernthing.com/how-the-word-tacky-originated-in-the-south-and-how-to-use-it-properly-2608593805.html. Accessed 1 Aug. 2020.

"Kitsch." *Wikipedia: The Free Encyclopedia*. Wikimedia Foundation, Inc., 30 Sep. 2021, en.wikipedia.org/w/index.php?title=Kitsch&oldid=1047289314.

Luesse, Valerie Fraser. "Things Mama Says Are Tacky." *Southern Living*, southernliving.com/culture/tacky-sayings-southern-mama. Accessed 1 Aug. 2020.

Neville, Brian, and Johanne Villeneuve. *Waste-Site Stories: The Recycling of Memory*. SUNY Press, 2002.

Viney, William. *Waste: A Philosophy of Things.* Bloomsbury, 2014.

Wilson, Charles Reagan. "Whose South?" *Southern Cultures*, vol. 22, no. 4, Winter 2016, n.p.

Wray, Matt, and Annalee Newitz. *White Trash: Race and Class in America.* Routledge, 1997.

Zimmer, Ben. "The Gauche Origins of 'Tacky.'" *The Wall Street Journal*, Eastern ed., 19 Jul. 2014, C.4

NOT YOUR MAMA'S TACKY

HUCKSTER STYLE AS SOUTHERN ENTERPRISE

CATHERINE EGLEY WAGGONER

*A*bout an hour and a half south of Memphis along Route 61, just outside of Clarksdale, Mississippi, in the heart of the endless Delta fields, sits an old cotton plantation turned bed and breakfast—or "bed and beer," as the owners tongue-in-cheek like to call it. The Delta, a region referred to in 1985 by southern scholar James Cobb as "the most southern place on earth" (xvii) and more recently by acclaimed author Jesmyn Ward as the "Mississippi-est part of Mississippi," is a diamond-shaped region in the northwest corner of the state renowned for cotton, catfish, blues music, extreme poverty, fervent religion, and lavish entertaining. Serving as a type of Delta shorthand, the Shack Up Inn (see Fig. 3) is a collection of forty-four or so renovated shacks and grain-bins-turned-hotel-rooms clustered around an old cotton gin, itself refurbished to be a funky concert space dubbed the Juke Joint Chapel. Guests check into shotgun houses once occupied by real sharecroppers, kick back on overstuffed couches on rickety front porches, swig cold beers, and take in the soulful blues of homegrown talent in an artful commercialization of culture that screams the "real deal."

"Real" or not, such sites constitute material manifestations of "southernness," serving important functions in a geographical area long in the crosshairs of controversies concerning regional identity.[1] Heated discussions over the removal of Confederate "Stars and Bars" from the Mississippi state flag and from undoubtedly one of the most

FIG. 3. Lobby sign in the Shack Up Inn. Photograph by Laura Egley Taylor.

venerable of southern institutions, NASCAR, as well as the dramatic removals of Confederate statuary from public grounds, are just the most recent examples demonstrating the high level of investment people have in defining the South. While quirky tourist sites such as the Shack Up Inn might appear to constitute less potent manifestations of southern identity than the serious business of flags and monuments, we are wise to remember that such sites are not merely entertaining regional renditions of a mythical past; they are rhetorical manifestations shaping cultural understandings with a significant component of their power couched within their visual aesthetics.

To even the casual observer, the Shack Up Inn represents a departure from stereotypical displays of southern culture. This bed-and-beer does not play to tourists' visions of a moonlight and magnolias Old South with its white-columned mansions and hoop-skirted belles, as seen in the Natchez Pilgrimage Tours, for instance, nor does it salute cheery down-home country charm à la Dollywood, both the kind of locales criticized for whitewashing the South's historical legacy. In contrast, the Shack Up Inn noticeably serves up "poor" for all to see, stylizing it in gender and race and proudly putting it out there in a bold assertion of cultural authority. Grounds for this claim include the place's prevailing aesthetics—parts rustic agri-chic, eclectic arty funk, voodoo vibe, boyish insubordination, and heartfelt tribute to good men and hard times, all offered up within an aura of exhibition-meets-hospitality. As that popular southern colloquialism goes: "We don't hide our crazy; we put it out on the front porch and offer it a drink."

These aesthetics of the Shack Up Inn beg for our attention in a spectacle suggestive of *tacky*, that conspicuous visual style historically aligned with poor white southerners. Characterized by the overblown use of cheaply made, mass-produced materials, *tacky* revels in the artificial (i.e., Why have "real" when "fake" looks just as good and lasts longer?) and conveys a sense of undisciplined excess (i.e., "More is always better than less.") in flagrant disregard of standards of good taste based on restraint. It is this dimension of *spectacle* that facilitates a general reading of *tacky* as feminine, even if not immediately recognized as such. We most often associate *tacky* with cheap women, not men, and their accompanying bad taste in accessories and decor. More obviously, of course, *tacky* is coded as "poor," its dimensions coming together to connote low socioeconomic status, shameless nouveau riche at its best and tasteless vulgarity at its worst.

Additionally, significantly, if not immediately apprehended as such, *tacky* is raced as "white," aligned with poor white culture and its "trash," and coded as southern from way back. From its early-nineteenth-century definition as a term referring to a small degenerate horse of little value, *tacky* evolved to connote *ill-breeding* and soon was tagged specifically to a distinctive subculture, *poor white*, consisting of white, economically disadvantaged farmworkers without their own property or slaves and who squatted on others' land ("Tacky"). This association stuck through the years, and while the concept currently is not exclusive to southerners, *tacky* nonetheless remains a hallmark of poor white southern culture as America's underclass, serving to solidify its low position in the social hierarchy while at the same time affording critical potential for escaping that abject station.[2] Recognizing the latter, many popular tourist attractions from the well-known Graceland and

Dollywood to the lesser-known Mammy's Cupboard, a Mississippi diner housed in the skirts of a giant replica of the beloved *Gone With the Wind* character, have capitalized on this regional association, embracing *tacky* and catering to tourists captivated by its kitschy appeal.

While the aesthetics of the Shack Up Inn exhibit shades of *tack*, a closer examination of that site reveals elements beyond *tacky* as conventionally defined. My analysis leads me to assert that the Shack Up Inn features a variation of *tack*, a complex visual aesthetic that draws upon sensibilities of and marshals poor white trash elements associated with *tacky* but stylizes them in gender and racial legacies distinctive to place. The result is more than merely a quirky sense of style tagged as lowbrow but rather a distinctive aesthetic enterprise that elevates poor white southern culture, ironically, via the very elements typically used to devalue said culture, pointing the way to a new understanding of "southernness." Let me show you what I mean.

THE RITZ WE AIN'T

When reading the Shack Up Inn's website (www.shackupinn.com), one gets the image of a fairly straightforward tribute to the sharecropping life, a version of the South seldom celebrated, overshadowed by tributes to the romanticized Old South. The collection of shacks is situated on the grounds of Hopson Plantation, a former cotton farm with historical significance; in 1944, the Hopson Planting Company produced the very first cotton crop taken from the seeds to baling by machine, reducing the need for manual labor. One of those laborers was Joe Willie "Pinetop" Perkins, pianist for the renowned blues artist Muddy Waters. The Shack Up celebrates Pinetop and other Black male sharecroppers, tempting guests to get a more intimate feel for this version of the South by staying overnight. The cotton gin/registration area doubles as a concert hall for local blues artists, as well as amateur pickers who bring their guitars and harmonicas for weeklong workshops and attend the popular Juke Joint Festival and other folksy gatherings. As such, the Shack Up Inn presents itself as *the place* to have an authentic live-in sharecropper experience via the lens of the Delta blues, and enthusiasts, primarily Europeans, heed the call and come knocking on this stop down the historical Blues Trail. Like I said, it all seems pretty straightforward.

On the other hand, to physically wander onto the grounds of the Shack Up Inn is to encounter a bit of unsettling ground-shifting as one takes in the cultural cues and tries to make sense of the place in which very little seems straightforward, actually. Perhaps this feeling of uncertainty is due to the overt poverty chic sensibility that pervades the place; shotgun shacks, once a symbol of destitution and hard times, now function as objects of desire at the price of one hundred dollars or so a night. Is this an appropriation that we should embrace, we might ask ourselves? Or perhaps the feeling of disorientation arises from the ubiquitous tongue-in-cheek tone that hangs in the air; religious artifacts, namely crosses and altars, are found in the midst of beer-induced revelry beneath a sign that reads: "Juke Joint Chapel/Prepare to Meet Thy God."

What are we to make of this send-up of religion, especially in the conservative Bible Belt? Whose joke is this, and who is being played? Add to this the supernatural air hanging over a place situated a stone's throw away from the infamous crossroads of Routes 61 and 49, where legend has it that father of the blues, Robert Johnson, traded his soul in a dark, dank Mississippi night to the devil in exchange for the guitar-playing genius that made him famous. That ethereal aura pervades the grounds of the Shack Up, materialized in artifacts redolent of voodoo culture. Might there be wandering haints captured in those vibrant bottle trees? The ensuing ambiance is one of finding yourself in a "slightly off" world of domesticity operating under an alternative logic, as objects that typically call up painful historical periods or seriously sacred values are loosened from those semiotic moorings to traffic in other meanings. It is a bit hard to find one's footing in this otherworldly place, to make sense of it all, but that is precisely the point: we are not supposed to make sense of it in rational terms; rather, we are meant to feel the sense of place outside of the parameters of rationality.

This alternative logic is carried on the backs of aesthetic sensibilities appealing primarily to emotions and grounded in localized cultural materials in a recasting of historical legacies for a contemporary audience. At the center of this recasting is class—poverty, to be specific—

conveyed materially as the sharecropper's experience but, meaningfully, stylized in a particular form of regionalized southern masculinity drawing upon sensibilities of blackness as it circulates whiteness. I classify this version of masculinity as huckster style, a mash-up between the likes of Mark Twain's iconic literary character, Huckleberry Finn, and Eshu, the trickster figure of African Yoruba mythology.[3] The result is a potent aesthetic of class and race awash in southern regionalism.

When all is said and done, visitors to the Shack Up Inn are encouraged to apprehend poor white southern culture in terms of gendered (manhood) and racial (blackness) sensibilities. I turn now to an explication of three aesthetic dimensions of huckster style: nostalgia, humor, and homage. I then contemplate huckster's critical implications for tacky in general and southern culture in particular, noting the potential in style as cipher.

NOSTALGIA

As is the case with most tourist sites of southernness, *nostalgia*, or a wistful longing for days gone by, is a palpable mood on the grounds of the Shack Up Inn, putting teeth into the oft-quoted words of Faulkner's fiction: "The past is never dead. It's not even past" (73). While most commercial sites of the South mobilize pining for a romanticized version of a "moonlight and magnolias" South with cavaliers, hoop-skirted belles, and white-columned mansions, the Shack Up Inn appeals to a different sort of imagined South: the view from the tractor shed, offering up a laid-back, rural life on the land with no role for ambition and its nagging pressures for upward mobility. To be sure, visitors to the inn see obvious *symbols* of work: rusty combines, broken-down plows, and various farm implements scattered in the yards and hung on the shack walls. However, upon closer inspection, there is no serious portrayal of *work* on this farm, historical or otherwise, with the exception of a single Blues Trail sign out front referencing the historical first of mechanized cotton farming. There are no lectures on planting or tours of cotton fields for guests, even though you can literally reach out and touch the bolls as you wander through the fields planted to augment the visual effect of the place. Indeed, there is no *work* defined as *labor* in this recasting of a plantation, an ironic statement for a former cotton plantation where sharecroppers labored in the fields and voiced musically their despair of endless oppressive work. Instead, we see the accoutrements of labor, farm tools and implements used as ciphers attesting to cultural authenticity although, significantly, detached from their connection to the actual bodies performing the labor, primarily those of Black men and women.

You might say that this is nothing new; recasting resulting in obscuration takes place in other tourist sites of southernness, where a focus on mansions and mint juleps at the expense of the slave labor upholding that leisured life essentially erases race, all in the service of a white nostalgia. But the semiotic muddying of work in the Shack Up Inn takes a different focus: this is a man-child's playground, marked by simple pleasures of beer drinking and guitar picking with no one harping on you to "get back to work." This is not a fancified, feminized, whitewashed version of the South but a gritty depiction of "life on the land" made up of actual homes (shacks) brought together in a familial concept of settling down often associated with women as the domesticators and, indeed, keepers of "home." Strikingly, however, there is nothing either domesticated or feminine about the Shack Up Inn. This establishment rejects the structured, mannered world of southern, cultured, white femininity. Guests are warned before their arrival that "the Ritz we ain't"; there is no cleaning service during a visit, but a side benefit is that the roof leaks "only when it rains." There is no room service, no fine linens, no wake-up calls, no need ever to get cleaned up or be on schedule. There is, however, "all the beer your liver can stand" and a funky concert space right across the lawn with buddies waiting for you.

These elicited feelings constitute nostalgia of a particular sort—a juvenile yearning for escape from adult responsibilities. Here, "poor" is tinged with a huckster vibe of freedom from the woman's world, and thus apprehended not as destitute but as release from the sissified conventions of civilization that suck the life out of men, trapping them in the never-ending treadmill of ambition and upward mobility. The Shack Up Inn exudes nostalgia for a made-up past, a yearning for an imagined life with no real responsibilities except, perhaps, for keeping enough cold beer on ice.

HUMOR

Not surprisingly, there is an impish tone in this adult playground, where nothing is to be taken too seriously, *poverty*, least of all. Life's troubles can be managed capably through clever resourcefulness within a spirit of rebellion, while imbibing a few cold ones, puffing on a harmonica, and belting out a good, sad song. This is huckster sensibility: no sophomoric fart jokes here, but rather a type of stylized pert wit characterized by lovable impudence.

A hefty portion of this *humor* is delivered subtly via a clever repurposing of "poor" items in a tongue-in-cheek sensibility long associated with poor whites forced to make do with what they had. Abandoned car tires are painted in vibrant colors and used as planters for petunias, for instance, and hubcaps and cut-up license plates adorn walls as art. Old wooden doors are hung horizontally over beds as headboards, and a kitchen spatula hangs in one shower, serving as a soap dish. Items of vintage farm culture appear throughout the place; grain bins are refitted to become charming cottages with gin loading docks used as patios, and various tools hang on the gin wall as decoration. Each shack has a porch (how could it *not*?), either open or screened, outfitted with cast-off items used as furniture; a ripped bench seat removed from an old, junked van, for example, when propped against the wall, serves as a front porch loveseat right next to an abandoned church pew. Overall, a spirit of childlike makeshift mischief is carried out via the resourceful and eclectic arrangement of repurposed "trashy" artifacts.

This clever, often irreverent, sense of humor takes form as well in the designated names and descriptions for each shack, visible on hand-scribbled signs throughout the grounds, as well as in artfully printed souvenir posters available in the "lobby." Guests are encouraged to take home a little spirit of the place, and what better form than a depiction of a shack with its bawdy and/or slightly inappropriate tag line? They might select from the Biscuit shack with its slogan: "If your biscuit don't rise, it's not the butter's fault," and the Fullilove shack, the "no-tell motel" with its cheeky motto: "Bring your wife or your girlfriend; heck bring both of em!" Such hetero-masculine messages point to a dark history of gender and racial politics in the South, wherein privileged white men could and often did get away from the restrictions of the "big house" to have their way with women, Black and white. Here, however, such messages are coded as harmless and amusing, yet, significantly, a touch old and grizzled (i.e., certainly not "young"), the sort of comments your slightly inappropriate uncle might say, lending much to an air of impertinent humor in accordance with huckster style.

HOMAGE

Complementing these sensibilities of *nostalgia* and *humor* is *homage*, discernable as genuine admiration for Delta bluesmen and romanticized Black male sharecroppers as cultural heroes. The place is a tribute to artists like Pinetop Perkins, the "boogie-woogie piano man" who lived on the premises, drove a tractor at Hopson, and played and sang away his hard times, teaching the greats like Ike Turner to play piano and eventually finding great fame and Grammy recognition himself. Pinetop and other blues stars are revered at the inn, their music in the form of vinyl 45s hanging on the walls of the shacks, along with their 8x10 black and white portraits. Check in, and you can live for a night or two like they did, playing the old piano in your shack's front room and perhaps catching a bit of their muse. Or reserve the flagship shack named for Robert Clay, a hardscrabble sharecropper who lived his whole life in that shack, raising several sons who never knew their daddy kept a whiskey still in the attic until after his death. Stories and artifacts like these are preserved in homage to the Delta bluesmen in a genuine and heartfelt appreciation, and it is no wonder why blues enthusiasts travel from across the globe to visit the Shack Up Inn and soak up the atmosphere. This is bromance, huckster-style.

Accordingly, the tribute to these men comes across as sincere, not merely marketing schticks to capitalize on European interest, although there is that, too. These are musicians historically relegated to the margins, only in the last forty years or so becoming "cool" as establishments along the Blues Trail mark their place in the wider American culture. The reverence for their contributions is palpable on the grounds of the Shack Up, perhaps the only part of the place meant to be taken seriously. Notably, however, the veneration at this site is not a typical commemoration of the bluesmen. There are no detailed plaques of their musical accomplishments, no statues or grandiose markers dedicated to their greatness. Instead, visitors are encouraged to immerse themselves in this sharecropper world of hard times, sit a spell on the front porch, listen to the tunes coming from the SiriusXM channel inside playing exclusively the blues, and perhaps even feel inspired to pick up a guitar and follow along in what might be the highest form of tribute. On the whole, what is celebrated in these artists is their art*form*, the blues as stylized despair generated from southern legacies of poverty and racial oppression, and that artform comes with a lifestyle of boozy escapism and release.

Correspondingly in the huckster style, the act of honoring such heroes takes an alternative form of worship with its own kind of prayers and liturgy, far from the sanitized veneration found in many mainstream places of worship, particularly those characterized as "white." As pilgrims, Shack Up Inn guests bring their guitars and harmonicas with the hopes of catching muses and replicating the former occupants' artistic flair, in music and person, if only for a weekend in this sacred space. Summoning spirits is not without risk, however. Several trees adorned with brightly colored, slim-necked bottles dot the ground, an affirmation of the African tradition of bottle trees poised to trap wandering evil spirits. After all, this is the region where Robert Johnson sold his soul to the devil for musical genius; perhaps that offer still stands today.

HUCKSTER'S IMPROBABLE POTENCY

Any explications of the aesthetic dimensions of huckster style begs the larger questions of its potency and relevance to *tacky*. In general, we know that the spectacular—even mesmerizing—dimensions of *tacky* are what initially captures the eye of critics seeking to understand its rhetorical power. *Tacky* is widely known to be gaudy, over-the-top, shiny, enormous, cheap, overly sentimental, and synthetic. Significantly, these spectacular aesthetics assume a gendered dimension when it comes to *tacky*, linked with femininity "gone too far," as in the case of women who embody overabundance like Dolly Parton with her big hair and ample bosom or younger versions of aesthetic overload, Jessica Simpson and Britney Spears, who exemplify emotional excess with their immoderate sentimentality redolent of childlike naïveté. We know that performative abundance aligns easily with femininity, a construction steeped in artifice and yet, ironically, perceived "naturally." Bell, for example, has gone so far as to say that performance is "the ground zero of the feminine," pointing to women's everyday enactments of feminine deportment and bodily adornments as evidence (351). In short, when we think of *tacky*, we do so in terms of traits and aesthetics apprehended as *excessively feminine*.

The huckster aesthetics at the Shack Up Inn, however, point critics in a different direction. This style is a variation of *tacky* marked as masculine, not feminine, and that regendering enables traction in a manner that *tacky* with its feminine footings does not. "Dixie, after all, is a woman's name," as McPherson reminds us, and, accordingly, southern studies aficionados have traced the ways in which the South has been feminized as a means for reconciling regional shame and loss (19). Within the powerful Lost Cause mythology, the South is rendered as white virtuous womanhood, worthy of honor but vulnerable, constantly in need of valiant protection.[4] Part of that protection entails chivalry, as white men engaged in actions ranging from good manners of opening doors to abhorrent acts of violence including lynching, all in the name of honoring their women. Another, less obvious means of protecting a regional form of femininity is the establishment and reinforcement of aesthetic codes that distinguish respectable womanhood high on the pedestal from its lowbrow version, cheap womanhood. *Tacky* is situated in the latter, of course.

Huckster style maneuvers a sidestepping of "cheap, fake, and garish," incorporating trashy elements in a new semiotic system that effectively rejects the feminine and mobilizes the masculine as *organic to the place*. This is a move made possible via masculinity's general theoretical position as being close to nature and "all things wild," while in contrast, femininity is aligned theoretically with domesticated culture.[5] In this vein, masculinity is mobilized via features viewed as *elemental* in southern culture, in substance and in style. Artifacts tinged with regionalized masculinity, including farm implements, hubcaps, and vintage gas signs, are not only local but decrepit, the rustier the better. Unlike the mass-produced materials of tacky valued for their shiny plastic newness as signs of modern progress, these artifacts have meaning in both their obvious state of decay and connection to locale. As such, they have "life," in that they appear to "grow" organically from the place, seemingly coming into completion by *entelechy*, a life-giving force rather than a fashioned design (Trilling 127). The "organic," folklore studies tells us, provides a well-worn avenue to authenticity, and with "authentic" comes higher aesthetic value.[6]

If *gender*—in particular, masculinity—redeems poverty at the Shack Up Inn, due credit must be given to *race*, as well. While not overtly announced, *race* is nonetheless present stylistically at this site, functioning as warrant for cultural authority. Huckster masculinity draws upon aesthetics of blackness, primarily in the blues style that pervades the place, but also in the prominence of bottle trees and voodoo sentiments, nods to African and subsequent African American slave culture. In short, huckster calls up Black culture sensitivities, marshaling the aesthetics for its own manifestation as an authentically "cool" style, an assertion of cultural authority that registers emotionally via a complex interplay of *nostalgia*, *humor*, and *homage*.

While scholars might be tempted to disparage this move outright as an appropriation of cultural style in unethical and/or hegemonic terms, we might pause to consider one aspect of critical potential: *style as cypher*. McPherson points to this promise in her assertion that style has the capacity to function as more than mere commodification of culture; as an example, she notes the stylistic dissidence in products of the African American-owned clothing company, NuSouth, where the Confederate Flag is turned on its head, sporting the blacks, greens, and reds of the African liberation movement (36–37).

While hard-pressed at this point to argue that huckster style constitutes such critical dissidence in a wholesale manner, I nonetheless submit that style as emplaced at the Shack Up Inn should not be hastily dismissed as either an unsurprising commodification of lowbrow culture or a straightforward co-optation of sensibilities of blackness. Rather, huckster style's very existence as a permutation of *tacky* suggests the complexity of a visual aesthetic perhaps too rashly assessed by critics as static and/or one-dimensional. Further, this display of huckster style showcases the ingenuity of southerners—in this case, *white* southerners—who, rather than being subjugated by a historical, popular association with *tacky*, demonstrate the creative resourcefulness to adapt it in the service of asserting and maintaining cultural authority. We would do well to take such rhetorical enterprise seriously if we are to understand the South beyond caricature.

NOTES

1. See Waggoner and Taylor for more on women and the construction of southern regional identities.

2. For more on poor white culture in the United States, see both Isenberg and Wray.

3. Lewis explains how trickster figures appear in the mythology of many cultures, often in the form of animal characters, using their power to transgress physical and social boundaries.

4. For an explanation of the Lost Cause mythology, see Tindall.

5. I find Ortner's early piece still to be very helpful in explaining this construction of gender.

6. For discussions of the role of *authenticity* in cultures, see both R. Cobb and Bendix.

WORKS CITED

Bell, Elizabeth. "Performance Studies as Women's Work: Historical Sights/ Sites/Citations from the Margin." *Text and Performance Quarterly*, vol. 13, no. 4, 1993, pp. 350–74.

Bendix, Regina. *In Search of Authenticity: The Formation of Folklore Studies.* U of Wisconsin P, 1997.

Cobb, James C. *The Most Southern Place on Earth: The Mississippi Delta and the Roots of Regional Identity.* Oxford UP, 1992.

Cobb, Russell. *The Paradox of Authenticity in a Globalized World.* Palgrave MacMillan, 2014.

Faulkner, William. *Requiem for a Nun.* Random House, 1950.

Isenberg, Nancy. *White Trash: The 400-Year Untold History of Class in America.* Viking, 2016.

Lewis, Hyde. *Trickster Makes This World: Mischief, Myth, and Art.* Farrar, Straus and Giroux, 2010.

McPherson, Tara. *Reconstructing Dixie: Race, Gender, and Nostalgia in the Imagined South.* Duke UP, 2003.

Ortner, Sherry. "Is Female to Male as Nature is to Culture?" *Women, Culture, and Society*, edited by M. Z. Rosaldo and L. Lamphere, Stanford UP, 1974, pp. 67–87.

"Tacky." www.etymonline.com/word/tacky (1 October 2021).

Tindall, George B. "Mythic South." *Myth, Manners, and Memory.* Vol. 4 of *The New Encyclopedia of Southern Culture*, edited by Charles Reagan Wilson, U of North Carolina P, 2006, pp. 126–27.

Trilling, Lionel. *Sincerity and Authenticity.* Harvard UP, 1972.

Waggoner, Catherine E., and Laura E. Taylor. *Realizing Our Place: Real Southern Women in a Mythologized Land.* UP of Mississippi, 2018.

Ward, Jesmyn. "The Mississippi-est Part of Mississippi." *YouTube*, uploaded by Off the Shelf, 10 August 2017, www.youtube.com/watch?v=QC31iya4jPY.

Wray, Matt. *Not Quite White: White Trash and the Boundaries of Whiteness.* Duke UP, 2006.

READING *LOLITA*
IN COAL COUNTRY

JIMMY DEAN SMITH

This essay contains accounts of child sexual exploitation. Its title alludes to both Vladimir Nabokov's *Lolita* and to Azar Nafisi's *Reading Lolita in Tehran*. Nafisi asserts that "the desperate truth of Lolita's story is not the rape of a twelve-year-old by a dirty old man but the *confiscation of one individual's life by another*" (33, italics in original). In this essay, I refer to that theme of enchantment and possession. But Nabokov's charming narrator is a monster, and Humbert Humbert's exploitation of a little girl devastates many readers no matter how pretty his prose. Like the episodes of child-rape in *Lolita*, the specimens of exploitation in this essay are fictional, but that does not mean they feel untrue.

*T*exts created by popular artists who are foreign to coal country, outsiders who choose to exploit the place-mythology of Appalachia, represent genres that are sometimes perceived as tacky, or even trashy—potboiler, exploitation film, sociological porn. Vladimir Nabokov's novel *Lolita* (1955) toys with the latter, as well as several other downscale genres, to create a ludic modernist art novel, while *The Trail of the Lonesome Pine* (1908) by John Fox, Jr., and the movie *Child Bride* (1938) aim putatively for sincerity, though the exploitative nature of these texts is never in doubt. The action of *Lolita* takes it across the United States, but the importance of coal country—its seldom acknowledged identification of Appalachia with the victimized child of its title—is central to its theme of exploitation. The two other texts are primarily set in coal country, near the "white hot center of cognitive Appalachia [where] the mythopoetic idea" of the region is strongest in the popular imagination (Smith 169). I aim to draw place-specific comparisons between rapacious industrialization and the monstrosity of sexual predation—that is, between the instrumentalization of Appalachia and that of the children who live among its resource-rich mountains. To do so, I use texts that revolve around three modes of child exploitation: grooming; child marriage; and rape.

The dating of my main texts extends into the mid-twentieth century, but they are all influenced by rhetorical moves practiced by nineteenth-century writers: sentimentalism, the promise of verisimilitude, the pleasures of uninspected myth. In his foundational study *Appalachia on Our Mind*, Henry D. Shapiro examines how, in the period of national self-examination following the Civil War, "local-color writers and . . . Protestant home missionaries" (xiv) developed a rhetoric that "made Appalachia seem a strange land inhabited by a peculiar people" (xiii), a backwards regional Other, "in but not of America" (xiv). To "integrate Appalachia into America" (xvi), "agents of systematic benevolence and . . . agents of economic modernization" stepped forward (xvii). Shapiro stops short of including outright profiteering among the results (or goals?) of coal country mythopoesis, but other theoretical frameworks make room for predatory capital. Arriving in the 1970s, for example, the "internal colony" model allows for an "understanding [of] the region's web of exploitation," writes Elizabeth Catte, that extends well into the twentieth century and "the domination of the coal industry" (122). In the early years of the industrialization of Appalachia, "[the word *exploitation* was] a nonpejorative" meaning the "absorption of the natural wealth of the region into the national economy" (McCauley 395). To exploit was to recognize and realize the potential of a mountain, river, or person. *The Trail of the Lonesome Pine, Child Bride,* and *Lolita* all embody this pattern of recognition-realization in the person of a pedagogue, an uplifter whose motives are suspect at best.

Shapiro notes how the post-Civil War "local-colorists" helped establish "a conventional view of the mountain region as an area untouched by . . . progressive and unifying forces," an area open to industry. But, "[b]y 1890," he writes, the mythologizing had begun focusing on "degradation and degeneracy" (5). An essay written in 1886 illustrates how those modes crossed paths. Once a popular novelist, in his travel writing the Bluegrass native James Lane Allen (1849–1925) explored the resource-rich Cumberland Mountains for urban readers, delivering tropes that are still valuable to exploiters of the region (Shapiro 26–29): "Here are some of the finest coal-fields in the world . . . a virgin growth of the finest economic timbers" (244). Untapped natural bounty would appeal to outsider capital, but, suggests Lane, ethical moneyed philanthropists *must* exploit (i.e., "use") nature's plenty because Appalachia's people will otherwise continue in squalor, "responding feebly to the influences of civilization" (228). Among the many types of coal country backwardness Allen notes are mountaineers' sexual practices: "There is among the people a low standard of morality in their domestic relations [and] the delicate privacies of home life" (236). The Victorian fussiness of Allen's travelogue obscures neither its winking voyeurism nor its innate rhetorical appeal to normative culture. For the sake of Christian decency, eastern capital must intervene in coal country.

Allen's essay arrived at an early peak of outsider enthusiasm for mountain stereotype, when expanded rail travel made it all the easier to encounter the degenerate Other. Essayists like Allen provided some of the stereotypes, while trains let tourists and extractive industrialists experience coal country up close. Capitalists took natural resources out of the mountains; tourists took souvenirs. "Since at least the 1890s," writes the cultural historian Patrick Huber, "vacationers have happily carted home cheap, gaudy, mass-produced souvenirs to commemorate their Dixie excursions" (72). By 2008, Huber's own collection of "tacky southern souvenirs [and] southern kitsch" already comprised "more than four hundred items, including hillbilly postcards; outhouse-shaped salt-and-pepper shakers; an 'American by Birth, Southern by the Grace of God' t-shirt," and so on (69), many of which toyed with—and institutionalized—the othering myths of coal country. Perhaps the most pernicious of those regarded aberrant sexuality. "[I]n the national imagination," writes Huber, "hillbillies . . . are often cast as savage barbarians with frightening sexual appetites. . . . including incest, rape, pedophilia, and bestiality" (76). Profiting from a mythopoetic loop, entrepreneurs of coal country kitsch created tacky icons of Appalachian eros, including "the crown jewel of [Huber's] collection," the Horny Hillbilly, "a small plastic figurine . . . that depicts a stereotypical southern mountaineer [with] a monstrous, erect tallywhacker" (69–70). What damage this grotesque humanoid (it "resembles West African fertility statues or some images of the Greek god Pan") could wreak in a one-room cabin is suggested by a joke Huber repeats: "Question: 'What's a hillbilly virgin?' Punch-line: 'An ugly third-grader'" (76).

Crass, unfunny, and clearly horrifying, that joke plays on premises useful to exploiters of children, of course, and also to exploiters of the land those children inhabit. In environmental writing about coal country, writes Allen Batteau, there are "certain elements we have come to expect in the image-making . . . most notably references to Appalachia as a bounded region, represented by a young girl . . . [a] lissome girl representing the land" (184). Metaphorically, the land is third-graders who are not "ugly"—who are "worth exploiting." As the mythology plays out in the texts below, the youth and fragility of the girl-children representing Appalachia are not cautions against victimization but invitations to despoil.

"HAVE YOU EVER BEEN A CHILD BRIDE?"

Today, the pageant of musty hillbilly tropes in *Kentucky Moonshine*, a comedy starring the Ritz Brothers (1938) seems typical of disposable Saturday afternoon fare, full of fake beards, 'shine, and feuding. But in 1938, a line a reporter speaks casually to the Appalachian female lead, "Have you ever been a child bride?" was up-to-the-minute humor. As Nicholas L. Syrett points out, in 1937, national newspapers reported the marriage of a nine-year-old girl to a twenty-two-year-old man in Tennessee (202), a sensational story that confirmed popular (titillating, horrifying) myths of backcountry debauchery. The Tennessee marriage inspired not only a one-liner in a forgettable movie (and an embarrassed flurry of legislation in Nashville) but also *Child Bride* (1938), a classic exploitation movie about the marriage of an eleven-year-old girl to a middle-aged man. The film putatively urges audiences to take a stand against the vile practice of child marriage, proffering a social justice project as a pretext for disturbing material, including child nudity and a plot turning on the (thankfully thwarted) legal rape of an eleven-year-old. (I say "legal" rape because, in the film, sex with girl-children is authorized by the state.)

An opening crawl frames *Child Bride* as both anthropology and activism: "In dramatizing life among these 'back yonder' folk—we aim neither to ridicule nor to defend their mode of living . . . and if our story will help to abolish Child Marriage—it will have served its purpose" (punctuation as in original). In fact, the movie persistently ridicules the people of "Thunderhead Mountain," spending the entirety of its sixty-two minutes both displaying and assailing their mode of life, which is based largely on state-sanctioned pedophilia. The theme of legal child marriage also appears in *Lolita*. Humbert Humbert notes that he could have married his victim in "some of the United States" (135): how can his fetish be abhorrent, he asks, if several states would sanction it? One character in *Child Bride*, the teacher Miss Carol, is a champion of progressive marriage laws, and several stretches of film show her assailing Thunderhead's retrograde practices. Many of the locals, both men and women, object: their whole social structure relies on child marriage. Perhaps the most famous recounting of child marriage in coal country, Loretta Lynn's *Coal Miner's Daughter* depicts an ecosystem, the coal camp, reliant on marriage practices that we would today find anachronistic (as did Lynn herself when she wrote her story in the 1970s). The wedding night itself is played for laughs—thirteen-year-old Loretta doesn't know better than to come to bed fully dressed—until it ends with a reminder of what child brides endured: "He really had a time with this little girl he married. He finally had to more or less rip off my panties" (51). Although *Child Bride* ends before such events come to pass, it titillates with the same possibility.

At the time the film was released, Syrett writes, Tennessee had already changed its laws, thus rendering moot the film's putative reformer purpose; *Child Bride* "exploits in the name of banning exploitation" (217). The film's exploitative centerpiece lies halfway through the film. Unencumbered by the production code that restrained studio movies, *Child Bride* features an infamous five-minute sequence that includes numerous shots of the protagonist, played by twelve-year-old Shirley Mills, swimming nude while Jake, the film's stereotypical hillbilly villain, a moonshiner and murderer, spies on her. Not watching, however, is Jennie's lifelong friend, Freddie, another pubescent child (who goes shirtless for minutes at a time). Today, for the first time, Jennie forbids him to skinny-dip with her and makes him turn his back when she undresses. "Freddie, you ain't going swimming with me no more," says Jennie. "So don't you take your clothes off. . . . [Y]ou can't see me without my clothes on." Freddie's responses—"We've always gone in swimming together" and "I know how you look without your clothes on. I've seen you lots of times"—balance playacted innocence and titillation, establishing for the film's viewers a long history of the little girl's unblushing nudity. That balance tips decidedly toward carnality when Freddie complains, "Now I can't kiss you no more," and Jennie replies, "Of course you can, silly. Only with my clothes on." Apparently, the children have kissed in the nude "lots of times" before. The dialog sequence concludes with Jennie admonishing Freddie, "Now don't beg."

The framing of the children's blossoming sexual lives has changed. How does Jennie know that it is wrong to go naked in front of Freddie? "Teacher says not to," says Jennie. "Teacher says that I shouldn't put bad ideas into your head." Although Miss Carol is native to Thunderhead Mountain, "Teacher" has "been out in the world, [has] gone to school" and thinks it her "duty" to uplift the locals. Representing middle-class morality, as well as the hope that education will modernize other children as well (predictably, Jennie is her star pupil), "Teacher" opens her students' eyes to their shame, reminding little girls that it is their fault if boys get "bad ideas." What Allen Batteau writes about Mary Noailles Murfree's fiction suggests how the local-colorist's mythologizing informs *Child Bride*: "[The] mountains are identified as feminine. . . . [T]he lissome girls, signifiers of the mountains par excellence, are linked to Nature [and] every case opposed to educated outsiders. . . . The Nature of the mountains and these lissome girls is opposed to the world of business and battles and government bureaus" (Batteau 50). With her boyfriend working to convince the governor to outlaw child marriage, Miss Carol is a potent foe of Thunderhead's "mode of living." During the swimming scene, Freddie says, "I wish that teacher would mind her own business." It is a complaint he shares with several other males on Thunderhead Mountain, including the Peeping Tom on the ridge. Jake controls a ring of middle-aged men who hate Miss Carol because "she's out preaching against us marrying young uns." Their toxic "mode of living" (feuding, moonshining, lying about) is based on the "master/slave" relationship they maintain with underaged wives. Harry Revier's script lets these men champion their way of life, and even Miss Carol argues against child marriage on biological and social grounds, as if the immorality of state-sanctioned statutory rape were not reason enough.

But debate takes a backseat in the film's prurient conclusion. Having murdered Jennie's father and framed Jennie's mother for the crime, Jake forces the girl into marriage. The middle-aged man and his child bride celebrate with a kiss. The action shifts to a scene at Miss Carol's house. Her "sweetheart" arrives in a car that also carries two lawmen. They have come to Thunderhead Mountain to post notices that eighteen is now the minimum age for marriage. Later we see Jennie, in Jake's cabin, slipping into a nightgown. Offscreen, Jake, with a note of irritation, tells her to "jump into bed." Only a fatal shot fired from outside saves Jennie from her fate. The child bride, now a child widow, reunites with Freddie. The corpse in the cabin—the children have no idea who shot Jake—is forgotten. "It's all right now," says Freddie. "You don't have to be *his* wife. Later [that is, when they are both grown], you can be mine." They kiss on the lips, Jennie in nightgown, Freddie's shirt unbuttoned to the waist, and the movie ends. In about five minutes of screen time, she has gone from newlywed to widow to just engaged. Her next marriage, however, will be uplifted, befitting a world of education, and laws, and sweethearts wearing three-piece suits and driving cars.

We do not see who fires on Jake—we do see that Freddie has stationed himself outside with a rifle but that it is not aimed into Jake's cabin—so once more Jennie is the subject of a voyeur's gaze, in this case the assassin's. By focusing on Jennie in a one-shot, we viewers are also made to bring our gaze to the girl in her nightgown, a shot that recalls one at the beginning of the film in which Jennie in her nightgown is backlit so her body's outlines are exposed. But we are nonplussed. As when we joined Jake, the bad voyeur, in spying on the naked girl, we are the *good* voyeurs, prurient outsiders with the excuse of anthropo-logical curiosity and the moral charge of uplifting the hillbilly.

"AND AS SPRING PASSED AND THE SUMMER CAME ON, THE LITTLE GIRL BUDDED AND OPENED LIKE A ROSE"

The phrase *little girl* appears eighty-four times in *The Trail of the Lonesome Pine* (1908). The female protagonist of John Fox, Jr.'s, novel is June Tolliver, a barefoot child of the mountains when readers first see her sitting "at the base of the big tree—her little sunbonnet pushed back, her arms locked about her knees, her bare feet gathered under her crimson gown and her deep eyes fixed on the smoke in the valley below" (1). She is gazing out on that "big world" (2) when its handsome emissary arrives. The male protagonist is Jack Hale, a college-educated "bluegrass engineer" who "comes to the mountains to make his fortune in coal but remains to fall in love with the region and with a simple mountain girl" (Pearce viii). Jack's first sight of June emphasizes her erotic connection with nature: her "crimson gown" reminds him of "a flaming bush of sumach [sic]" (7). To his greeting of "Howdye [sic], Little Girl?" her silent response is startlingly on the Freudian nose: "One bare toe went burrowing suddenly into the sand, one finger went to her red mouth" (10).

A romance so beloved it has been turned into three feature films and an outdoor drama, *The Trail of the Lonesome Pine* shares with Nabokov's *Lolita* an obvious (in *Trail*'s case, even more flagrant) focus on the pubescent form as object of desire. Likewise, each novel congratulates its male protagonist for spotting the local talent. Humbert explains that he can see past the unremarkable looks of certain "demoniac" "maidens" "[b]etween the age limits of nine and fourteen" (Nabokov 16) to "the fey grace. the elusive, shifty, soul-shattering, insidious charm that separates the nymphet" from other little girls (17). Jack is not, like Humbert, "an artist and a madman, a creature of infinite melancholy" (17), but in these parts he might be something better: a university-trained land speculator with "the vision of a seer" (Fox 41). Like the most infamous pedophile in literature, Jack has an eye for nymphet possibility: "a sculptor would have loved the rounded slenderness in the curving long lines that shaped her brown throat, her arms and her hands, . . . and her dangling bare leg. . . . . Some day that little nose would be long enough, and some day, he thought, she would be very beautiful" (81–82). And Jack has designs on the mountains, too, readily discerning that "the Gap" is the best place in the world to exploit "the four raw materials for the making of iron" (42). His industrial project climaxes in an erotic vision: "[T]here lay before him a beautiful valley. . . . the heaven-born site for the unborn city of his dreams, and his eyes swept every curve of the valley longingly" (44). June will be an improvement project, too: "The little girl . . . was born for something more than slow death in that God-forsaken cove . . . why not help her to it if he could? With this thought in his brain, he rode down from the luminous upper world of the moon and stars toward the nether world of drifting mists and black ravines. She belonged to such a night—that little girl—she was part of its mists, its lights and shadows, its fresh wild beauty and its mystery" (87). The prose in *Trail of the Lonesome Pine* is often like that: swoony, overmodified, not quite subject to any sort of internal logic. Although the novel takes clichéd turns into feuding and moonshining (or, per Shapiro, helps those clichés flourish), at heart the book is about Jack grooming a girl-child named for the month spring becomes summer.

Mid-century American novelists like Augusta Jane Evans (*Beulah* [1859]) and Susan Warner had written similarly pedagogical novels in which an older man, spotting a girl's potential, makes it his mission to educate—and then marry—the child. The catchphrase "little sister" in Warner's *The Wide, Wide World* (1850, reissued 1895) even prefigures Jack Hale's "little girl." Although Fox, too, is often assailed for sentimentality, such criticism does not obtain to nearly the degree that it does with Evans and Warner—perhaps because of his gender, or his locale, or his propensity for balancing sentimentality with such eruptions of stereotypes of toxic masculinity as feuding and moonshining. In any event, Jack Hale decides to refine "that little girl." He sends her to the first of several schools, this one near his office in town, and he visits often. Soon, June tells classmates who tease her that she thinks of Jack as her "beau" (176). She is ashamed, but Jack "[takes] her in his arms": "'You mustn't, little girl,' he tells her. 'I'm proud . . . little sweetheart—' She was clinging to him and looking up into his eyes and he bent his head slowly. Their lips met and the man was startled. He knew it was no child that answered him" (179–80). For readers, the kiss comes with a sense of relief: no, we have not been imagining that there is sexual chemistry between the handsome young engineer and the little girl. The deviance is in the novel, not in our own minds. That night, Jack "found himself strangely stirred. She was a child, he kept repeating to himself, [but] he knew she was no child among her own people, and that mountain girls were even wives who were younger still" (180), invoking the child-bride myth to mitigate the age-difference taboo. As for June, "Her nature had opened precisely as had bud and flower that spring. . . . [T]he little girl had answered as a young dove to any cooing mate" (181). In the last chapter, grown up and refined, June confesses that she has loved Jack since first seeing him (407). She is dressed in "a smart cloth suit of black" (411) but changes into "the last crimson gown of her girlhood." Here costume change signifies that June, once *only* an unexploited resource, is now both refined woman and "submissive child" (406):

> "Here I am," [she cried] . . . her hair braided down her back as she used to wear it. . . . She blushed as his eyes went downward toward her perfect ankles. . . .
> "You're mine now, little girl, mine—do you understand that?"
> (412–13, italics in original)

Humbert Humbert describes an early sexual experience with Dolores Haze as "Lolita had been safely solipsized" (Nabokov 60). And here is stalwart Jack Hale, finally the possessor of his own little girl, going "Mine, mine."

Jack's exploitation of the land and the little girl would not have worked had he lacked allies in Lonesome Holler. John Fox, Jr., writes Henry D. Shapiro, "freely acknowledged his intellectual debt to [James Lane] Allen and . . . took personal inspiration from Allen's successful exploitation of Appalachian themes" (30). Fox's mythologizing requires an Appalachian insider who is willing to modernize, to accept outsider philanthropy both for the region's own good and to show outside philanthropists (and buyers of melodramatic mountain novels) that their efforts are not in vain. The third major character in *The Trail of the Lonesome Pine* serves these purposes. There is "no more famous character in all the hills" (26) than June Tolliver's father, the noted feudist and moonshiner Devil Judd. In the novel, Judd can be diabolical when the need arises, but when we first see him, he is looking to get out of the mountain myth game. To that end, he coyly brags to Jack, whose entrepreneurial ambitions precede him, about the excellent coal—"five feet thick!" (25)—on Tolliver land in Lonesome Cove. Jack is flabbergasted ("Heavens! What a find!" he thinks) to see the vein of "'bird's-eye' cannel" Judd proudly displays and begins immediately negotiating with Jack (34). (Even with university degrees, Jack is staggeringly incapable of understanding that Judd has been playing him for hours.) Less obviously, even to himself, Jack has begun brokering guardianship of June, insisting the unschooled girl needs a real education (27). Judd was able to open the mine with primitive tools, but Jack needs a modern industrial tool to exploit the seam's full potential. In a paragraph-long interior monologue that begins with Jack lamenting little June's coal country fate—"What a life for . . . that keen-eyed, sweet-faced child!"—the engineer reveals the tool he needs: "a steam drill" (35). The image is ineptly brilliant, linking land and little girl in a nightmarish eco-phallo-industrial symbol. Judd Tolliver is as happy to pimp out his land as his daughter—and Jack knows just the tool to use.

Through an examination of the Fox family papers, Darlene Wilson established that from 1890 and 1905—the time of his greatest fame as a novelist and greatest influence as a self-professed expert on Appalachian goings-on—John Fox, Jr., "may not have been physically 'in the mountains' more than six months out of fifteen years, and only then for very brief visits to his family's home in the controlled environment of Big Stone Gap" (30). Fox, that is, was not so much an embedded witness (or "local color correspondent" [Wilson 8]) as tourist, seduced by—and seducing readers with—"the security of pure cliché" (Fussell 38). Narrative artists continue to evoke the stereotypes of coal country in consumer culture-inspired narratives of child exploitation. The Loretta McCready arc of the neo-western TV series *Justified*, author Laura Albert's truck stop performance art hijinks (as JT LeRoy), and Scott McClanahan's faux-trauma memoir *Hill William* all link the victimizations of person and place. But an example of high art that alludes to different kinds of low art demonstrates best how coal country myths of transgressive sexuality continue to resonate.

Lolita is the story of a middle-aged serial rapist and the pubescent victim he destroys. Among the novel's allusions are those linking Dolores Haze with coal country: her father's family has Appalachian roots (Nabokov 148); she was born and lived in a "coal . . . producing area" (154) before her mother brought her to New England; Humbert last sees her in "a small industrial community" called Coalmont (267). Though not as explicitly as in the nearly allegorical *Trail of the Lonesome Pine*, the exploited child is linked to the exploited region, and the exploiters of both June and Dolores are linked as visionaries. Even when Dolores is disguised as a New Englander, Humbert can tell how ripe his Appalachian girl is for exploitation. Dolores is not an attractive child. She leaves dirty socks in the dining room (39), picks her nose (165), and ought to "wash her hair once in a while" (43). But, like the stout engineer Jack Hale, Humbert Humbert is blessed with the power of recognizing potential: "You have to be an artist and a madman . . . to discern at once . . . the little deadly demon among the wholesome children" (17). He exploits girls, that is, because he can magically tell which ones to exploit. Others, not artists or madmen, lack Humbert's supernatural vision: a "normal man . . . asked to point out the comeliest [schoolgirl] will not necessarily choose the nymphet among them" (17).

If "normal men" are, so to speak, "tourists" among schoolchildren, satisfied with the obvious and cliched, Humbert Humbert is a "bewitched traveler" (16). Compared with tourists, who seek stereotypical experiences, travelers are drawn to "the excitement of the unpredictable" (Fussell 39), "bewitched" not by normality but by deviance. This is how Humbert presents himself, so suavely that it is sometimes difficult to register just what a pathetic monster he is. Even while providing cover for the many months he and Dolores spend on "that wild journey of ours" (174)—a jaunty term for her kidnapping and exploitation—the road trip they take is not bewitching but touristic, with a "battered tour book" (154) as guide. Pedagogical Humbert claims to want "a sound education" for Dolores (111), but the instructional Grand Tour he arranges as cover for his interstate crime spree is sordid and sad. The novel catalogues tourist attractions along America's "smooth amiable roads" (152): Magnolia Gardens (154), "a cave where three southeastern states have a family reunion" (155), "a collection of guns and violins somewhere in Oklahoma, a replica of the Grotto of Lourdes in Louisiana" (151), shrines to tackiness, including souvenir stands where bewitched travelers buy such consumer crap as "Indian curios, . . . copper jewelry, [and] cactus candy" (148). (Though not mentioned specifically, Horny Hillbillies would not be out of place, although it is surely a coincidence that the priapic figurine shares initials with Nabokov's monster.) Their touristic motto could be "We had been everywhere. We had really seen nothing" (175). Repeatedly, Humbert and Dolores end up in "Functional Motel[s]—clean, neat, safe nooks, ideal places for sleep, argument, reconciliation, insatiable illicit love" (145). They are tacky places with nature-leaning names like "Sunset Motels, . . . Hillcrest Courts, Pine View Courts, Mountain View Courts, Skyline Courts, Park Plaza Courts, Green Acres" (146) where "every night, every night," he hears Dolores sobbing.

WORKS CITED

Allen, James Lane. "Through Cumberland Gap on Horseback" (1886). *The Blue-Grass Region of Kentucky and Other Kentucky Articles.* Harper and Brothers, 1892.

Batteau, Allen. *The Invention of Appalachia.* U of Arizona P, 1990.

Catte, Elizabeth. *What You Are Getting Wrong About Appalachia.* Belt Publishing, 2018.

Child Bride. Directed by Harry Revier, Astor Pictures, 1938. *Amazon Prime,* *www.amazon.com/Child-Bride-Shirley-Mills/dp/B001NFNQHA.*

Fox, John, Jr. *The Trail of the Lonesome Pine.* Grosset and Dunlap, 1908.

Fussell, Paul. *Abroad: British Literary Traveling Between the Wars.* Oxford UP, 1982.

Huber, Patrick. "The Riddle of the Horny Hillbilly." *Dixie Emporium: Tourism, Foodways, and Consumer Culture in the American South,* edited by Anthony Joseph Stanonis, U of Georgia P, 2008, Pp. 69–86.

Kentucky Moonshine. Directed by David Butler, Twentieth Century Fox, 1938.

Lynn, Loretta, with George Vecsey. *Coal Miner's Daughter.* 1976. Vintage Books, 2010.

McCauley, Deborah Vansau. *Appalachian Mountain Religion: A History.* U of Illinois P, 1995.

Nabokov, Vladimir. *Lolita*. 1955. Knopf Doubleday, 2010.

Pearce, John Ed. Foreword. *The Trail of the Lonesome Pine*. By John Fox, Jr. 1908. U of Kentucky P, 1984. Pp. vii–xvi.

Shapiro, Henry D. *Appalachia on Our Mind: Mountaineers in the American Consciousness, 1870–1920*. U of North Carolina P, 1978.

Smith, Jimmy Dean. "White for the Harvest: Hicksploitation TV and the Colonial Model of Appalachian Exploitation." *Small Screen Souths: Region, Identity, and the Cultural Politics of Television*. Eds. Lisa Henrichsen, Gina Caison, and Stephanie Rountree. Louisiana State UP, 2017. Pp. 166–83.

Syrett, Nicholas L. *American Child Bride: A History of Minors and Marriage in the United States*. U of North Carolina P, 2016.

Wilson, Darlene. "The Felicitous Convergence of Mythmaking and Capital Accumulation: John Fox Jr. and the Formation of An(Other) Almost-White American Underclass." *Journal of Appalachian Studies*, vol. 1, no. 1, Fall 1995, pp. 5–44.

EAT DIRT AND DIE, TRASH

TACKY, WHITE SOUTHERNERS IN THE GOLDEN GIRLS *AND* MURDER, SHE WROTE

JILL E. ANDERSON

hen *House Beautiful* announced maximalism as 2018's top designer trend, they noted that it is the "epitome of power, passion, and joy," embracing the "more-is-more" aesthetic (Heath). Since "there are no rules" to maximalist design, according to *Architectural Digest*, adherents are free to espouse "fantasy," but sticking to a cohesive narrative keeps the design from becoming "sloppy" or "a hot mess" (Wanger). Martinique, C. W. Stockwell's classic design, is maximalism writ large, the excessively overgrown banana leaf motif first introduced in 1942 into the corridors of the Beverly Hills Hotel. Since then, the design has popped up everywhere, from high-end designers to big box stores; sundresses to stemless wine glasses and metal water bottles; backpacks and throw pillows; all the way to a "Jungalow" line from Band-Aid designed by Instagram influencer Justina Blakeney, who takes the maximalist approach to boho-chic. In fact, the wallpaper and its accompanying overblown pattern shows up as the iconic backdrop in Blanche Devereaux's bedroom in the half-hour sitcom *The Golden Girls* (*GG*), which ran on NBC from 1985 until 1992. The matching bedspread, made with fifty-dollar-a-yard fabric, became so popular on the *GG* set that designer Ed Stephenson took it home with him to prevent theft by the crew (Keller). Katy Polsby, current CEO at Stockwell, notes: "What

Blanche Deveraux lacked in her taste in men, she certainly made up for with her exquisite taste in decor!" (Keller). The banana leaves, like Blanche, are at times *too much*, garish and over the top, tacky in a way that centers impropriety and makes it beautiful to behold and impossible to ignore.

Martinique, and its copycat designs, is now ubiquitous to the point of saturation. Polsby notes, "The brand is very much about being accessible and high design at once. [. . .] There are a lot of people who feel intimidated by design, and they shouldn't—There's no exact science. If the pattern makes you happy, it's the right thing to do!" (Keller). Occupying this middle ground—making "high" design accessible to the masses—means that Martinique—and its many knockoffs—is showing up everywhere. But what none of these articles mention is the historical inflection of a pattern labeled "Martinique." An obvious reference to the island in the West Indies, which is still a French colony, the name of the design cannot be separated from its plantation roots. Slavery officially ended on the island in 1848, but the glorification, reuse, and remanufacture of a banana leaf pattern that names but does not distinguish this history is troubling. That it appears so prominently in Blanche's bedroom seems an important piece of her southernness. Perched behind Blanche's ever-occupied, hectic bed, the banana leaves signal her fevered, excessive sexuality, the steaminess of her bed, her stickiness—and her very pointed obliviousness of the implications of a plantation pattern.

While this essay is not specifically about Blanche's wallpaper or whether Martinique is "too much" or in bad taste (full disclosure: I don't like it), it does take on the televisual inflections of southernness. Images, patterns, and words meant to signal and transmit "the South" also serve as a sort of shorthand for a tacky whiteness that exceeds perceived boundaries, much like Blanche and her exaggerated, overly sexual southernness. Another wildly popular show from the 1980s and 1990s was the hourlong CBS murder mystery *Murder, She Wrote* (*MSW*), in which Jessica Fletcher, played by the inimitable Angela Lansbury, also serves as a conduit for images of southern whiteness. Since like *GG*, *MSW* is not a show *about* the South, Jessica only plays the poised, good-natured, but never self-effacing foil for the translation and transmittal of these images of southern whiteness. As the introduction to the essay collection *Small-Screen Souths* argues, images and representations of the South "provide a televisual shorthand" that "is as dynamic as it is static, a space that offers remarkable fluidity through evolving media while it maintains a set of narrative forms, recurring tropes, and familiar themes that render it recognizable" (2, 3). Zooming in on Jessica and Blanche, the primetime audience witnesses their white privilege, class, and educational status as a seeming antidote against and frame for the tackiness levied against southernness by the wider culture. Tackiness *needs* an audience, some kind of objective approach from which to zoom out to confirm—but not necessarily judge or evaluate—its presence.

In many ways, both shows transmit images of tacky whiteness to a wide, prime-time audience by introducing but ultimately stepping away from serious political and social issues by neatly resolving conflict, as is often the case in this sort of television. Complex issues of the modern southern political and social landscape are translated into easily digested, familiar southern character types, neat, ordered plotlines, and familiar guest stars and character actors. Blanche's immersion in and Jessica's detachment from are evidence that "the televisual South allows us to see, at a distance, and paradoxically, it allows us to zoom in on the micro-machinations of home, region, nation, and globe" (Hinrichsen 2). By attaching derision to southern stereotypes, in Blanche's case, or dressing down the seriousness of murders done by southerners in Jessica's, the shows help their audience to elide and decenter the more serious, haunting aspects of southernness that the shows ultimately dismiss.

"Tacky," then, functions as a descriptor for the intersection of whiteness and trashiness. When enmeshed with stereotypes, the tacky traffics in exaggeration, in being unbounded by convention, and sometimes, frankly, in ugliness. Monica Carol Miller's treatment of ugliness and social rebellion in the writing of southern women makes a case for treating the "problem in southern culture at the level of the ordinary rather than in more hyperbolic registers" (32). Far from suggesting that Blanche is in any way physically ugly—she makes sure to repeatedly remind her friends that she is, in fact, "stunningly gorgeous"—I use Miller's definition of "ugliness" to point to the behavioral aspects of tacky, white southerners: "ugliness functions as a marker of defiance against social standards and expectations" (22). Since, as Miller notes, "the ugly does not so much explode or reinforce boundaries as it does threaten, irritate, and call them into question" and the "shock" that ugly effectively registers as a reaction, I read tackiness as a means of shaking up social categories and behaviors (22).

I will spend the rest of this essay focusing on a few specific episodes of *MSW* and *GG* that provide shorthand for the tackiness of a ruling class in the South, the (privileged) white experience reimagined for a wide television audience, ranging from representations of a nostalgic, romantic Old South fighting over inheritances to the tracing of the "pure" white heritage of Old South families as well as the country music industry. Set and costume design transcribe essential southernness and act as signposts of tackiness. Dialect, spoken through affected southern accents of dubious origin, are essential to broadcasting and demarcating these white southerners as acceptable—because of their whiteness— at the same time they misbehave, exceed the boundaries and expectations set for them, and act tacky through deception and downright lying. Both shows manage to do this while glossing over more crucial matters of racism, class, collective history, sexual assault, and, at least in Jessica's case, murder. Despite their attempts to engage with social justice issues, both shows ultimately throw out the possibility of challenging cultural inferiority and tackiness in favor of replicating more stable distinctions between classes through the vehicle of these white, privileged, self-possessed women. Because of this, any time someone exceeds the boundaries of perceived propriety or defies expectations in some way, they can be perceived as acting like trash. But given the nature of these televisual representations, we are not meant to take the implications of these excesses too seriously. The shows, by wrapping them up neatly at the rolling of the credits, frame tackiness as merely another significant and silly feature of the region and little else.

Blanche, who fashions herself as enormously appealing and stylish, often provides the TV audience with a primer on how to "be southern," at least stereotypically so. After all, in the aptly titled episode "Nice and Easy," Blanche explains, "Embellishment's one of the oldest traditions in the South. Tall tales and tall drinks," and then later notes that a lady never makes her guests "ill at ease" because "that's UN-SOUTH-ERN." But since her southernness is so transparent and unapologetic, we have to take it seriously even as we laugh at it. Through her firm rejection of acceptability in a seemingly culturally void, whitewashed version of Miami, Blanche represents the tension between her own version of refined, classy southern womanhood and how her heritage and sexuality are perceived as cheap, vulgar, and excessive by others. Whether through her southern identity or the expression of her open and overt sexuality, Blanche transmits images of tacky southernness.

Blanche occupies a mediary position in the southern tacky landscape. Both fully *of* the tacky and somehow in a position to zoom out and observe it, her perspective is essential to the mapping of tackiness. In an episode titled "Till Death Do We Volley," Blanche utilizes southernisms in order to revel in nostalgia for a lost past—both personal and historical. When Blanche recalls a time when she was "a blossoming belle who'd just won the Miss Magnolia Pageant," Dorothy, acting as the fed-up, intellectual foil, interjects: "I'm in no mood to hear a story about some yahoo cracker with four first names." "Pardon me, Dorothy," Blanche responds, "but we can't all come from places as socially acceptable as *Brooklyn*" (emphasis in original). After Dorothy cautions Blanche to "try to shy away from words like 'tarnation' and 'catfish,'" Blanche tells her tale of betrayal by a former best friend. After the girl had slept with Blanche's father (whose name is Big Daddy, a clear reference to Tennessee Williams's *Cat on a Hot Tin Roof*), her mother was given a new Cadillac to shut her up, forcing Blanche to conclude: "Ya' know, my family had a few dollars, and I loved them dearly but when you get right down to it, basically they were trash." Blanche's admission—that "basically" her own family, despite their wealth, was "trash"—indicates their mores and behaviors lay outside of social expectations and somehow reflected badly on their position in society. They are, for all intents and purposes, white trash, despite having "a few dollars." Blanche seemingly flips the notion of white trash on its head since "poor" typically accompanies the term. When she reframes "trash" to correlate with her wealthy white family, she makes them appear to be the opposite of "socially acceptable." We are able to laugh, along with the studio audience, at Blanche's foibles because the stakes are so low, and because "trash" often functions as one of Blanche's favorite maliciously charming put-downs (from which this essay gets its title). The dry, irascible, and deeply cynical Dorothy often questions Blanche's reliance on southern stereotypes by reinserting her own. Her quips are meant to highlight Blanche's backwardness, to make her trashiness legible to the TV audience, and to offer a comforting alternative to what might be classified—as it often is, given the space of thirty or so years—as nostalgia for a racist past that isn't exactly past.

But within critical whiteness studies, the stakes are much higher. Whiteness serves as an invisible norm, allowing for and promoting unearned privilege predicated on and perpetuated by the oppression of others. "White trash" not only provides a "useful [. . .] naming practice that helps define stereotypes of what is and is not acceptable or normal for whites in the U.S." but also critiques iterations of "social power," according to Annalee Newitz and Matthew Wray (4). Wray further articulates that the notion of "white trash" becomes "an expression of fundamental tensions and deep structural antinomies: between the sacred and the profane, purity and impurity, morality and immorality, cleanliness and dirt," and in doing so "names a disturbing kind of liminality: a monstrous, transgressive identity of mutually violating boundary terms, a dangerous threshold state of being neither one nor the other" (Wray 2). So if "tacky" signals "persons of low ideas and vulgar manners, whether rich or poor" who exhibit "an absence of style," who are "cheap and yet pretentious," we must acknowledge that they are words of degrees, of course (qtd. in Zimmer). They attach whiteness to tackiness in order to make these images more digestible. Tackiness gains a foothold in whiteness because whiteness is, as a disciplining norm, acceptable while tackiness is, as an emblem of excess, an ugliness, the auxiliary to whiteness. But to see something as tacky, we need to have a frame of reference, something seemingly objective on which to fix our gaze. This is how Blanche's family can be both privileged and trash—they are both and neither, but since they are white, they have access to the privilege afforded them by their position in society, their class, *and* their race. In other words, they can *afford* to be tacky, and Blanche can gleefully recall their trashiness, but only through the safety of Dorothy's gaze. Without that frame—which is

Jessica's role throughout *MSW*—we get dangerously close to accepting tacky is as tacky does.

Blanche's Big Daddy demonstrates his tackiness even as the "most respected and beloved" man in her hometown by destroying her expectations for his behavior. In the opening of the episode entitled "Big Daddy," Blanche declares that he "has truly been a father to everybody in our town," but she warns her uncouth, nonsouthern friends that he is "an old-time Southern aristocrat who is used to fine manners and gentility" (cue Dorothy's eyeroll). Blanche's expectation—that Big Daddy will provide an example of fine southern breeding—gets turned on its head when he arrives for a visit in a full white linen suit and black string tie and straw hat, a lá Colonel Sanders. He's "lost the stuffing out of his comforter," Blanche sulks when he reveals he's sold Twin Oaks, their family's home, to launch his country music career. But for Blanche, this is just as much a loss of social status as her personal legacy: his excessiveness, his trafficking in the clownish, unserious world of country music in a Miami bar, is a clear sign of senility and a betrayal of everything she'd been raised with. "I know I'm not any good," Big Daddy admits to his daughter, a confirmation that his amateur status will remain that and he is ultimately saved from permanent tackiness. Before the episode wraps and father and daughter are singing together in harmony, we come to understand that Blanche's perception of her father's rejection of his legacy and her inheritance is the unforgivable (at least for a moment) sin.

No one would ever accuse Jessica Fletcher, the best-selling mystery writer from Maine who merely visits the South occasionally, as being tacky. Throughout *MSW*, she reveals herself to be much more ready and able to engage with white southerners of a certain ilk because she plays the educated Yankee interloper. The audience is protected from directly engaging with any tacky cultural stereotypes since the filter of Jessica's gaze and observational powers is important to processing the cultural symbolism of her murder suspects and victims. Jessica's power lies in not only her ability to become *anyone's* confidant, slipping into and out of situations as it suits the plot, but also the control of her sometimes-intrusive gaze, disguising it as open, comforting, and homespun otherness. But Jessica, never excessive or socially unacceptable in behavior or appearance, serves as an urbane, sensible lens through which the audience views the tumult of the affairs in the messy and grotesque, often tacky, and even romantically nostalgic South.

Jessica is slightly detached as she fulfills the role of the Yankee outsider, a familiar trope in local color or regionalist literature, in which the outsider is able to visit the "foreign" country but does not have to stay. As Jennifer Rae Greeson explains, the South "is an internal other for the nation, an intrinsic part of the national body that nonetheless is differentiated and held apart from the whole," and Jessica's role as Yankee interloper allows her the distance to observe the shortcomings of the South's people while still feeling herself fully part of the goings-on (1). Jessica functions as the white frame narrator, speaking in a detached, non-vernacular voice, to control the portrayals of quainter and less accomplished types in the inside story, while "[t]he double structures are designed to highlight the gap between simple and 'peculiar' folk and the educated, superior framing voice" ("Southern Writers and Local Color"). Jessica is a willing participant in the tackiness of her friends, serving as a foil for the ugly, overreaching behaviors of other privileged whites.

Jessica's own encounter with a tacky country music scene takes place in Nashville via a country star (who is seemingly modeled on Dolly Parton) named Patty Sue. Played by a post-Brady Florence Henderson, the often denim-clad, sequin-bedazzled, big-haired Patty Sue draws Jessica to Nashville on the pretense of a concert but then embroils her in a family drama involving her stepdaughter's inheritance: "Defective genes. She got them from her mama." "Ballad for a Blue Lady" presents a version of the South as "a region fitted for nothing other than subordination," to invoke Greeson's terms (5). This means that bourbon, the drink referred to as "what makes the South the South," is the vehicle for the strychnine that poisons Patty Sue's husband, the washed-up songwriter played by the legendary Jimmy Dean. Jessica must swoop in to right the wrongs, even if that means implicating her longtime friend in his murder (via a botched suicide setup). From a safe, nonjudgmental distance, Jessica manipulates the tacky machinations of this scene, a device borne out in Jessica's interaction with Nashville PD's Lieutenant Jackson. Clad, as Big Daddy was, in full white suit, black tie, and cowboy hat, Jackson insists on serenading Jessica with his frankly laughable country songs throughout the investigation. It is a familiar trope: despite a clear occupation, everyone is actually just a country star waiting to happen. "I write books, not songs," Jessica laughingly tells Jackson, establishing a sort of writerly hierarchy in which country music is, well, the tackier option.

Because the southerners in another *MSW* episode, "Mourning Among the Wisterias," are of a certain class—educated, literate, and socially equal to Jessica—we are invited to view their affairs as only mildly nefarious. In this episode, Jess travels to Savannah, Georgia, at the invitation of her old friend, the bourbon-soaked, perennial bachelor, Pulitzer Prize-winning Eugene McClenden. The episode is again reminiscent of Tennessee Williams's *Cat on a Hot Tin Roof*, with Eugene in the role of Big Daddy, the dying patriarch, and the family gathered in the former plantation big house to fight over his fortune. Within this former plantation house, the specter of race is nearly erased (save for the innocuous, mostly silent presence of one faithful retainer, Ola Mae, played by Beah Richards) in favor of focusing on the squabbling of the wealthy white folk. Jessica's part as invited interloper in this drama allows her a level of intimacy to the southern patriarch, and she slides into this role with very little effort. In the opening scene Jessica sits on the plantation home's wide portico on an oversized wicker, listening to a reading of Eugene's latest play, dressed in a cool peach shirtdress, fanning herself and drinking iced tea. In fact, we learn that Eugene has invited Jess to his home to convince her to marry him—part of his scheme to not only stave off his family's schemes to get his money (his niece-in-law is slowly poisoning him with arsenic) but also protect his play's integrity.

Jessica's role as civilizing outsider plays off the devious, desperate, scheming people behind the machinations of the McClenden drama. Eugene describes Crystal, his nephew's wife, as a "girl with air in her head and fire in her drawers who can't wait to become a rich Savannah matron" (never mind the fact that she's murdered her uncle's lawyer because he assaulted her in the kitchen). When Deidre, Eugene's washed-up, too-old lead actress and former muse, observes that all southern women are "starved for sex," Jessica quips, "Well, I wouldn't know. I'm from Maine." Later, Deidre complains, as she listlessly fans herself, "I may play a Southern belle, but I've never gotten used to the beasties that thrive in this Southern climate." Drawing attention to her overheated body and suggesting that southern women—even privileged ones—should be accustomed to insects invading the home, Deidre plays up the stereotype of the sensual yet excessive southern belle. And Captain Thorne, the police detective clad in another outfit reminiscent of Colonel Sanders, tells Jessica in a backhanded compliment to further distance her from the goings on in his jurisdiction, "[F]or a Yankee, you don't miss much."

While Jessica, as Yankee outsider, is mere witness to others' tackiness, Blanche's direct engagement with matters of the flesh signals the raw threat of her tacky, social unacceptability. In "Witness," an episode that aired in March 1991, her obsession with reproduction, family lines, and heritage leads her to seek out membership in The Daughters of the Old South, which is a "club [that] is a link to the proudest of all heritages." Recalling when she and her friends used to "pretend to be Confederate belles" to receive gentleman callers, Blanche admits that one night she received seven callers, prompting Dorothy to point out that Atlanta is the location of the Centers for Disease Control. "Coincidence," Blanche shrugs, dismissing the connection between her sexuality and her trashiness. But later in the episode, Blanche's purity is called into question when she discovers she cannot "celebrate" or "prove" that she comes from "100% pure Southern Confederate stock" because she has a Jewish great-grandmother from Buffalo, New York. When she is forced to admit this fact during her "lineage presentation" in front of the members of the Daughters of the Old South, she is called out—"Yankee!" "Traitor!" Blanche's worthiness as a "true southerner" is called into question, and the invocation of her dishonor signals the other women's regard for her as trash. But she displaces this label, attacking the assembled women by declaring herself "just as Southern as the fruit on a scuppernong arbor growing on the banks of the mighty Mississippi." After giving an abbreviated version of Shylock's speech from *The Merchant of Venice*, Blanche hurls the last insult she has as she storms off stage: "Oh, you lost the war. Get over it!" Later, when she concludes, "Those small-minded peckerwoods aren't real southerners," she exposes the real rub: that their tacky behavior for condemning her for impurity is the real problem here. "I'm a real southerner," Blanche argues, "Real southerners are compassionate people, they're wise and gentle. They sit around on porch swings and regale with stories of Abraham and Moses . . . and all the other people who worked on the plantation."

Of course, we could make the argument that Blanche's casual, tossed-off racism is the tackiest thing there is, or that attempting to murder your uncle for his hard-earned playwriting fortune is mere ugliness, but for now, let us not form a hierarchy of tackiness. In fact, neither woman is taken to task for her own white, educated privilege until separate series come along. Blanche is finally forced to confront the racist inflections of her own life in "Camp Town Races Aren't Nearly as Much Fun as They Used to Be," an episode of the short-lived *GG* spinoff *The Golden Palace*. The Daughters of the Traditional South are planning to stay at the Miami hotel co-owned by Blanche, but her Black colleague, Roland (portrayed by Don Cheadle), declares, "Those bonnets and bigots aren't staying in this hotel." Blanche then dances into the dining room in full nineteenth-century dress, singing "Dixie," and when she attempts to hang a Confederate flag in the lobby, Roland invokes the Nazi flag. While Blanche sees it as "just a flag," Roland points out that the flag actually represents violence and discrimination that is, in fact, not just a historical relic of a bygone time: "The legacy of that flag is alive every time I'm walking down the street with a group of my friends, and I see a white person cross over to the other side because they're afraid. So please don't tell me about that flag; I've battled that flag all my life." When she finally sees Roland's side, Blanche realizes that her whole life—her family, her memories, everything she loves— is "tarnished [. . .] by the truth" of racism (though the word is never used explicitly in the scene). "White people are going to have to start making positive assumptions about people of color," Roland declares, and as is the custom with half-hour sitcoms, a hug and a handshake bring them back together and erase these social ills.[1]

When Jessica discovers that she is descended from slaveholders in the 2001 made-for-TV *MSW* movie *The Last Free Man*, she must confront her own association with a racist South. Jessica learns of Sarah McCullough through a Black historian played by a post-*Cosby*

Phylicia Rashad, who is working to clear the name of her own ancestor, Samuel Pinckney, an enslaved man who is (falsely, it turns out) accused of murdering a plantation owner. Through flashbacks, we see Lansbury as Sarah, a Virginia aristocrat who is slowly unraveling the mystery of who actually killed the slaveholder. Samuel dies during his attempt to run away but not before he apologizes to Sarah for causing her trouble, pointing out her decency, so that Sarah can declare she is proud to be associated with him. From the distance of about 150 years, Jessica helps bring to light Samuel's innocence, declaring him "finally free" in the closing scene of the movie. It is, like the scene between Roland and Blanche, intended to assuage Jessica's guilt for her ancestral racism, and the onus of the collective reckoning, as so much reckoning is, is placed on the oppressed.

Since the shows don't ultimately confront the collective damage done by historical racism or take seriously the South's seemingly inherent tackiness, I'll close here with something each show does well—what Natalie Atkinson calls a "low-flying feminism." Both Blanche and Jessica play "the widow with equal parts charming comedic airs and take-no-bullshit feminism." Far from helpless, desexualized, "dotty," or even too old to have an adventure, each woman is self-possessed and navigates a sticky world with verve and intelligence. Blanche's power lies in her ability to defy conventional notions of upstanding womanhood and embrace her tacky whiteness, while Jessica finds influence in her ability to become *anyone's* confidant, slipping into and out of situations as it suits the plots—even when they include some real trash.

NOTES

1. Despite being available to stream on YouTube for years, this episode recently resurfaced online at the end of June 2020, amidst the Black Lives Matter protests that were a response to Breonna Taylor's and George Floyd's (amongst many others') murders by police in March and May 2020. Roland's reaction to the Confederate flag echoes the calls for monuments and statues to Confederate leaders to be taken down each day across the country. In fact, on June 30, 2020, Mississippi became the final state to remove the obvious Confederate emblem from their state flag in a belated acknowledgement of the destructive power of this symbol. Just two days before that, in another move toward racial reconciliation, Hulu pulled a 1988 episode of *The Golden Girls* titled "Mixed Bless-

ings" that's since been labeled the "blackface" episode. In it, Dorothy's son Michael brings home his Black fiancée, Lorraine, but it's quickly apparent that despite Dorothy's surprise at Lorraine's race, her real complaint is that Lorraine is much older than Michael. When Blanche and Rose appear in the living room in front of Lorraine's family in mud masks, Rose declares: "This is mud on our faces. We're not really black!" There is debate about whether this is truly blackface or not, and while I do not have the space here to lay out the arguments for and against, my point is that Hulu removed, rightly or wrongly, an episode of a thirty-plus-year-old television show that not only featured some of the few Black characters in the entire series but also grappled with questions of race (as well as ageism). And, as Steven W. Thrasher points out in a piece for *Vulture*, this scene isn't even the most racially offensive or even generally problematic one in an episode that reveals that Michael was conceived when Stan drugged and raped Dorothy in the backseat of his car.

WORKS CITED

Atkinson, Nathalie. "'I couldn't help but notice . . .': *Murder, She Wrote*'s Prime Time Feminism." *Cléo: A Journal of Film and Feminism*, vol. 3, no. 1, 2015.

"Ballad for a Blue Lady." *Murder, She Wrote*. Written by William Bigelow, directed by William Jameson, Universal Television, 1990.

"Big Daddy." *The Golden Girls*. Written by Barry Fanaro and Mort Arthur, directed by Terry Hughes, Witt/Thomas/Harris Productions, 1986.

"Camp Town Races Aren't Nearly as Much Fun as They Used to Be." *The Golden Palace*, written by Marc Sotkin, directed by Lex Passaris, Witt/Thomas/Harris Productions, 1992.

Greeson, Jennifer Rae. *Our South: Geographic Fantasy and the Rise of National Literature*. Harvard UP, 2010.

Heath, Olivia. "How to Embrace Maximalism in the Home." *House Beautiful*, 18 Jul. 2018, www.housebeautiful.com/uk/decorate/looks/a21729800/maximalism-interior-design-trend/.

Hinrichsen, Lisa, et al. "Introduction: The Televisual South." *Small-Screen Souths: Region, Identity, and the Cultural Politics of Television*, edited by Lisa Hinrichsen et al., Louisiana State UP, 2017, pp. 1–22.

Keller, Hadley. "'Golden Girls' Producers Had to Confiscate Blanche's Bedding." *House Beautiful*, 2 July 2019, www.housebeautiful.com/lifestyle/a28264526/golden-girls-blanche-bedspread/.

Miller, Monica Carol. *Being Ugly: Southern Women Writers and Social Rebellion*. Louisiana State UP, 2017.

"Mourning Among the Wisterias." *Murder, She Wrote*. Written by Peter S. Fischer and Richard Levinson, directed by Walter Grauman, Universal Television, 1988.

Murder, She Wrote: The Last Free Man. Directed by Anthony Pullen Shaw, CORY-MORE Productions, 2001.

Newitz, Annalee, and Matthew Wray. "Introduction." *White Trash: Race and Class in America*, edited by Matt Wray and Annalee Newitz, Routledge, 1997, pp. 1–14.

"Nice and Easy." *The Golden Girls.* Written by Stuart Silverman, directed by Terry Hughes, Witt/Thomas/Harris Productions, 1986.

"Southern Writers and Local Color: A Regional Twist on a National Trend." *Publisher's Bindings Online*, University of Alabama, bindings.lib.ua.edu/gallery/southern_color.html. Accessed 22 Dec. 2017.

Thrasher, Steven W. "The Real Mud on *The Golden Girls.*" *Vulture*, 2 July 2020, www.vulture.com/2020/07/the-real-mud-on-golden-girls.html.

"Till Death Do We Volley." *The Golden Girls.* Written by Susan Harris, directed by Terry Hughes, Touchstone Television, 1989.

Wanger, Shoko. "Maximalists, Rejoice: Here's How to Keep Your Space from Looking Sloppy." *House Beautiful*, 17 July 2017, www.housebeautiful.com/uk/decorate/looks/a21729800/maximalism-interior-design-trend/.

Whitt, Jan. *Dangerous Dreams: Essays on American Film and Television.* Peter Lang, 2013.

"Witness." *The Golden Girls.* Written by Susan Harris, directed by Zane Buzby, Touchstone Television, 1991.

Wray, Matt. *Not Quite White: White Trash and the Boundaries of Whiteness.* Duke UP, 2006.

Zimmer, Ben. "The Gauche Origins of 'Tacky.'" *Wall Street Journal*, Eastern ed., 19 July 2014, pg. C4.

REDNECKS ON REALITY TV

THE COMMERCIAL ACT OF
REPRESENTING RURAL WHITENESS

AARON DUPLANTIER

henever I think of The History Channel's reality show *Swamp People*, the unmistakable image of an overweight, bare-chested white man wearing denim overalls is the first thing that comes to mind. The man's name is Bruce Mitchell. Long, flowing hair under a stars-and-stripes do-rag, he's perched at the front of his tiny flatboat, holding his shotgun, with his free hand resting on the square of his pointer dog's back. Mitchell and his peers featured on *Swamp People* hunt alligator. Each episode of the show is focused on the drama that unfolds around that dangerous pursuit. Casually watching the show in the past, I never much considered who Mitchell was besides this cartoonish character, even as a Louisiana native myself. Mitchell hails from a small town called Ponchatoula not far from New Orleans. His accent is thick, similar to my Cajun relatives, but his grandiosity and esoteric embrace of the bayou lifestyle are unfamiliar. On his personal website (brucethealligatorman.com) are photos and YouTube videos of him alongside his wife and children. There's a write-up on the opening page that details how he met his wife in junior high, the birth of his children, how he learned to run a turtle farm from his father-in-law, and his daily routine of eating oatmeal at 4 a.m. before going out on the hunt. I'm pretty sure he didn't write this biography—it feels like the invention of Janet, his wife, because of its continual nods back to her professional contributions—but it's revelatory nevertheless. Culturally, rural, white southern identity inhabits an uneasy space in the popular imagination insofar as its stereotype predominates over any notion of the complexity of these people's actual lives. Bruce Mitchell signifies that problem for me, and maybe because of our shared geography, it's an even deeper, personal problem. And, certainly, reality TV is a venue where we see this play out in a particularly explicit way. But the motivations for individual participation in a reality program are not as simple or straightforwardly degrading as one might imagine. How the dynamics between "real" performers and the production forces behind the scenes play out, too, can serve to illustrate the complexities of white, rural identity in the twenty-first century.

First, it's important to consider that reality TV's cultural designation as "trash TV" means that it's a format that holds the same perceived value as a rural white southerner in the popular imagination. This is not to say that every rural white person participating in the reality TV enterprise is self-consciously "aware" of this function, but whether *latent* or *overt*, reality shows act as a sort of perverse affirmation for their identity as "lesser," "humble," or "unpretentious." To explain what I mean by *perverse:* Even when exploitation value is at its most undeniable, the person appearing on camera is still communicating, "I am here," offering audience visibility to a specific, codified identity in a way that social media or other venues for self-display may not afford. Importantly, it is not a question of awareness but, rather, simply participation. Part of this activity is when reality performers try and capture something tangible, true, and authentic on-screen—something that they or the viewer believes is "real." John Corner, a reality TV scholar, refers to this as "selving" by which "true selves" emerge from the "performed selves" on reality television (51). It can be an unforeseen emotional outburst, a compulsive action, a fart, a fight. Because of the format's well-known negotiation of truth, people who appear on-camera operate as part of a continuum of reality and what that constitutes, what's "real" and "what isn't." This is an ideal conversation for a rural white person to penetrate. Many of these folks insist their lifestyle is grittier and more palpable than that of a person living on one of America's coasts, in a big city, or in the North. This aura stems from generations of rural whites asserting their ties to the agrarian way of life, emphasizing it over immaterial pursuits of the mind favored by some Yankee. John Wilbur Cash was one of the vocal early-twentieth-century figures who rejected the idea of a pro-intellectual "Southern Aristocracy" in favor of a "world in which horses, dogs, guns, not books and ideas and art were [their] normal absorbing interests" (qtd. in Cobb 170). *We are more real,* they might argue. *Salt of the earth.*

More often than not, reality fare starring rural, white people like *Here Comes Honey Boo Boo, Buckwild,* and *Duck Dynasty* (all three I will be writing about here) features something other than "performances," asserting a veracity not true of similar shows featuring a different demographic. We have been told, emphatically, that reality TV is *fake.* Fakeness, though, comes with the stipulation that a person ought to engage with reality TV as if it were the same as a sitcom or drama. From the reality performer's perspective, this is to believe how you appear on the show is separate from how you "really are." What you are "off-camera" is sacred, meant to be held close. It's the same methodology the rich kids of MTV's *The Hills* and *Laguna Beach* deployed when those shows aired for seven years. The final moments of the on-the-nose 2010 finale of *The Hills* features a limousine carrying one of its star players who hops out to be greeted with a sound stage, surrounded by camera operators, a set and props, and professional stage lighting. The production team of TLC's *Here Comes Honey Boo Boo* made no attempt at this sort of *wink-wink* self-referentiality and encouraged the opposite; they wanted those redneck off-camera selves to permeate their edited, tidy narrative because their performers were already interesting and ignorant and funny to look at when they found them. And the cast would never dare represent themselves as anything but themselves or else be confused with some "Hollywood elite."

It's not shocking that *Here Comes Honey Boo Boo* (2012–2014) was a success for its basic cable network. Its pilot episode titled "This is My Crazy Family!" smartly captures the internal conflict of this televised, real-world family and the complexities of how they *know* they appear on-camera, never mind the show's wicked humor and watchability. In confessional footage early from that episode, seated in front her family, Alana Thompson, who is the titular Honey Boo Boo and young-est child, shouts emphatically, "Yes, we are rednecks!" with a suitable twang. Her family disagrees in unison: "No, we're not!" And here, the crux of the internal conversation these folks conduct daily is on full display for the cameras and audience, a contradictory self-awareness that delights in and also denies the identity they propound. Much is made of reality TV's exploitation value, and what TLC's producers did to the ignorant white participants on this show and other shows, some still airing today. However, I'd argue that the exploitation here is willful, not some easy to narrativize exploitation with a tidy victim and perpetrator. I think someone from McIntyre, Georgia, the home of Alana and her mother Mama June, might dispute its backwoods characterization on TLC if they didn't also eagerly celebrate an annual gathering called "The Redneck Games" in East Dublin, a short thir-ty-minute drive down the interstate. Bobbing for pigs' feet and belly flopping into mud pits, Alana and her family also participate in those games in the pilot episode.

What's interesting, too, at "The Redneck Games" is that Mama June and family openly mock and ridicule the other country folk there, talking about how ugly and unkempt they appear, how overweight they are, among a variety of insults. At other moments on the show, the family say the same about themselves and to each other. In confessional footage from season two, episode five, appropriately titled "Chubby Chaser," Alana's sisters criticize each other's appearance, saying: "Put your fat back in!" Mama June functions as the heart of the show; she has the most screen time of all the family members and provides more confessional footage, or direct address to the camera, than anyone else. "Hold on, I'm scratching my bugs," she says while digging her fingers in her hair with a delighted, satisfied chuckle. Performatively, Mama June knows what she's doing and what expectations her audience has for her, possibly even informed by the physically present production staff. Considering the audience's perspective, the innuendo of complete fakery ("Tsk, everyone knows they're feeding those people lines!") is the stuff of reality TV mythos—the sort of thing fans debate about on anonymous internet message boards, part of the machinery that used to keep these shows *hot*. Such speculation has waned in popularity over the years. To reiterate: Mama June is not someone who's ignorant of how she appears in contrast to everybody else in America, but the full depth of that juxtaposition and what it signifies is more than likely lost on her. And this is part and parcel of the family's disagreement as to *what* they really are, rednecks or not. That this exploitation is willful doesn't make it fully understood by its beneficiaries.

From here, the viewer is left to wrestle with the family's contradictions: I am not the maligned identity, but I am. I love what I am, but I also hate it. Mama June addresses the camera in the pilot: "We just don't care. We love our little life. And we're having fun doing it." The verbal nuances here are telling—"our *little* life," and that "We just don't care," meaning her family shrugs off other people's judgements, already proven untrue. She's acknowledging their shortcomings but also trying to unearth some measure of pride therein. This is the root of self-awareness for many people in poor, white rural communities in America nowadays. Because of the prevalence of social media, film, and television, there is no longer "pure ignorance" when it comes to the victimhood and blame of "redneck identity." There is a knowingness alongside the twang that also sometimes finds an unease in existing as this maligned, notoriously "dumb" identity. And it's a fact this show and its gleeful characters openly accept, deny, then accept again. Professor of Media at Lund University and reality TV thinker Annette Hill calls *Here Comes Honey Boo Boo* a "feaux reality celebrity experience" because structurally it wants to be like MTV's *The Osbournes*, harmless and easy to commercialize, but Mama June's family were already suffering from the domestic squalor associated with poor, southern whiteness when TLC found them, not the petty life concerns of rich Los Angeles celebrities (95).

In 2014, TLC canceled *Here Comes Honey Boo Boo* while it maintained solid viewership due to Mama June's publicized and previously undiscovered involvement with an ex-lover, Mark Anthony McDaniel, who was indicted for sex crimes against a minor. That minor was also Mama June's oldest child. McDaniel happened to be the father of two of Mama June's children (France). A batch of season five episodes went unaired for a few years before TLC aired them, salaciously titled as the "lost episodes." Season two, episode three, "It's Always Something with

Pumpkin," features a crude animation made by the TLC production staff narrativizing and essentially making light of middle child Pumpkin (birth name Lauryn) being struck by lightning, subsequently changing her "brain," noticeably for the worse. Since the incident, Alana says Lauryn is now "stupid." This family quirk is the subject of much back-and-forth on the show, and Lauryn reminds the audience about her misfortune frequently. These silly familial anecdotes the show is built around hide a darker truth about their life that TLC either purposely chose *not* to portray on camera or couldn't capture. More important, their production team could not anticipate the collision of that off-screen truth (which would eventually disrupt their lucrative advertising revenue, the soul of basic cable's monetary value) into the well-maintained narrative they'd designed. Whatever the circumstances, replacing cartoonish buffoonery with the actual problems of this family was a false dream of the producers.

Mama June's impetus for signing on with TLC was opportunistic. And, certainly, the family she muscled along may well have been less willing. Her continued participation in the reality TV enterprise via the WEtv network's *Mama June: From Hot to Not* (2017–2019) and *Mama June: Family Crisis* (2020) was evidence of her money-grubbing spirit and speaks to the ostensible sanctity of her on-screen performance. But it's worth considering that the vehicle of reality TV can serve to "actualize" misunderstood identity through its vivid platform, no different than it did when Pedro Zamora appeared on MTV's *The Real World: San Francisco* in 1994 and represented AIDS victims. Long on the forefront of representing the underrepresented, MTV's single-season phenom *Buckwild* (2013) focused on a group of young adults recently graduated from high school in the hills of Sissonville, West Virginia, one of America's poorest states. Like Mama June, these kids "know how they appear" on camera but the through line of that awareness and the desire for television success is not overtly laid bare. The direction for where their lives will go, why they're participating in this show, and what's happening don't seem to be as self-consciously assessed by the cast beyond the knowledge that, yes, their bodies will eventually show up on TV.

MTV's *Buckwild* conveys the anarchistic, careless energy of drunk rednecks shooting their guns into the night sky, at traffic signage, into mailboxes. In the show's intro, we are told by the cast through voice-over that "West Virginia is a place founded on freedom. The freedom to do whatever the fuck you want! Around here, you live by your own set of rules," setting the tone for its televisual chaos. In the show's second episode, its young participants set up a makeshift pool using a blue tarp and the rear of a borrowed dump truck. They do flips off the roof of a two-story house into it. The cast is regularly shown starting fires and going "muddin'" in their lifted, tricked-out pickup trucks, which ostensibly are the only objects of value for the young men on the show. They love their potato guns, too. Mustachioed garbageman Shain Gandee is the youthful native whose family comes from Wolfpen Holler of Sissonville, where the cast spend much of their documented time. He drives a four-wheeler, loves to hunt deer and squirrel, and puts his life in danger regularly. MTV uses his penchant for lunacy, often incited by his buddy Joey, as a device for the show and includes a parental warning before every episode cautioning viewers not to "recreate or re-enact" the activity featured, à la MTV's notorious *Jackass*. Shain rolls himself up in an oversized tire and flops down a hill, then brags about swimming downstream of a power plant later that same episode. He rejoices in his stupidity.

A popular criticism slung at reality TV participants is their lust for fame. On MTV's *The Real World* or CBS's *Big Brother*, for instance, it's not so uncommon to see players identifying their prior pursuits as actors or fashion models; a starring role in this reality program might serve as a performer's "big break," as it has for others. Mama June knew this. The kids on *Buckwild* seemed to be operating under a different assumption, though. As popularity for the show peaked and West Virginian politicians came out against it and its dubious depictions of their constituents, Gandee and Shae Bradley (the show's blonde female lead) went on a press junket where much was made of "how little" they had, reiterating their lower-class status and the raw intent behind the show. It felt less like advertising for *Buckwild* and more of a defense of their lifestyle choices, which manifests itself in the narrative of the show as well. Executive producer John Stevens wanted to "change people's perspectives" and "get people talking" with the show's unique illustration of rural life (Rice). In an *Access Hollywood* interview filmed near Times Square in early 2013, Gandee cheerfully recalls his first-ever plane ride from the day before, arriving at JFK airport, and his tourist venture to the Statue of Liberty. Neither Gandee, with his bulbous camouflage jacket and ratty hat, nor Bradley exerted that aura of future Hollywood talent. These were not aspirational, young up-and-comers. These were fish out of water who would inevitably return to their bowl.

Buckwild was canceled immediately after its first season aired, when Shain Gandee died in a mudding accident. He and his uncle had been drinking at a local bar near Wolfpen Holler and, in the early morning hours, plunged their 1984 Ford Bronco haphazardly into a mud pit. Unable to drive it out, their exhaust pipe became submerged. Along with Shain, three people inside the vehicle died of carbon monoxide poisoning (Memmott). Figuring this alongside the reality TV program that profiteered on Gandee's brash life, the exploitation value is without question, which is why MTV didn't hesitate to cancel the show or else end up with pie on its face. The show's production company failed to reboot the premise with MTV's *Slednecks* a year later, which took place in Wasilla, Alaska. It's worth considering, here, the idea of a "dupe" in New Media discourse. At the heart of a lot of revered digital content inhabits someone getting worked over, cheated, made fun of, or scammed. A great example is YouTube prank videos, one of that platform's most prevalent genres. The prank/scam can serve to teach a lesson to the viewer but more often functions as schadenfreude. As evidenced by their interviews, the kids on the show had bought into a conversation wherein the production staff had framed *Buckwild* as a "revelation" of the West Virginian way of life; *Buckwild* was meant to rectify some misunderstanding about redneck living and get people to *change their perspective.*

I'd argue, though, that the presence of cameras and the recursive awareness of all its participants, whatever the supposed "thesis" the show's producers were trying to upsell, generated a feedback loop for redneck living in the digital age. There is no distinction between reality and representation when it comes to a dirty hick from the boondocks. They are exactly what we imagine, and have been fed via popular media platforms, because of how little has been done to dispute this conception—and, frankly, because of these folks' own willingness to resubstantiate the legitimacy of this "harmful" stereotype. Only, the actors in this scenario don't see it as harmful. This display of self is liberating. The redneck stereotype is cruel, and anyone who might actively perpetuate it in their life choices is a problem, but taking pleasure in your own ignorance and making that defiant act as "visible" as possible means that, sadly there will be a dupe—like the kids of Wolfpen Holler—waiting for a camera to show up. As television scholars Anita Biressi and Heather Nunn note, "the display of self on the internet and Reality TV has, if anything, actually re-invoked the cultural emphasis on the individual subject as the guarantor of ontological knowledge" (34). If the "redneck" is repeatedly codified via its on-screen representation, and viewers imbibe its "spectacle of actuality," then the cycle of negative stereotyping persists (Jermyn 74). However, the paradox of wanting to be considered anti-intellectual but also, somehow, a serious person with intrinsic goals and of value to larger American society persists, too.

For me, the *Duck Dynasty* clan communicates the most problematic and overt relationship to the reality TV paradigm and representation of rural, white southern identity. They are not "downtrodden," socioeconomically or from a societal perspective. They are successful capitalists. And when they associate themselves with "lower-class" folks, it truly does serve as a kind of "slumming," but replaces the urban housing project with a trailer park. This isn't a behavior somehow unique to the Robertson family but certainly one that is distressing as visible as it was when their TV show aired. It's true nowadays that rich, white southern folk often enjoy the same cultural items as those of their poorer ranks; it serves as proof they share the same geographic territory and ideological sentiments but certainly not the same "material" space. The two groups' *comfort* differs tremendously, and this is indisputable. Further, just because someone is *maligned* does not make that person *marginal*. Rednecks still have white skin—meaning that they still have the highest predisposition to succeed in America—even if reviled by many, so when Christian conservatives and rural whites peg themselves as an ostensibly disenfranchised group in America, it raises valid questions.

The Robertson family portrayed on-camera in A&E's discontinued

Duck Dynasty (2012–2017) can do a lot to help illustrate why this is so. Anyone who's watched Fox News knows that a dominant narrative of wealthy, successful, rural white folks argues they are an oppressed class under the thumb of coastal elites. This is a *narrative*, to be clear. Opioid abuse, existential dread, religious hysteria, domestic and sexual violence all plague poor, rural white communities of the deep South and the American elsewhere (see: Pennsylvania/Ohio). It's not fair to say that having a cultural relationship with this identity means you're the same as someone who has an economic, material relationship with this identity. And this is part of the appeal of participating in reality TV, too, because it "authenticates" the "realness" of these rich folks' white, rural southerness. For the Robertsons, appearing on reality TV was very much a self-conscious exercise in communicating to their hometown of West Monroe, to other good Christians, to other southerners and "real" Americans, that they were *just like them*. They were already the brand managers and owners of the Duck Commander duck call property, with assets in the millions.[1] Biressi and Nunn assert, "The politics of reality TV is a cultural politics. It is usually implicit rather than explicit, concerned with 'social difference' rather than with the 'working class,' concerned with the politics of identity rather than with the politics of collective action or solidarity" (3). Here, Anita Biressi and Heather Nunn emphasize that the worth of a person's cultural representation in reality TV is not overtly its political or economic value but simply the identity markers of its existence (example: "Look, that guy Willie Robertson is a duck hunter—I am too!" a viewer might think). It makes no difference that the Robertsons just so happen to be filthy rich and nothing like the majority of their target demo; that's not the point for their audience, at least not explicitly.

Thinking about them in tandem with *Buckwild* and *Honey Boo Boo*, the Robertson family's participation in reality TV is also meant to rectify some "misunderstanding" about their rural white culture, identity, life. It makes this specific identity fully visible. Television offers a richness and depth not afforded by contemporary social media. Again: these peoples' active, willing participation says, "We can revel in this lifestyle, no matter what you think," in a perverse affirmation of their life choices and cultural background, circling back to an earlier idea from this essay. Except, for the Robertsons, it's not so perverse. Documentary theorist Bill Nichols writes extensively on the high "indexical quality," or its "uncanny sense of a document or image that bears a strict correspondence to what it refers," of the moving visual image over any other form of representative output, be it the photograph or written account, etc. Assuredly, *Duck Dynasty* is merely a "representation" of white, rural living, but it is a show judged by the "pleasure it offers" its specific audience, and—by that measure—it succeeds as a *better* reality to contrast with some poor, abject white viewer's daily life (35). This is not schadenfreude, and if meant to be, it's weak. In West Monroe, a glimpse inside Willie and Korie's (his wife's) palatial TV house: adorned with luxury shiplap, exposed finished concrete floors, brushed copper appliances, plush leather furniture, oak tones. It has that rustic feel but exudes wealth like a good HGTV model home ought to. It's the reality minus the fantasy because Willie is showing us and everybody else, he's already got what they intrinsically desire. And we all just accept it as a matter of fact. A workday, as portrayed on *Duck Dynasty*, consists of drinking sweet tea and quitting the day early to hunt.

The Robertson family does well to codify their particular version of uncouth redneck: spoiled by money but never forgetting the wild roots of their poor, white ancestry. This dichotomy is meant to charm their audience. In season ten, episode seven, the Robertson clan face rising flood waters in West Monroe, Louisiana. With the roads blocked and electricity down, the family sit around using flashlights inside patriarch Phil and his wife Kay's humble elevated modular home and reflect on their life before financial success. "Remember when we were poor?" Willie asks his mother Kay. "We used to burn our garbage in the front yard. I didn't know what 'new socks' were till I got to college." It's imperative, here, that the audience know they *were* poor at one point, so they carry that authentic aura; they're not "slumming it" as a lower cultural class for the viewer. This communicates that the Robertsons rose above that economic status but being "rich" has not changed them; the nondenominational Christian family prayer held around the dinner table at the end of each episode reinforces that image. Further, *Duck Dynasty*'s easy-to-digest episodic narrative, often following a sitcom arc where all conflict is resolved by the episode's conclusion, means that this is an image of country bumpkin living very easily contained/ controlled. And this ought to be when the average viewer really "feels" the show as a marketing ploy for the Duck Commander merchandise, for the A&E channel, for all the production forces behind *Duck Dynasty* that might benefit from bandying about white, rural identity as a meaningful and marketable distinction. And yet, for loyal devotees of the Duck Commander and *Dynasty* brand, no such revelation apparently happened.

The direction of the family's relationship with the A&E Channel was symptomatic of a rude, white southern bedfellow. Phil Robertson, the original architect of the Duck Commander duck call brand and the sole reason for which the family was handed a TV show, poisoned the well as he made public statements that were antigay and against the ideological grain of A&E. Infamously, Phil gave a December 2013 *Gentleman's Quarterly* (*GQ*) interview where he contemplated why a gay man would prefer a "man's anus" over a "vagina." Phil goes on to say on the matter: "It's just not logical, my man" (Magary). His later defense was that, well, *I'm Christian.* More questionable comments followed in other venues. Of note, too, is that Phil's participation in the *Duck Dynasty* television show dropped off significantly over time. In seasons one through four, he was on-camera frequently, but—in tandem with his off-screen controversies—seasons five through eleven (2014 on) saw him as more of a secondary participant. Following that interview, A&E initially suspended Phil from the show but faced backlash from their viewership, reversing the decision. Some advertisers pulled from the show. Willie, Phil's son and "modern" capitalist entrepreneur, was the face of his company and (I guess) knew better than to make flippant comments about people's sexual preferences. It was one thing to visibly pray around the dinner table but quite another to point at a person's genitals and make judgments. In one sense, you *could* read the show as Willie's economic pursuits falling victim to his father's purist ideology, if it didn't all work out for the Robertson clan in the end. Eleven seasons of any TV show is no disappointment. And the popularity of the *Duck Dynasty* brand persists among the Christian Industrial Complex of the Bible Belt, where Phil and Willie's faces still adorn t-shirts, caps, Monopoly games, and bowie knives at local

Wal-Marts, Pilot gas stations, etc. Even if Phil Robertson was dogmatic in his conviction, Willie's capitalist flexibility was always the superior opponent.

In episode eleven, season one of *Duck Dynasty*, Phil and Kay are in a small boat collecting logs to build some duck hunting structure. Kay pesters him with chitchat. And that's literally the crux of the entire scene: Phil and Kay annoy each other. That's how I would describe *Duck Dynasty:* a litany of banal scenarios punctuated by good-old-boy sayings, the sound of interspersed nondiegetic fiddle, and the aesthetic of redneck living. I'd emphasize the "aesthetic aspect" here. *Duck Dynasty* has that "hermetically sealed quality" of what media critic Mark Andrejevic isolates during the reality TV boom at the turn of the millennium, when reality TV shifted its "attention on the apparatus of celebrity production" (5). The scraggly beards, the copious camouflage, the lifted trucks—*Duck Dynasty* is merely an aesthetic. Because I recognize these people as "genuine" rednecks, there's no need for these performers to take that extra step, go that extra mile. Reality television fulfills its promise when it gives the viewer "selving," raw openness, moments where you know participants did not want to be filmed.

In contrast, looking at episode five of *Buckwild*'s doomed first season, Shae Bradley confronts her cheating boyfriend Jessie J. in a troubling scene filmed at his trailer home. She'd returned to collect a few things left during previous overnight stays; he's visibly angry, yelling and cursing. Anticipating this reaction, Shae had brought along a female companion, Anna, as a physical buffer. If the cameras were not present, this may well have evolved into a domestic violence incident not uncommon in the region or unfamiliar to Shae and Anna. Understandably, throughout this heated exchange, Shae is scared, crying, and keeping a purposeful distance from Jessie J. Outside its participants' lack of real wealth, *Buckwild* captures a poverty of mind and spirit that can generate empathy in its viewership, and if not that, then pity. Whatever people who watch the MTV show think of their individual choices, it undoubtedly features downtrodden young, white folks arrested by their material conditions. *Duck Dynasty* endears its fans through a mere cultural identification; its popularity means that the human representational standard for its audience is fairly low. The transgression of the productive forces behind *Buckwild* in making something exploitative, by virtue, ended up capturing something "more real" than *Duck Dynasty* because it communicates a tangible truth about the people who populate these lesser-known corners of America. The Robertson clan don't actually represent rural whites but are instead an extravagant anomaly; it just also happens to be a reassuring one.

NOTE

1. This figure is according to third son and CEO Willie Robertson, which he based on numerous outdoor store contracts who were carrying their duck call merchandise prior to the reality show's filming (Owens and Scholz).

WORKS CITED

Andrejevic, Mark. *Reality TV: The Work of Being Watched.* Rowman and Little-field, 2004.

Biressi, Anita, and Heather Nunn. *Reality TV: Realism and Revelation.* Wallflower Press, 2005.

Buckwild. Parallel Entertainment and Zoo Productions, 2013. *MTV,* www.mtv. com /shows/buckwild.

"Chubby Chaser." *Here Comes Honey Boo Boo,* season 2, episode 5, TLC, 31 July 2013. *Amazon Prime,* www.amazon.com/gp/video/detail/B00E0H0R98/ ref=atv_ dp_season_select_s2.

Cobb, James C. *Away Down South: A History of Southern Identity.* Oxford UP, 2005.

Corner, John. "Performing the Real: Documentary Diversions." *Reality TV: Remaking Television Culture,* edited by Susan Murray and Laurie Ouellette, New York UP, 2004, pp. 45–62.

"Daddy's Got a Gun." *Duck Dynasty,* season 1, episode 11, A&E, 2 May 2012, play. aetv.com/shows/duck-dynasty/season-1/episode-11.

France, Lisa Respers. "Mama June Admits Relationship with Another Sex Offender." CNN, 13 Nov. 2014, www.cnn.com/2014/11/13/showbiz/celebri- ty-news-gossip/mama-june-sex-offender-honey-boo-boo/index.html.

Hill, Annette. *Reality TV.* Routledge, 2015.

"It's Always Something with Pumpkin." *Here Comes Honey Boo Boo,* season 2, episode 3, TLC, 24 July 2013. *Amazon Prime,* www.amazon.com/gp/video/ detail/B00E0H0R98/ref=atv_dp_season_select_s2.

Jermyn, Deborah. "'This is about Real People!': Video Technologies, Actuality, and Affect in the Television Crime Appeal." *Understanding Reality Television*, edited by Sue Holmes and Deborah Jermyn, Routledge, 2004, pp. 71–90.

Magary, Drew. *Duck Dynasty's Phil Robertson Gives Drew Magary a Tour of West Monroe*. *GQ*, 18 Dec. 2013, www.gq.com/story/duck-dynasty-phil-robertson.

Memmott, Carol. "Autopsy: *Buckwild* Star Gandee's Death Accidental." *USA Today*, 2 Apr. 2013, www.usatoday.com/story/life/tv/2013/04/02/buck-wild-shain-gandee/2045783/.

Nichols, Bill. *Introduction to Documentary*. Indiana UP, 2001.

Owens, Ryan, and Jim Scholz. "'Redneck' Millionaires Built 'Duck Dynasty' in Duck Call Business." *ABC News*, 20 Mar. 2012, abcnews.go.com/Entertain-ment/redneck-millionaires-built-duck-dynasty-duck-call-business/story?id.

Rice, Lynette. "*Buckwild* Producer Defends Show by Saying It's Not a 'Train Wreck.'" *EW.com*, 7 Dec. 2012, ew.com/article/2012/12/07/buckwild-produc-er-defends-mtv-show/.

"Shain Gandee's—one of his last interviews." *YouTube*, uploaded by R.I.P. shain gandee, 1 Apr. 2013, www.youtube.com/watch?v=ovMmCeKyj1Y.

"There Will Be Flood." *Duck Dynasty*, season 10, episode 7, A&E, 27 July 2016, play.aetv.com/shows/duck-dynasty/season-10/episode-7.

"This is My Crazy Family!" *Here Comes Honey Boo Boo*, season 1, episode 1, TLC, 8 Aug. 2012. *Amazon Prime*, www.amazon.com/Here-Comes-Honey-Boo-Season/dp/B008V6Q2YS.

SOUTHERN WOMEN DON'T WEAR SWEATPANTS

SOUTHERN MOTHERS AND THE DECEPTIVE POLICING OF APPEARANCE

MONICA CAROL MILLER

*A*ctress Reese Witherspoon has frequently noted in interviews that proper southern women are acutely aware of their appearance in public. She cites her own rule of never appearing in public in sweatpants as an example of the myriad rules to which a particular model of southern womanhood is expected to adhere. In a 2016 interview with *Women's Wear Daily* about her own fashion company Draper James, for example, Witherspoon discussed how her no-sweatpants rule is one that her own grandmother impressed upon her.[1] Along with Witherspoon's maternal warnings, in articles such as "Things Mama Says are Tacky" and "10 Things Every Southern Woman's Asked Her Momma," popular southern-themed media outlets such as *Southern Living*, *Garden and Gun*, and *The Bitter Southerner* all use the threat of "tackiness" as a boundary of appropriate behavior and appearance. Specifically, these boundaries are used to delineate a particularly conservative and even retrogressive aesthetic and identity of southern white womanhood under the guise of well-meaning and even fun advice and directives.

This essay focuses on the rhetoric of "tackiness" as it is deployed by media outlets such as those listed above, as well as other recent popular written texts such as Witherspoon's own 2018 lifestyle guide *Whiskey in a Teacup: What Growing Up in the South Taught Me About Life, Love, and Baking Biscuits*. Specifically, I focus on the way that the image of motherhood is used in this aesthetic- and behavior-enforcing rhetoric, as being frequently referenced in these guides as the teacher, arbiter, and final authority on what constitutes "tackiness." As charges of "tackiness" can imply excess or laziness in a general failure of discipline, I will particularly focus on the significant role that gender plays in these remonstrations, and the ramifications of tackiness as both a delineation of acceptable behavior as well as a pressure valve for occasional relief from the unattainable expectations of successful white womanhood, expectations which I will ultimately argue are built upon a foundation of deceit.

The behavior of white women in the American South has traditionally walked a fine line between control and catharsis. Such white, maternal femininity was exemplified by the image of the nineteenth-century plantation mistress, who faced nearly impossible-to-achieve expectations. As Catherine Clinton explains in *The Plantation Mistress: Woman's World in the Old South*, "plantation mistresses were familiar with all facets of farm management," regardless of whether their husbands were living or not, or present on the plantation or not (32). Such duties, however, had to be carried out without legal recognition of their role: even as a plantation mistress might be "ready to make full use of her talents as household manager and domestic laborer, the society—ruled by males in the legislature and in the courts—deprived the plantation mistress of her own legal identity" (33). In other words, a woman might be able to succeed, but she was not allowed to take credit or even ownership of her successes.

Successful white, southern femininity, then, has its roots in the kind of misrepresentative appearances that would a century later be characterized by the metaphor of *Steel Magnolias*, the 1987 Robert Harling play adapted into the 1989 blockbuster, star-studded movie. As the title metaphor demonstrates, the ideal southern white woman must be as strong as steel but look like a fragile flower. Women are expected to be in full control: of the household, of their children, of their communities, and of themselves. But even more important, this control must be executed under complete subterfuge and disguise, what Tara McPherson characterizes as the "conscious yet compulsory nature of white southern women's masquerades" in the film (166). That is, in fact, what tackiness is: letting the appearance of effortlessness slip. Showing that your hair is dyed, that your clothes are new, or that you might actually have an appetite for something other than passive agreement. Southern womanhood requires strict stage management in order to hide the mechanisms behind the scenes.

And yet part of the enjoyment of *Steel Magnolias* is that it does pull the curtain back somewhat on the very work that successful southern womanhood requires. With scenes set in a beauty parlor and in preparation for a wedding, we see just how much work goes into seemingly effortless beauty. As the beautician Truvy (played by Dolly Parton in the film adaptation) acknowledges in the first scene of the play, "There is no such thing as a natural beauty" (Harling I:1). Indeed, the contradictory celebration of southern tackiness by the very women who disdain it personally makes sense if it is understood as something of a pressure valve for such women. Southern white women use the occasional foray into tackiness—a meeting of their Red Hat Society club, for example, or an accent pillow in their she-shed with a Dolly Parton quote on it—as a conscious breaking of the rules, a momentary carnivalesque foray that ultimately reinforces the rules rather than challenges them.

In general, "tackiness" describes activities that may be enjoyable but are not allowed for women who aspire to this certain image of white, upper-middle-class, southern femininity. In the *Southern Living* article "Things Mama Says Are Tacky," Valerie Fraser Luesse acknowledges how southern mothers stereotypically use "tackiness" to discipline the behavior of everyone around them, noting that "Southern girls who smoke still hide it from Mama." Drawing from a *Facebook* poll of *Southern Living* readers, Luesse's feature breaks up these judgments into categories of "Personal Grooming," "Fashion," "Thanksgiving Hospitality," "Christmas," "Funerals," "Houses of Worship," and "Basic Human Decency." Many of these dictums are about keeping control of things: "'Snow at the North Pole.' If we may quote Weezer from *Steel Magnolias*, 'Have your roots done!' Retouch, retouch, retouch." Indeed, Luesse's summative statement about what "Things Mama Says Are Tacky" demonstrates how maternal dicta regarding tackiness are both discipline as well as self-preservation: "Anything else than that suggests Mama failed in raising you. Always remember. Tacky is as tacky does."

Tackiness is both a blight on one's own character as well as a poor reflection on one's upbringing. However, the seriousness of these pronouncements is undercut by the use of humor in their delivery, as we see in their frequent appearance on novelty items. For example, the *Garden and Gun* magazine website sells "Southern Expression Cocktail Napkins" which include ones that read, "If Mama Ain't Happy, Ain't Nobody Happy."[2] There is also a tea towel reading "Don't Be Tacky" sold by the *Down South* website, which includes the explanation that its slogan is "What your mama told you when you tried to set the Thanksgiving table with paper plates." Both outlets promote southern-themed goods that employ a certain sense of humor about essentializing southern identity, while still affirming a sense of southern exceptionalism. The *Down South* website, for example, which sells primarily kitchen- and entertaining-themed goods such as dishtowels, cloth napkins, coasters, and napkin rings (along with T-shirts and tote bags emblazoned with humorous southern-themed slogans), describes its mission as making "high quality goods for Southern women at reasonable prices. We make products that come from a clean and traditional Southern aesthetic" ("Who We Are"). They describe their products as being "Suitable for Southerners with resolute characters and gracious dispositions." As with much of the evocations of tackiness in popular media, there seems a thread of lighthearted humor running through these descriptions, but a humor that acknowledges an undercurrent of seriousness.

It can often be difficult to judge what balance of humor and seriousness is meant to be understood in many of these descriptions; in fact, one aspect of their popularity may very well be this lack of clarity, as I expect that the people who purchase these goods may be buying them with different levels of irony or lack thereof. A particularly good example of this is the "Pretty Little Gloves" product sold on the *Down South* website, as their product description could be read with any number of valences of irony effectively: "These white cotton gloves are what Emily

Post would have called 'serviceable.' They are made of a good sturdy cotton jersey with a double set of seams on the fingers. The wrist has a very delicate zig-zag trim that makes it look a little dressier than what you normally see. On the Daughters of the American Revolution scale, they are perfect for chapter meetings, grave markings and daytime paging at Continental Congress. If you are marching down Constitution Hall behind the President General during the flag drop, you will need something fancier" ("Pretty Little Gloves"). A reader can imagine actual members of the DAR ordering these gloves and having various pairs to wear, depending on the formality. One can also imagine someone buying this as a gag gift of some sort, making fun of the women who wear such accessories seriously. The language of the product description is such that either interpretation is a viable one (and such ambiguity, one would imagine, is likely good for business).

Throughout the website are references to "Grandma" and "Memaw," in addition to the product description about Mama. These more-or-less serious references to mother figures emphasize the central role that mothers play in popular notions of a particular image of white southern femininity. In her study of young women in the American South in the mid-twentieth century, Susan K. Cahn discusses the role that mothers played in reinforcing the class- and race-based norms of appearance in their daughters, what she describes as the "bodily lessons of class": "For middle class girls this often consisted of instruction in control and propriety" (145). Cahn identifies "tacky" as a descriptor used by mothers in policing their daughters' behavior, one on a continuum of warning words: "Even more pejorative than 'common' was the term 'tacky,' which sounded nearly like 'trashy,' the most severe insult to describe poor whites" (138–39). Importantly, the continuum from tacky to trashy that Cahn invokes is one of whiteness, whose valence is based on class.

In Cahn's characterization, this continuum appears hierarchical, with tacky seeming to be less of an indictment than trashy is. Indeed, the racially marked term of "white trash" is one of active failure, both material and moral. In *White Trash: The 400-Year Untold History of Class in America*, Nancy Isenberg discusses how "marginalized Americans were stigmatized for their inability to be productive, or to produce healthy and upwardly mobile children—the sense of uplift on which the American dream is predicated" (xiv).[3] In the context of tacky existing on a continuum with trashy, tacky functions as a warning about the potential of falling into the failure of trashy. An occasional foray into the tacky might be allowed, as a pressure valve or an experience of a frisson of danger, an encounter with the forbidden. However, it might also function as a gateway to trashiness, a condition of both moral and aesthetic failure.

So, while an occasional flirtation with tackiness may be allowed to those with more secure socioeconomic status—wearing a sequined red hat to an official Red Hat Society Meeting,[4] for example—it is only allowed because the woman wearing the hat is fully aware of the norms of appearance that her flashy hat is violating. In this way, conscious flirtation with tackiness is a form of slumming.[5] An occasional foray into the tacky—through a busy holiday-themed sweater, for example—ultimately reinforces the norms that they momentarily violate. In order to break the rules governing appropriate behavior, appearance, and decor, however, one must first understand what the rules are and when they apply. Wearing a sequined red hat to a Red Hat Society luncheon with others of your social set who are similarly dressed is an afternoon of fun. Wearing the same hat to a PTA meeting would be looked at askance. And wearing it to a funeral would generally break serious rules of decorum. And where are young women expected to learn these rules? From their mothers.

In the make-believe world of southern femininity, a girl's best friend is her mama, whose disciplinary ways should ultimately win her loyalty as she molds her daughter into a new image of herself. The South as a sorority of white womanhood, drawn together by common values and aesthetics, is the vision of so many southern lifestyle brands, including that of Reese Witherspoon. Witherspoon's admiration for both her mother and her grandmothers is a through line of her book *Whiskey in a Teacup*. Explaining the book's title, Witherspoon quotes her grandmother Dorothea, who explained that "it was a combination of beauty and strength that made southern women 'whiskey in a teacup.' We may be delicate and ornamental on the outside, she said, but inside we're strong and fiery. Our famous hospitality isn't martyrdom; it's modeling. True southern women treat everyone the way we want to be treated: with grace and respect—no matter where they come from or how different from you they may be. Dorothea taught me never to abide cruelty or injustice. The Golden Rule, she said, applies to everyone" (10). This "whiskey in a teacup" metaphor is similar to the "Steel Magnolias" one in its implication that successful southern womanhood has deceit at its heart. This is a lifestyle of erasing any appearance of effort, error, or weakness. Whether steel masquerading as a fragile flower or a teacup hiding liquor, the metaphors at the heart of white southern womanhood are ones of deceit.

Indeed, such deception is directly related to the continued deployment of illusion and false history in the very concept of southernness, especially retrograde understandings of the South as a region of white southern belles and hospitality. I'm drawing here directly from the work of Anthony Szczesiul's *The Southern Hospitality Myth: Ethics, Politics, Race, and American Memory*, in which he argues that "southern hospitality has functioned primarily as a white *mythology*, produced by whites, directed to a white audience, and invested in the project of maintaining white status and privilege" (7, emphasis added). Just as Szczesiul demonstrates that the defining characteristic of southern hospitality is, in fact, a myth that has produced and reproduced a fallacious image of a South that erases its complex history of racism and race-based violence, so, too, is the "sacrificing and maternal . . . Dixiefied angel on the veranda" ideal communicated by *Steel Magnolias* doing similar cultural work (McPherson 166).

These myths and deceptions of both southern hospitality and all-knowing southern mothers serve a similar purpose of reproducing and controlling appearances. For example, a May 2012 issue of *Southern Living* included a Mother's Day tribute, "ask[ing] fellow Southerners—from musicians and chefs to actors and writers—to share pearls of wisdom that came straight from the women who raised them" (Glock). The centrality of control in southern womanhood emerges in the title, "Make the Effort":

OF ALL THE POSSIBLE sins of my childhood, being lazy was the worst. Imprudent choices (dating that guy who blew his fingers off with a firecracker), fibbing (she hit me first!), failing (all maths), and premature flirting (at a church retreat) were all, if not welcomed, generally forgiven.

Not so laziness. My mother's mother cooked three meals a day from scratch in full, camera-ready makeup and Jackie O ensembles. Idleness was to be avoided like lice. Worse than ungodly, it was tacky. Sloth was for folks with no self-respect, the Snookis of the world, none of whom would have survived a day in the Appalachia of my kin, where money was tight but pride thick as honey.

As a girl, I wondered why it took my mama an hour to "put on her face." Why we had to iron linens. Why we had to be the ones making homemade caramels for every single family at Arlington Congregational. I later realized the point was not the result, but the exertion.

Make the effort. Life is not to be phoned in. That was why you shaved every day and spot-treated your shirts and sang in church. Why my mother never left the house with a hair askew, even if only to get the mail. It was not vanity (well, not entirely). It was dignity. It was gratitude. It was a way of saying thanks to the Almighty for the opportunity to have a life in the first place, and a promise that as long as my mother had a say, none of her babies was going to waste it. (Glock)

This focus on "making the effort" and keeping things under control are seen as very much related to appearance. *Southern Living* readers included several appearance-related dicta in their responses to the question of "Things Mama Says Are Tacky":

Visible bra straps. Mama wouldn't say "bra straps," of course— not in mixed company anyway. She would say "exposed foundation garments."

Sheer skirt, no slip. Sinful in a house of worship and scandalous everywhere else.

Pink plastic hair curlers worn in public. The good people at
Conair have made amazing advances in big hair technology, so
turn on, poof out, and join the electric age. (Luesse)

Indeed, *Garden and Gun's* "You Know Your Mama is Really Southern
If . . ." column is all about discipline, appearance, and control, including characteristics such as:

Everything you owned before age five was smocked.

Your first words were *Mama, Daddy,* and *Yes, ma'am,* in that order.

She asks you, 'Wouldn't you feel better with a little lipstick on?

You know better than to leave the house without wearing clean
underwear—and it's monogrammed.

She tries to defeat the humidity with Aqua Net hairspray.

You've got home training and know what it means.

She uses "tacky" as the ultimate insult.

In all of these rules, tackiness is kept at bay through a firm control
over one's appearance.

And, to return to Reese Witherspoon, her stories about her grandmother's rules governed by the fear of being deemed tacky are ultimately about the ways in which white southern womanhood is defined
by the control of appearances. Witherspoon's grandmother told her that
"presenting yourself well is a way to show others you care about them"
(49). This is the source of her rule about being seen in sweatpants.
According to Witherspoon, "I guess she is why I have a real mental
block about wearing workout wear all day long. I think you gotta get
up, gotta work out, and then you gotta get dressed in a real, proper
outfit by ten in the morning. I would never judge anyone for doing
otherwise. But if I did it myself, I just know my grandmother would
haunt me with that line she always said: 'Only wear sweatpants when
you're supposed to be sweating'" (49). Her grandmother had weekly
standing appointments for hair and nails, too, as another strategy in

keeping her appearance under control (50). The sweatpants dictum is not limited to Witherspoon, however. In "Things Mama Says Are Tacky," a *Southern Living* reader included, "Athleisure. No, no, no. Why wear gym pants to the Piggly Wiggly? Are you planning to hurdle the Vidalias or put them in your buggy?" (Luesse).

A slide into a tacky appearance is a surrender of control, an admission of failure to properly take care of everything and everyone. It's important to note the strong connection that tackiness has to judgmental southern mothers—primarily white southern mothers—to see the significantly gendered dimension of tackiness as a threat to propriety.[6] By recognizing the ways that tackiness is deployed by women as a strategy of controlling other women's behavior and appearance, we can better understand the meanings of the celebration of southern tackiness as a potential pressure valve for women who wish to momentarily shrug off their responsibilities. With tackiness as a marker of what's unacceptable for southern women, southern mothers use it to both delineate expectations of their children and exercise their privilege in breaking the rules—as long as it's clear what the rules are.

NOTES

1. The article also has a video clip of Reese Witherspoon talking about her mother, confirming Witherspoon's characterization of the maternally enforced mores within which she was raised and continues to be involved.

2. Other variations offered are "That Dog Can Hunt" and "Gimme Some Sugar," reflecting the lifestyle magazine's understanding of southern identity as one encompassing cordiality, hunting lifestyles, and appreciation of humorous vernacular.

3. That Isenberg equates production with procreation in this description highlights the important role that mothers play in the literal reproduction and sustaining of the norms and mores of the "acceptable" white society through child-rearing.

4. The "Red Hat Society" is a social organization for women over the age of fifty, based on the Jenny Joseph poem "Warning," in which the speaker fantasizes about being old enough to be secure to wear the color purple "with a red hat which doesn't go, and doesn't suit me" (Joseph 1–2). Under the auspices of chapter meetings, women don garish red hats and even feather boas, otherwise tacky accessories in their taking what the Red Hat Society's website describes as "an occasional 'recess' from the cares and duties of everyday life" ("About Us"). Though they are an international organization, they are frequently featured in and advertise in magazines such as *Southern Living* (see, e.g., "The Red Hat Society Celebrates Friendship Over (and Under) 50").

5. Here I'm using the definition of "slumming" from George Chauncey's *Gay New York: Gender, Urban Culture, and the Making of the Gay Male World, 1890–1940*: "Going slumming in the resorts of the Bowery and the Tenderloin was a popular activity among middle-class men (and even among some women), in part as a way to witness working-class 'depravity' and to confirm their sense of superiority" (36).

6. I have yet to see any significant discussion made in popular culture about tackiness and southern fathers. Most discussions about southern fathers generally focus on food, cars, and sports.

WORKS CITED

"About Us." *Red Hat Society*, www.redhatsociety.com/page/about_us#. Accessed 13 Sept. 2020.

Cahn, Susan K. *Sexual Reckonings: Southern Girls in a Troubling Age*, Harvard UP, 2007.

Chauncey, George. *Gay New York: Gender, Urban Culture, and the Making of the Gay Male World, 1890–1940*. Basic Books, 1994.

Clinton, Catherine. *The Plantation Mistress: Woman's World in the Old South*. Pantheon Books, 1982.

"The Don't Be Tacky Tea Towel." *Down South*, downsouth.house/products/the-dont-be-tacky-dishtowel?customer_posted=true&variant=7252271136834#contact_form. Accessed 18 Apr. 2020.

Glock, Allison. "Make the Effort." *Southern Living*, May 2012, p. 106.

Harling, Robert. *Steel Magnolias*. Dramatists Play Service, 1988.

Huckaby, Darrell. "At Christmas, Tacky Depends on How You Look at It." *Online Athens*, 8 Dec. 2019, www.onlineathens.com/lifestyle/20191208/huckaby-at-christmas-tacky-depends-on-how-you-look-at-it.

Isenberg, Nancy. *White Trash: The 400-Year Untold History of Class in America*. Penguin Books, 2017.

Joseph, Jenny. "Warning." 1992. *Scottish Poetry Library*, 2020, www.scottishpoetrylibrary.org.uk/poem/warning/.

Luesse, Valerie Fraser. "Things Mama Says Are Tacky." *Southern Living*, www.southernliving.com/culture/tacky-sayings-southern-mama. Accessed 18 Apr. 2020.

———. "25 Things Only a Southern Dad Says." *Southern Living*, www.southernliving.com/culture/southern-dad-quotes. Accessed 1 July 2020.

McDonald, Jorie Nicole. "12 Quotes About Southern Women That Are So True." *Southern Living*, www.southernliving.com/culture/southern-women-quotes. Accessed 18 Apr. 2020.

McPherson, Tara. *Reconstructing Dixie: Race, Gender, and Nostalgia in the Imagined South*. Duke UP, 2003.

"Pretty Little Gloves." *Down South House and Home*, 2020, downsouth.house/products/pretty-little-gloves?variant=32082946261058. Accessed 4 July 2020.

"The Red Hat Society Celebrates Friendship Over (and Under) 50." *Southern Living*, 24 June 2019, www.southernliving.com/culture/red-hat-society.

Ritterhouse, Jennifer Lynn. *Growing Up Jim Crow: How Black and White Children Learned Race*. U of North Carolina P, 2006.

"Southern Expression Cocktail Napkins by Garden & Gun." *Fieldshop by Garden and Gun*, www.ggfieldshop.com/southern-expression-cocktail-napkins-by-garden-gun. Accessed 4 July 2020.

Szczesiul, Anthony. *The Southern Hospitality Myth: Ethics, Politics, Race, and American Memory*. U of Georgia P, 2017.

"Who We Are." *Down South House & Home*, 2020, downsouth.house/pages/about-down-south. Accessed 4 July 2020.

Witherspoon, Reese. *Whiskey in a Teacup: What Growing Up in the South Taught Me About Life, Love, and Baking Biscuits*. Touchstones, 2018.

"You Know Your Mama Is Really Southern If . . ." *Garden and Gun*, 11 May 2018, gardenandgun.com/articles/know-mama-really-southern.

II.
Revolutionary Tackiness

TACKY WHITES AND ELEGANT CREOLES

THE COLOR OF TASTE IN NINETEENTH-CENTURY LOUISIANA

JARROD HAYES

*I*n their first encounter in *The Silence of the Lambs* (1991), Hannibal Lecter tells Clarice Starling, "You know what you look like to me with your good bag and your cheap shoes? You look like a rube, a well-scrubbed, hustling rube with a little taste. Good nutrition has given you some length of bone, but you're not more than one generation from pure white trash." This brutally accurate assessment of Jodie Foster's character decodes her class heritage by "reading" cues that signal a lack of fashion. In this essay, I will consider how translatable these cues might be across the French-English language divide in the US South of the nineteenth century. When I first saw this film just after relocating to New York City from the South, I must admit to feeling relieved upon realizing that, unlike Clarice, I was *two* whole generations away "from pure white trash." During my childhood in the North Carolina Piedmont, an entire apprenticeship of our cherished working-class taste taught me to associate the tacky South, like the label *white trash* in Lecter's mouth, with a specific place, Upstate South Carolina, where my father grew up in Spartanburg County, adjacent to Dorothy Allison's Greenville in *Bastard Out of Carolina*. During our annual visit to a place only two and a half hours away by car, my more or less solidly working-class mother made it clear that "white trash" was not just something one should attempt to climb *out* of; it was also something you could fall back *into*.

The very expression *white trash* suggests that taste is racialized in the South. While I was urged to distinguish myself *from* tacky whiteness, white *taste*—even of a working-class variety—was something I was urged to aspire *to* with admonitions like "Act white!" or rewards like "That's mighty white of you!"[1] The contradiction central to a notion of taste with which one distances oneself from a tacky whiteness by working even harder at being white ultimately finds a recognizable counterpart across the divides that separate the Anglo South I grew up in and the French-speaking context of nineteenth-century Louisiana on which I have focused my research for about fifteen years. This context otherwise offers a number of *contrasts* with the Anglo South, not least of which is the way in which white and Black are defined as racial designations. One key difference in this regard was the caste of free people of color that flourished in Francophone Louisiana under a racializing regime that considered them to be neither Black nor white. In this context, white Americans (read white *Anglo* Americans) were seen by white Creoles and Creoles of color alike as tacky, and the taste and beauty of free women of color were often considered to be a standard worthy of imitation by the wealthiest white Creole women and against which even white female beauty could be judged. While Creole women of color in *plaçage* relationships—or contractual relationships with wealthy white men—were more economically privileged than Clarice's parents, the tacky/stylish distinction that defined their social context nonetheless bears some resemblance regarding its racial implications.

In this essay, therefore, I will consider how a class hierarchy of taste might be mapped onto the racial landscape of nineteenth-century Louisiana. In particular, I will examine Sidonie de La Houssaye's four-volume *Les Quarteronnes de la Nouvelle Orléans* or *The Quadroons of New Orleans* to unpack the seemingly contradictory opposition between presumably positive aesthetic associations with the racializing category

"quadroon" and its quite negative *moral* associations.[2] Set in the 1820s
and 1830s and published in the 1890s, these novels stage the institution
of *plaçage* and the infamous "quadroon balls" that served as their prelude
by excessively repeating numerous racist clichés, though ones often
unrecognizable as such from a contemporary Anglo American perspective. Indeed, in de La Houssaye's discursive universe, the *quarteronne* is
more beautiful (even often more light-skinned) than the wealthy white
women with whom she competes for men. She has an excessive taste
for luxury and takes an excessive pleasure in displaying her wealth. As
Michel Fabre states in his contribution to Werner Sollors's *Multilingual
America*, the Creoles of color of New Orleans were the "aristocrats of
manners" (29). In fact, a few tacky white Creole characters in these
novels will attempt to become less tacky by copying stylish *quarteronne*
characters. Yet, because white Creoles ultimately owned the means
of production for the stylish original that they copy, while the racial
implications of any French counterpart for a tacky Anglo South may
differ, its class implications remain remarkably similar.

Although these novels are too complex to summarize in detail, my
readers might find it useful to consider a brief summary of the first
volume (the simplest as well as the shortest), *Octavia la quarteronne*, as
an example of how "juicy" de La Houssaye's stories are. This novel
recounts the tragedy that its eponymous "heroine" sets in motion for
her lover Alfred D. after he dumps her to take on a "legitimate" (read
white) wife, Angèle. After the married couple has two children, Octavia
kidnaps their daughter, takes her to Havanna, alters her civil status to
pass her off as her own illegitimate daughter, raises her as a *quarteronne*
renamed Mary, and "pimps" her out to wealthy white men. Meanwhile,
Angèle dies of sorrow leaving behind her remaining child, Léonce. Years
later, Octavia brings Mary back to New Orleans and incites Léonce to
fall in love with his biological sister. To pay Octavia the price she has
demanded to "place" Mary, Léonce forges a check from his grandfa-
ther. Octavia then alerts the bank, the police, and Alfred, who rushes
to discover his son and daughter in a compromising embrace about to
consummate the *plaçage* contract. In this climactic scene, Alfred shoots
Mary and himself. As a result, Léonce loses his sanity and spends the

rest of his days in an asylum. In a letter to George Washington Cable dated 29 March 1887, de La Houssaye delightfully sums up, "It's licentious, immoral, demimonde."[3]

Indeed, when Mary turns twelve, Octavia throws a birthday party that the novel describes as scandalous: in imitation of the infamous "quadroon balls" of the period, guests consist of little girls of color and white boys. The resulting to-do is described as tacky, not because of this particular racial mix but because the same "good" families, whose adult men flock to the grown-up equivalents, refuse to let their younger boys attend. Instead, Octavia must rely on the economic sway she holds over the city's white shopkeepers and artisans to send *their* sons, because they rely on the business of wealthy women of color. Despite the elegance of the "real deal" it seeks to copy, therefore, this ball is considered distasteful, so that Mary's birthday party becomes only a pale imitation, indeed a parody, of its intended original. The novels offer numerous examples of similarly tacky behavior on the part of both white and *quarteronne* characters. Because the length of this chapter will not permit a detailed discussion of all of these examples, I will focus on a scene in which several white women sneak into a masked "quadroon ball" so as to copy the latest fashions. I will argue that the counterintuitive association of tackiness with whiteness and taste with *quareteronne*-ness in de La Houssaye's novels results in a *symbolic* capital that only *seemingly* inverts the association of economic capital with whiteness. In fact, while *quarteronnes* are beautiful and personify aesthetic value, the cultural capital they represent nonetheless remains the property of white folks.

Indeed, although the set of fashion clichés that de La Houssaye uses to dress and define her eponymous characters make them significant status symbols, these clichés also explicitly racialize her title characters: "Their luxury was astonishing and ravishing. Their elegance was innate, as was the sensual grace that made them so attractive. They were always dressed in all the richest and newest that fashion had to offer" (*Octavia* 44). Given that de La Houssaye also describes the palatial abodes of many of her primary *quarteronne* characters as "dens of debauchery and perdition" and "scum-ridden lairs" (*Violetta* 258), the glowing terms with which she characterizes their sense of style is all the more surprising. And even these abject place descriptors, which contribute to metonymic representations of their residents' moral character in de La Houssaye's first two volumes (featuring *quarteronne* characters worthy of scorn), give way in the third and fourth volumes (featuring virtuous *quarteronnes* whom the novels urge us to pity rather than scorn) to descriptions of a more positive nature: "The house was furnished and decorated with great elegance and exquisite artistry. During her last years in the convent, Dahlia had embroidered upholstery to give her father. It was a real masterpiece; bouquets stitched in chenille on pearl-gray velvet. And Jean Lebon, high society's cabinetmaker, had mounted each piece onto tulipwood with fine gold filaments, just as Dahlia had instructed" (*Dahlia* 389). This sumptuous residence is described in the series' fourth volume; the third contains the incident that will serve as this chapter's main example, but the house of the sympathetic character named in the third volume's title, *Gina la quarteronne*, is not the one where this episode takes place. Rather, it is set in the mansion of a more reprehensible secondary character, Adoréah, whom readers first encountered in the first volume and who, in the third, organizes the aforementioned soiree upon completion of the construction of her new home as stipulated by her *plaçage* contract with the wealthy Dr. Fleury. After an exquisite, detailed description of the mansion's decor, de La Houssaye introduces two, semianonymous "illustrious beauties of the time whose names and follies are still known today" (293): "Best friends, though rivals in beauty and whimsy, Madame Suzon R. et Madame Sylvie Y. swore that they would gain entrance to Palace Adoréah and dance at the famous soirée. After putting their heads together, here is what they resolved to do: Suzon R. is the one who took on the task of writing Adoréah to request an invitation" (*Gina* 293).

Given that, in de La Houssaye's discursive universe, white Creole women and Creole women of color almost never mix, in part because the latter's "dens of debauchery and perdition" and "scum-ridden lairs" are viewed as morally contagious when it comes to white female virtue and purity, this episode is quite astonishing. While considering that such a request would lower their social status on the one hand, on the other Suzon assumes that Adoréah would be so honored by their presence that she would happily accept. Therefore, a subterfuge is devised by which the party will be a costume ball, at which only men (and they will all be white) will have to present their invitations; the women (in principle, all Creoles of color) will not. Suzon and Sylvie may thus enter without being recognized as white Creoles, since individual identity, not visible difference determines race here. This is a crucial moment, particularly in the historical context Monique Guillory describes in her essay titled "Under One Roof: The Sins and Sanctity of the New Orleans Quadroon Balls": "[D]espite their popularity among the upper echelon of New Orleans socialites, the balls were covert, underground treasures, and many patrons donned masks in order to protect their identities" (83). So what de La Houssaye presents as idiosyncratic on the part of Suzon and Sylvie was apparently a common practice historically. Guillory also states, "Many white women were so possessed by . . . fear that they started attending the balls themselves to check up on their husbands or even possibly to find husbands" (87).

In contrast, de La Houssaye frequently represents white women's purity by stressing their ignorance (in the etymological sense of the term) of the very existence of *quarteronnes*, much less the "quadroon balls." The only previous instance in which a white woman even steps foot in the house of a woman of color requires considerable rhetorical acrobatics: in *Violetta la quarteronne*, after Pierre Saulvé has abandoned his wife and children for his mistress Violetta, whom de La Houssaye presents as the most evil of the *quarteronne* characters, and his dying youngest child asks to see him, Saulvé's virtuous eldest daughter Marie, named after the Blessed Virgin herself, must inquire as to Violetta's address before going there to transmit her brother's request. Her appearance at Les Violettes, as Violetta's mansion is called, is ruthlessly exploited by de La Houssaye for all its shock value. Marie's virginal purity brings all Violetta's guests to tears, even those who are presented as immoral in other passages, and Violetta, alone unmoved by the pathetics of this episode, goes so far as to throw a temper tantrum because Marie has dampened spirits at her soiree. Indeed, when de La Houssaye speaks of "these infamous creatures whose name a respectable woman can't pronounce without blushing" (*Gina* 130), she presents herself as precisely such an *honnête femme*. Yet not only does she name these women, but she does so to excess. In fact, one might read Suzon and Sylvie as stand-ins for the presumably white narrator herself, who exhibits a remarkably similar curiosity for *quarteronnes*, the knowledge of whom challenges the very purity that is supposed to define her white womanhood.

And in fact, what Suzon and Sylvie witness is nothing less than the inauguration of a new fashion trend: "To Adoréah the quarteronne goes the glory of having first, before any other, instituted buffets in New Orleans: her example was followed quite quickly, and a fortnight later, Suzon R. threw a party during which she introduced the buffet to the Crescent City's high society" (*Gina* 303). This passage interests me because it strengthens a characteristic of de La Houssaye's novels that I have often spoken of, their inversion of the Anglo American convention of the passing narrative.[4] Indeed, this novel explicitly points out that it is Suzon and Sylvie who are passing for women of color: "Excited by wine and the novelty of the situation, Suzon and Sylvie kept bursting into laughter and joking as if they were actually among their equals. And, an odd sight to behold, a stranger who might have observed this little scene would have certainly mistaken our grand dames for *quarteronnes*, and the *quarteronnes* for two ladies belonging to the highest of societies" (*Gina* 304). If we compare this passage to an Anglo American notion of passing in which the one who passes does so by copying some supposed white original, here, what Suzon and Slyvie may think they are copying, some counterpart that would be a *quarteronne* original, is undone. For they are now face-to-face with what would normally constitute that original, but that supposed original now defines itself in opposition to Suzon and Sylvie's supposed copy. A white performance of *quarteronne*-ness thus reveals itself to be the original, not the copy, and the racial difference it purports to assert is revealed to be a white invention.

Indeed, the taste and elegance of *quarteronnes* did not go unnoticed by English-speaking visitors to New Orleans. In his 1806 *Travels in America*, Thomas Ashe "wrote a most incredible account of their fantastic dress. He pictures them in petticoats ornamented at the bottom with gold lace or fringe, over which was worn a velvet jacket fitted close to the shape, laced or buttoned in front, with long points hanging down quite round the petticoat and trimmed at the end with pearl tassels.

Their slippers were of gold embroidery and their stockings interwoven with gold (if we are to believe his account) and their most usual headdress either a handkerchief of gold gauze braided with diamonds or chains of gold and pearl twisted in and out through a profusion of fine black hair" (Brink 413). This fashion description is quite worthy of the pages of *Elle* and *Jardin des Modes* to which Roland Barthes devotes such lavish attention in his 1967 *Système de la mode*. While Barthes's high-structuralist indulgences as regards the analysis of fashion might seem outmoded to us today, rereading his semiology of fashion in conjunction with de La Houssaye can contribute to a close reading for racial signifiers, especially in a context in which white Americans (read white *Anglo* Americans) were seen by white Creoles and Creoles of color alike as tacky.

Système de la mode also parallels another, contemporaneous study, Colette Guillaumin's 1972 *L'Idéologie raciste: Genèse et langage actuel* [Racist Ideology: Genesis and Current Language], which engages in the close reading of a corpus of newspaper articles that rivals Barthes's meticulous and almost mathematical readings of fashion magazines. If Barthes theorizes fashion as a system of signs, for Guillaumin as well, "'race' is a signifier" (64). And in sociology, "Race [. . .] becomes visible not as biological reality, but rather as biological *form* used as SIGN" (3). Guillaumin thus engages in a teasing out of stereotypes remarkable for its time, since what are increasingly called racial "dog whistles" in the left-leaning media of the US are already singled out, even if not named as such in her work. Yet Barthes nonetheless adds something to Guillaumin's understanding of racism when he writes that "this signified is in fact tautological: Fashion can only be defined in relation to itself, because fashion is only an article of clothing and Fashion's clothing is nothing more than what Fashion decides that it is" (287). He hereby names a rather tautological logic underlying fashion that one can recognize in de La Houssaye's eponymous characters, who are *quarteronnes* in part because they are well-dressed. Race itself thus depends on a similarly tautological logic that might be boiled down to the formulation *all x are y; z is x because s/he is y.*

That this tautological logic might tell us something about race is hinted in Homi K. Bhabha's reading of Frantz Fanon's *Peau noire, masques* blancs (1952) [Black Skin, White Masks]—perhaps the most important French contribution to critical race studies. In a famous passage, Fanon famously tells the story of an encounter with a French mother and her child in a train during which the latter labels him with a racializing epithet: "Regarde, le nègre! . . . Maman, un nègre!" (91) ["Look, a Negro! Maman, a Negro!" (93)]. In this primal scene of antiracist consciousness, Fanon also states, "I . . . discover my livery" (94). And this is but one of two mentions by Fanon of Black skin as a kind of livery, in which he compares Black skin, never a biological covering but always constructed through cultural "epidermization," with clothing, thereby suggesting that a semiology of fashion might contribute to the theorization of racialization. The Fanonian livery imposed on the racialized body, the body racialized through that very, sometimes *violent* imposition of a livery, might also be said to work through a Barthesian tautology—all x (Blacks) are y (cloaked in Black skin); z (as an individual) is x because s/he is y. The rather banal incident of racial profiling related by Fanon might thus be considered paradigmatic because the very racial distinctions that its white participants claim merely to recognize as a preexisting fact are, in fact, imposed through the deployment of this tautology. De La Houssaye's own sartorial tautologies, as well, are another manifestation of such profiling.

In one of his most extended discussions of Fanon, "Interrogating Identity: Frantz Fanon and the Postcolonial Prerogative,"[5] Bhabha also quotes Barthes, specifically the latter's notion of the "effet du [sic] réel" (48) or reality effect,[6] in his theorization of the relation between Black and white, Colonized and Colonizer. Furthermore, it is in relation to Fanon that Bhabha develops one of the characteristic notions for which he quickly became renowned—mimicry—which might otherwise have been understood as a colonized Other (here a Black person) escaping the stain of stereotype by imitating a colonialist Self (white people), by attempting to pass for white, in other words. Reiterating Fanon's title, Bhabha describes such passings as "the white man's artifice inscribed on the black man's body" (Bhabha 45), yet in his particular reading of the relation between Fanon's white mask and Black skin, Bhabha complicates that notion of passing by stressing that "[i]t is not the colonialist Self or the colonized Other, but the disturbing distance in-between that constitutes the figure of colonial otherness" (45), thereby deconstructing the white/black binary upon which any such notion of passing relies. In fact, each side of this binary is produced through a "rhetoric of repetition or doubling that . . . displays the art of *becoming* through a certain metonymic logic" (54).

Bhabha more explicitly links the metonymic logic that characterizes mimicry with his understanding of stereotype in another essay, which also references Fanon throughout, "The Other Question: Stereotype, Discrimination and the Discourse of Colonialism."[7] Here, he describes stereotypes as "not the setting up of a false image which becomes the scapegoat of discriminatory practices. It is a much more ambivalent text of projection and introjection, metaphoric and metonymic strategies, displacement, over-determination, guilt, aggressivity" (81–82). If we return to the tautological formula that I have used already, we can adapt it to such a metonymic logic linking part to whole and whole to part so as to account for precisely the kind of relations that allow for stereotyping: z (the individual) is a member (a part) of group x (the whole); all (members of) x (the whole group) are y; z is therefore y. If the part (black skin) is what is allowed to define blackness as racial identification in general (the whole), and if that skin is a white mask worn like an imposed livery, where does the metonymy of skin stop? Would the livery of race not then become an extra layer of epidermization, like an onion layer that cannot simply be peeled off to reveal some core of racial essence? When de La Houssaye writes that her *quarteronne* characters "were always dressed in everything richest and newest that fashion offered" as a way of asserting that "their elegance was innate," she is therefore dressing them up in a rather Fanonian mask of race.

Now I am certainly not the first to explore a link between fashion and systems of racialization. As early as 1985, scholars have considered the relation between taste and fashion on the one hand and slavery on the other.[8] In her 2010 *Trading Places: Colonization and Slavery in Eighteenth-Century French Culture*, Madeleine Dobie offers examples of slavery's *material* culture and provides the background for some of the many items of furniture that de La Houssaye lists in her *quarteronne* characters' palatial abodes and the male Creole characters of color who created them. Indeed, studies like Dobie's detail the material culture that both made slavery and was made by it; it was produced from the raw materials extracted from slave-based colonies, and it signified the taste and distinction of the slave-owning class, thereby situating Adoréah's taste within the slave system that produced it. In short, whereas one might be tempted to believe that the elegant Adoréah offers the original that the tacky Creole *white* women desire to copy in the key episode in which Suzon and Sylvie attend Adoréah's soiree, if one returns to Adoréah's childhood in the same volume, one learns how Adoréah came to acquire such admirable taste.

Before "coming out," Adoréah was named Jeannette, and Jeannette and her sister Gothe were, as slaves, adopted by their master's daughter Léontine as her goddaughters. This "adoption" also involved an education in not only reading and writing but also dancing, music, and painting. Very quickly, however, it becomes clear that this education is given to Jeannette and Gothe not for their benefit but for Léontine's:

> Whenever Léontine went to the theater, she always took Jeannette and Gothe with her and had them sit by her side, where everyone could see them in the front of her booth, for she was convinced in advance that their extraordinary beauty and their costumes, just as luxurious as they were picturesque, couldn't fail to attract the attention and admiration of everyone there.
>
> And her darlings accompanied her during her coach rides, and it was a pleasure for the young girl, whenever she had company, to call the young girls into the salon and have them perform sometimes the minuet, sometimes a *pas-de-deux*, or the catchucha, the Cracovian, the hornpipe, or another of the latest dances they had learned. (26)

So we can see here that it is actually from her white patron and godmother that Adoréah learned to perform her elegance and fine taste.

Furthermore, by being taught to perform as a musician for a white audience, Adoréah is taught to perform her *quarteronne*-ness. Race, therefore, is a white production here; although *quarteronne*-ness is produced as having aesthetic value, even as being the standard of beauty against which white female beauty is judged, the cultural capital it represents remains the property of white folks. The young Adoréah-to-be thus constitutes the proof of Léontine's taste and distinction, no matter how much others disapprove of her protégées' education. The fact that she is the property of Léontine's family when she is taught how to become a *quarteronne* thus reverses the relation between original and copy, thereby confounding any attempt to apply the Anglo American concept of passing to these novels. In short, Suzon and Sylvie may *appear* to be the tacky ones at Adoréah's party, but when they copy the latest fashions and bring them home for their own soirees, they are merely reasserting ownership over an aesthetic system that both creates and is created by an economics of slavery that gave rise to the tripartite racial system to which de La Houssaye's characters of all races belong.

NOTES

1. For an interesting reading of this expression in conjunction with my primary texts, see Harris 55ff.

2. *Quarteronne* is only roughly translatable as "quadroon." Henceforth, I will therefore only use the French term because de La Houssaye's novels teach us that racial designations can only be incompletely translated. Many of the clichés that the label *quarteronne* conjures up are more consistent with the archetypal octoroon in Anglo American literature. For example, despite his project of theorizing "circum-Atlantic performance" involving both French and English Americas, Roach concentrates not on *quarteronnes* but on octoroons, in part because the only literary texts associated with New Orleans that he examines are in English and were *Anglo* observations of Franco Louisiana racialization.

3. Qtd. in Perret 198. All translations of de La Houssaye, like all other translations for which no reference is made to a published translation, are my own.

4. I have given a number of lectures on this topic, but for the most recent, see Hayes.

5. *Location of Culture* 40–65.

6. With this expression, Barthes refers to reality as an effect of realist narrative, not something that could pre-exist it (see Barthes, "L'Effet de réel"). For Bhabha, therefore, racial difference would be one such reality effect.

7. *Location of Culture* 66–84.

8. See Mintz; Kritz; Buckridge; Logan.

WORKS CITED

Allison, Dorothy. *Bastard Out of Carolina*. Plume, 1992.

Barthes, Roland. "L'Effet de réel." *Communications*, vol. 11, 1968, pp. 81–90.

————. *Système de la mode*. Seuil, 1967.

Bhabha, Homi K. *The Location of Culture*. Routledge, 1997.

Brink, Florence Roos. "Literary Travellers in Louisiana between 1803 and 1860." *The Louisiana Quarterly*, vol. 31, no. 2, 1948, pp. 384–424.

Buckridge, Steeve O. *The Language of Dress: Resistance and Accommodation in Jamaica, 1750–1890*. U of the West Indies P, 2004.

Cable, George Washington. *Strange True Stories of Louisiana*. 1888. Pelican, 1994.

Dobie, Madeleine. *Trading Places: Colonization and Slavery in Eighteenth-Century French Culture*. Cornell UP, 2010.

Fabre, Michel. "The New Orleans Press and French-Language Literature by Creoles of Color." *Multilingual America: Transnationalism, Ethnicity, and the Languages of American Literature*, edited by Werner Sollors, New York UP, 1998, pp. 29–49.

Fanon, Frantz. *Black Skin, White Masks*. Translated by Richard Philcox, Grove Press, 2008.

————. *Peau noire, masques blancs*. Seuil, 1952.

Gikandi, Simon. *Slavery and the Culture of Taste*. Princeton UP, 2011.

Guillaumin, Colette. *L'Idéologie raciste: Genèse et langage actuel*. Mouton, 1972.

Guillory, Monique. "Under One Roof: The Sins and Sanctity of the New Orleans Quadroon Balls." *Race Consciousness: African-American Studies for the New Century*, edited by Judith Jackson Fossett and Jeffrey A. Tucker, New York UP, 1997, pp. 67–92.

Harris, Christine Elizabeth Koch. *Liminality in Gender, Race, and Nation in Les quarteronnes de la Nouvelle-Orléans by Sidonie de La Houssaye*. 2006. Louisiana State U, Ph.D. dissertation.

Hayes, Jarrod. Lecture. "The Spectacle of Race in Nineteenth-Century Louisiana." 18 July 2017, Monash University, Melbourne, Australia.

Kritz, Kay Dian. *Slavery, Sugar, and the Culture of Refinement: Picturing the British West Indies, 1700–1840*. Yale UP, 2008.

La Houssaye, Sidonie de. *Dahlia la quarteronne*. Tintamarre, 2014. Vol. 3 of *Les Quarteronnes de la Nouvelle-Orléans*.

————. *Gina la quarteronne*. Tintamarre, 2009. Vol. 2 of *Les Quarteronnes de la Nouvelle-Orléans*.

————. *Octavia la quarteronne*. Tintamarre, 2006. Vol. 1 of *Les Quarteronnes de la Nouvelle-Orléans*, pp. 41–141.

————. *Violetta la quarteronne*. Tintamarre, 2006. Vol. 1 of *Les Quarteronnes de la Nouvelle-Orléans*, pp. 143–339.

Logan, Tanya Camela. *Dressing Masculinity among Black Men in Paris since the mid-1970s*. 2014. U of Michigan, Ph.D. dissertation.

Mintz, Sidney W. *Sweetness and Power: The Place of Sugar in Modern History.* Viking, 1985.

Perret, Joseph John. *A Critical Study of the Life and Writings of Sidonie de La Houssaye with Special Emphasis on the Unpublished Works.* 1966. Louisiana State U, Ph.D. dissertation.

Roach, Joseph. *Cities of the Dead: Circum-Atlantic Performance.* Columbia UP, 1996.

The Silence of the Lambs. Directed by Jonathan Demme. Strong Heart Productions, 1991.

HE'S NOTHING BUT A TACKY

TACKINESS AND TRANSGRESSION IN
FRONTIER HUMOR SKETCHES

KATHARINE A. BURNETT

The 1891/1892 short story, "The Tenderfoot," begins like many other western shorts popular in the nineteenth century. Set in the 1850s far West, it features a mining town characteristic of the Gold Rush era. Told from the perspective of an unnamed miner, it's also written entirely in western dialect: "Back in the '50s, we old miners didn't hev much respect fur them weak-kneed, white-handed chaps, thet you call 'dudes' now. They was rank pisen to us an' one of 'em never struck our camp without hevin' so many tricks played on him thet arter awhile he was glad enough to git away." Like many of the local color stories of the same era, the dialect is an easy nod to authenticity, a demonstration that the story is, indeed, of the region. Yet, the fact that it is written makes it a deliberate construction of identity, a choice on the part of the author to create an image for the reader through coded language.

As a result, this overt and rather forced use of dialect reads like a performance. The performance is only emphasized by the fact that the dialect suddenly disappears for several lines later in the story: "'Mebbe Mulligan's gang has struck the camp again,' said Tom Haydon, laying his hand on the butt of his revolver as he spoke. Every other man instinctively made the same movement as the thought flashed across their minds; for another visit from Tim Mulligan's dare-devils wasn't a very pleasant outlook." The language is refined in comparison with that first paragraph, and such a radical contrast is jolting. It would be easy to read this moment as a simple technical error—and perhaps (or probably) it was. But the slip only lasts for a line or two, and the dialect returns immediately, remaining consistent throughout the rest of the story. It reads as a small wink to the reader, an acknowledgment that the performance of western identity is tongue-in-cheek, and we're all in on the joke.

The story's authorship makes this performance doubly interesting: it was written by Paul Laurence Dunbar, an African American author from the Midwest whose work has been read by popular audiences and critics almost exclusively in terms of racial realism. "The Tenderfoot" was the first short story that he sold in 1891 to the A. N. Kellogg Newspaper Syndicate, and it was part of a general fascination Dunbar had with the West.[1] Yet it is also an outlier, for Dunbar's most recognized work, at least with contemporaneous audiences, was his dialect poetry and fiction set primarily in the South and Midwest.[2]

It seems incongruous to mention Paul Laurence Dunbar in relation to a western regional story. It's even more incongruous to include him in a collection on southern tackiness. Dunbar was neither western, southern, nor particularly tacky, at least according to the popular definition. Yet the performance of identity in "The Tenderfoot" raises questions about how tackiness functions as a cultural and aesthetic trope. The nudge-and-nod usage of the dialect highlights the story's manufactured westernness, and, for the very reason that it is so over-the-top and forced, it becomes a tacky performance. And like most tacky representations, the story relies on a contract between astute readers and the author, in which a select group is in on the performance, but the performance itself is not overtly acknowledged.

Drawing from southern modes of representation, in this case popular frontier humor stories from earlier in the century, Dunbar's story uses tackiness to blur the boundaries that normally demarcate racial, regional, and class-based identities. Here we have a midwestern Black author whose work was almost always heralded as the epitome of artistic representations of Black life in the South and Midwest, who dons and doffs the identities of white, lower-class, and western characters—and it is up to the readers to correctly interpret that performance. This shell game of cultural performance then becomes a way in which Dunbar, through a simple regional tale, undermines the very cultural markers that define the story and its author for readers to create a more interesting—I'd argue more sincere—presentation of identity at the end of the nineteenth century. In this case, tackiness in "The Tenderfoot" is a two-way gatekeeping device: the performance of region through dialect marks the subjects of the story as othered to the presumably middle-class, East Coast, white readers. Yet the tacky performance also filters out who can recognize the performance for what it is, who is perceptive enough to properly read and interpret the many layers at work in the story: from regional demarcations, to class, to race. Tackiness exports and modifies distinctive identities and recasts them in new and more subversive ways.

My use of the term "tacky" in relation to "The Tenderfoot" requires some explanation, because the story does not fit the characteristics normally associated with the term in popular culture. As discussed often in this collection, the *OED* identifies the term emerging as a noun at the beginning of the nineteenth century in reference to poor whites in the southern Appalachian region but was also used to describe "a degenerate, 'weedy' horse." Only later in the century was "tacky" used as the adjective more common now, a descriptor for something cheap or tawdry.

But how did the term make that journey, from a regionally- and contextually-specific noun, to an amorphous, abstract term that (much like pornography) most people can't define but know it when they see it? The simple explanation would be an association between the definition of "tacky" as a shoddy horse with those who often rode such horses. Perhaps tackies were tacky because they rode tackies, and the term spun off from there.

Another answer, one that better captures the diffuse quality of tackiness as a concept, lies in how "tacky" is adopted, utilized, and further, perceived. Like many aesthetic models, tackiness is reliant on audience reception for its functioning. There is no inherent quality that makes something or someone tacky; it always involves an exchange between the tacky subject and the perceiver. That subjective and fluid quality makes tackiness even harder to define, and perhaps one of the best corollaries lies in the concept of the uncanny outlined by Freud. Normally we raise the idea of the uncanny in literary studies to discuss gothic literature. An oversimplified definition would be something that is familiar, yet unfamiliar, where the dissonance creates a sense of discomfort and fear. In gothic representations, especially in eighteenth-century British novels, there are ominous settings, disguised or doubled figures, psychological uncertainty—all contribute to the gothic uncanny.

Tackiness draws from the same principles of the uncanny but to different ends. As with the gothic uncanny, tackiness is imitative but just a little off. As Freud describes it, the uncanny "is in reality nothing new or foreign, but something familiar and old—established in the mind that has been estranged only by the process of repression" (13). Similarly, the adjective "tacky" becomes a way of identifying something that transgresses established norms, like a tracing that doesn't quite match up. Not repressed, necessarily, the object imbued with tackiness is only so because the viewer connects with it as something they recognize, but it deviates in some way from the common understanding of that representation. In either case, an audience is necessary to produce the feeling of tackiness or uncanny. Thinking of tackiness this way connects the early definitions from the *OED*. On these terms, the noun versions of tacky as horse and tacky as person are very similar: both are imitative of a norm but just a little off. In both cases, tackiness functions as a way to cordon off non-normative behavior, wherein a nontacky observer witnesses and interprets tackiness from a distance. There's an implicit hierarchy in which the observer is elevated above the tacky person or thing because of their lack of tackiness.

Despite the uncanny quality of tackiness and its function as a sorting mechanism in American culture, tackiness also enables greater moments of sincerity that transcend the categories it supposedly creates and delimits. Because, to return to the definition of tacky as uncanny, in order for something or someone to be labeled as tacky, it first must be familiar or recognized by the observer. Through this exchange, the moment of recognition, the tackiness of the subject becomes something real, sincere. In these moments of sincerity, there is a form of authenticity in which the ability to perform and interpret tackiness brings forth the knowledge on the part of observers (like us) that we are not part of this, and that we'll never completely understand it. In these moments, tackiness reverses the implicit power dynamic, and the ability to read and perform tackiness becomes a way to elevate the tacky person or thing above the normative observer. In this sense, tackiness and the term "camp" go hand in hand. In her "Notes on Camp" (1964), Susan Sontag comments that camp is an aesthetic mode, the whole point of which is to "dethrone the serious. . . . More precisely, Camp involves a new, more complex relation to 'the serious'" (10). And perhaps not coincidentally, Sontag identifies the origins of camp in the eighteenth century with gothic novels. In tacky, uncanny, and campy representations, the serious—usually synonymous with the normative—is undermined by the tongue-in-cheek quality of the performance.

"The Tenderfoot" and its literary forebears trace out the evolution of the term tacky: from the "poor white" of the southern region in the early nineteenth century, to the shoddy horse, and finally, to the aesthetic exchange that upends normative cultural perceptions and representations. By laying out the epistemological routes of the word, the story also traces the geographic path of southern tackiness: from the US South, to the far West, then beyond. The trope of tackiness— one could even say the genre of tacky—begins with the most popular representations of the early South associated with the noun tacky: frontier humor stories published in the 1830s, '40s and '50s. These are the representations that bring tackiness into the mainstream in the nineteenth century and connect the *OED* definition to the general use of "tacky" as an adjective in contemporary culture. Frontier humor sets up a paradigm taken up in later stories like Dunbar's "The Tenderfoot," wherein the tacky uncanny interrogates social categories and brings forth more sincere representations.

One story in particular demonstrates the patterns of tackiness that emerge in the late nineteenth century: Augustus Baldwin Longstreet's "The Horse-Swap," published in his 1835 collection, *Georgia Scenes.* Longstreet's collection is probably the most well-known or well-studied of the earlier frontier humor writing, often called southwestern humor tales. In doing a simple term search, this story is also one of the few that uses the word "tacky" directly—in this case the literal, noun definition for a horse.

The traditional interpretation of southwestern humor, especially Longstreet's stories, is to view them as forms of representational containment. In *Georgia Scenes*, the stories usually begin with a frame narrative as told through the perspective of a middle-class, well-educated observer who witnesses events set in motion by the lower-class "tackies" populating the South. This frame allows for a sort of Bakhtinian transgression, where the actions of the lower-class characters critique social, economic, and gender categories touted by middle-class America, while still being contained literally and metaphorically in the story.

"The Horse-Swap" is no exception. In the story, the middle-class narrator observes a horse trade between two locals: Yellow Blossom (as he calls himself) and Peter Ketch. Blossom, who proclaims himself an exceptional horse trader, presents Bullet, a "peculiarly interesting" horse of gangly and odd dimensions who also appears to be very skittish (26). Ketch offers Kit, a stolid, well-formed horse, who is "monstrous mean" and also blind (27). The men reach an agreement, and at the end, Blossom reveals that Bullet has a horrendous sore under his saddle— the cause of his "skittishness." But Blossom's triumph is undercut by the revelation that Ketch's horse is not only blind but also deaf. To the narrator's amusement, the trade is a wash. By all accounts, the story fits with the traditional interpretation of southwestern humor: the locals perform their hijinks while the more middle-class narrator stands by, uninvolved.

Understanding "The Horse-Swap" through the lens of tackiness as uncanny or even campy offers a different, more complicated perspective on the layers of transactions occurring in the story. Each horse is both a literal tacky (in the noun form) and also embodies the adjectival form as defined by the uncanny: appearing normal but just a little off. But the tackiness of the horses symbolizes the way in which the men involved in the swap use the uncanny qualities to their advantage. As Peter Ketch comments on his own horse while the men examine him, "he's nothing but a tacky," an observation that seems to both encompass and excuse any of the horse's defects (27). It implies that everyone in the exchange knows what they're getting into and can read the situation for what it is. Rather than a simple con in one direction, the tackiness of the horses—and the men's own tackiness—puts them on equal footing with one another, with Yellow Blossom just as duped as his counterpart Peter Ketch.

Tackiness also puts the two traders on equal footing with the narrator, and by extension, the reader, thus achieving that moment of sincerity, the complication of "serious" social norms. The ability to read and perform tackiness becomes an advantage in this exchange, and by extension in the South more generally. The narrator, unable to interpret the tackiness, or the off quality of the horses and the men, only sees at face value. Until the minor deceptions are revealed at the end, he is in the dark, and the story implies that if he had taken part in the trade, his misreading of the tackiness would have made him—and by extension, the reader—a victim of the con. Indeed, the story hints at that possible outcome, for Yellow Blossom approaches the narrator first in an attempt to trade, perhaps sensing his lack of perception.

Stories like "The Horse-Swap" create a pattern of tacky representation in which the performance and ability to read tackiness becomes key to achieving a sincere form of representation that can exist outside of mainstream normative standards. This ultimately allows the term tacky to transcend the regional origins of the definition and carries it to the frontier of the far West, another space in which social categories are in flux. Of course, this occurs first in literal terms through actual physical migration from the South to western areas (Texas, California). Many of the southern humorists document this in their fiction.

It also occurs through the adaptation of literary form and genre. Dunbar's "The Tenderfoot" picks up the patterns established in stories like "The Horse-Swap" but pulls them even further from the historical and regional origins of tackiness. Those adaptations of form become a way of blurring the lines between the most inviolable social categories and distinctions: in the case of nineteenth-century cultural norms, that category is race. As an early form of literary tackiness, Longstreet's story highlights a pattern in how the concept is traditionally understood: in reference to white, lower-class communities and culture. The trend largely stems from the origins for the word, which locate tackiness in the "poor white" space of Appalachia and the South, where "The Horse-Swap" takes place. "Tacky" and "white trash" were usually synonymous throughout the nineteenth century and became racialized in the context of debates over slavery. Mary Boykin Chesnut, the member of a wealthy South Carolina plantation family, even connects the two terms in her Civil War diary, describing a member of a local poor white community as a "perfect specimen of the Sandhill 'tackey' race" (401).[3] As a result, the use of the term "tacky" continues to be associated with lower-class whites of the South: think of the ubiquity of Dolly Parton, popular representations of "hillbilly" culture, or the quasi glorification of the redneck in everything from stand-up comedy to Netflix miniseries.[4]

"The Tenderfoot" and its employment of tackiness through the structure of frontier humor throws this essentialist understanding of race and racialized class out the window. To return to the story, that dialect-heavy first paragraph immediately evokes several indicators of performance and authenticity that tap into a form of tackiness as uncanny. First is the adoption of the presumably white "old miner" persona by a Black, educated, middle-class author. The narrative persona and overuse of dialect establishes distance between the represented and the reader, and the multiple layers of performance and imitation create an effect that is just a little off. The result is a representation of identity that unmoors it from the nineteenth-century understanding of race or racialized class as fixed and inherited. Instead, identity in "The Tenderfoot" is more akin to eighteenth-century understandings of race, when "writers used *race* to denote a sense of human somatic difference (albeit, and indeed, one that could change) influenced by environmental factors, not one in the blood" (Chiles 10). Through the tackiness employed in the story, Dunbar reveals the instability of race at a moment when it was being codified in US legal institutions and social life, particularly the US South; *Plessy v. Ferguson* was decided just a few years later in 1896, and the laws that limited the lives of Black Americans integrated an essentialist understanding of race into the fabric of US society.[5] Tackiness in Dunbar's story, and the concept's reliance on performance, allows for the sort of mutable interpretation of identity that existed prior to the nineteenth century and defies the process of racial systematization taking place contemporaneously in the Jim Crow South.

Building on the story's imitation of earlier frontier humor, the plot of "The Tenderfoot" is concerned entirely with the performance of authenticity: namely, who is a "real" miner and who is a tenderfoot. The story revolves around a tenderfoot named Fred Bender who enters the camp. During his first appearance in the local tavern, the seasoned miners read him in the same way that Peter Ketch and Yellow Blossom read each other's horses: "He was togged out in a rough workin' suit, *but his hands give him away*, fur they looked soft an' tender an' there wasn't nothin' like sunburn on 'em to spoil their whiteness" (456, my emphasis). Bender himself has the uncanny quality of tackiness—he seems fine at first glance but is just a little off. But unlike the middle-class spectator/narrator in "The Horse-Swap," Bender is just as capable of reading the other miners as they can read him. In response to taunts from the locals, Bender is able to respond with his own sharp rejoinders—that, coupled with his size and brawn, show that he's no mere tenderfoot. Likewise, the narrator positions himself as one of the miners, rather than a casual observer, through his adoption of dialect. Thus, a writer imitating and performing in a tacky style features characters adeptly imitating and performing tackiness.

The slightly off imitation continues with the plot of the story. One of the locals, Tom Haydon, is eager to humiliate the newcomer and challenges him to a wrestling match. Bender, further proving that he can hold his own, wins the fight, humiliating Haydon. The plot draws from an earlier frontier story by Longstreet called "The Fight," which was also published in *Georgia Scenes* alongside "The Horse-Swap." However, unlike Longstreet's fight, which ends with the men ripped to shreds, this story makes amends between the two men through a senti-mental act of heroism: Bender saves Haydon's daughter from a runaway horse. "The Tenderfoot" ends with a neat, sentimental story rather than the double-con that ends most frontier humor stories. Therefore, the story amplifies its tacky uncanny quality by veering further from the original source material. And like "The Horse-Swap," the tackiness of "The Tenderfoot" leads to an ultimate moment of sincerity—where the men are on equal footing by the end of the story.

While it seems odd, thinking of Dunbar's western writing as part of the genre of tackiness reveals how the term allows for the transgression of normative categories as it relates to class, gender, *and* race—and how a historical understanding of the term can make it more useful in discussions of contemporary culture. In this representation, tackiness is not used to reinstate easy, normative definitions of identities but instead raises questions about the foundations of those identities. In turn, this literary context has more far-reaching implications for the use of tackiness. If Dunbar, like the earlier southern humorists, could harness tackiness to achieve a new form of sincerity, how can it be done in representations even more disconnected from the historical origins of the term? In this sense, the moment of sincerity in the story applies to Dunbar's act of authorship, wherein the tackiness in simply writing a story like this—that is, in performing an authentic identity that's just a little off—creates a new space for authorship beyond the easy categorization of "Black author who writes about Black culture." Once we as readers know that it's Dunbar, we are left with an uncomfortable, uncanny feeling, because it takes away our ability to read him and the story—by taking away that easy categorization. Identifying Longstreet's and Dunbar's stories as part of the genre of tackiness reveals how much of what we normally think of as tacky is such a celebration of a particular form of whiteness and social class. But seeing both as moments of sincerity on the continuum of tackiness also complicates those definitions. Just as Longstreet's and Dunbar's stories utilize tackiness to belie culturally enforced categories, contemporary tackiness can bring forth moments of sincerity not relegated to upending class hierarchies and reinforcing social or racial norms.

Dunbar's "The Tenderfoot" subverts the concept of tackiness and its usage by revealing a new dynamic, in which the story plays with the readers' expectations of normative definitions of regional, class, and finally, racial identities at the end of the nineteenth century. In this sense, understanding the evolution of tackiness as a term, and tracing it through a wide variety of contexts beyond regional boundaries, highlights tackiness's dual function in both establishing and confusing social categorization in life and artistic representation. It also opens up the possibilities of what we can consider tacky—and why that matters.

NOTES

1. Between 1899 and 1900, Dunbar spent time in Colorado to recover from tuberculosis, though "The Tenderfoot" reveals his interest in the far West went back further than that short visit. Later in 1900 he published *The Love of Landry*, a novel set in the state. For more on Dunbar's biography and the publication history of his short stories, see the foreword and introduction to *The Complete Stories of Paul Laurence Dunbar*, edited by Gene Andrew Jarrett and Thomas Lewis Morgan, with the foreword by Shelley Fisher Fishkin. The quotes appear on pages 455 and 456 in that same volume, respectively.

2. In a now famous (or infamous) review of Dunbar's poetry collection, *Majors and Minors* (1895), realist author William Dean Howells praised Dunbar for his "direct and fresh authority" in regard to Black southern dialect, while another review of a reading Dunbar gave at the Library of Congress in 1901 was titled, "Poetry of the Negro" (see Howells, "Life and Letters" in *Harper's Weekly* [1896] and the *Washington Post* [16 June 1901]).

3. See Isenberg, and Jolene Hubbs's essay in this collection on tackiness and poor whites in late-nineteenth-century local color literature.

4. Consider the unprecedented popularity of the Netflix documentary series, *The Tiger King* (2020).

5. See Hale.

WORKS CITED

Chesnut, Mary Boykin. *A Diary from Dixie, as written by Mary Boykin Chesnut.* Edited by Isabella D. Martin and Myrta Lockett Avary, Appleton, 1905.

Chiles, Katy L. *Transformable Race: Surprising Metamorphoses in the Literature of Early America.* Oxford UP, 2014.

Dunbar, Paul Laurence. "The Tenderfoot." 1891/2. *The Complete Stories of Paul Laurence Dunbar*, edited by Gene Andrew Jarrett and Thomas Lewis Morgan, Ohio UP, 2005, pp. 455–58.

Fishkin, Shelley Fisher. Foreword. *The Complete Stories of Paul Laurence Dunbar*, edited by Gene Andrew Jarrett and Thomas Lewis Morgan, Ohio UP, 2005, pp. ix–xi.

Freud, Sigmund. "The Uncanny." 1919. *The Standard Edition of the Complete Psychological Works of Sigmund Freud*, translated by James Strachey, vol. 17, Hogarth Press, 1953.

Hale, Grace Elizabeth. *Making Whiteness: The Culture of Segregation in the South, 1890–1940.* Pantheon, 1998.

Isenberg, Nancy. *White Trash: The 400-Year Untold History of Class in America.* Viking, 2016.

Jarrett, Gene Andrew, and Thomas Lewis Morgan. Introduction. *The Complete*

Stories of Paul Laurence Dunbar, edited by Gene Andrew Jarrett and Thomas Lewis Morgan, Ohio UP, 2005, pp. xv–xliii.

Longstreet, Augustus Baldwin. "The Horse-Swap." *Georgia Scenes.* 1835. Edited by M. E. Bradford, J. S. Sanders & Co., 1992, pp. 23–31.

Sontag, Susan. "Notes on Camp." 1964. Picador, 2019.

OUTHOUSES AND OTHERS

THE OZARK TACKY NOVELS OF
DONALD HARINGTON

JOSEPH A. FARMER

*J*n *Hill Folks: A History of Arkansas Ozarkers and Their Image*, Brooks Blevins refers to the Ozarks as "that other Southern mountain range" or "Appalachia West," a region "obscured, even eclipsed, by myth and stereotype" (5). Cartoonists, folklorists, and filmmakers alike cannot seem to resist trafficking in tacky representations of barefoot, illiterate, promiscuous, and incestuous poor white hill people. Studies of hillbilly iconography seem to reflect America's ambivalence toward its backwoods, frontier past, though they may disagree on the target demographic for these images and the kitschy collectibles that enshrine them for posterity. Marketing specialist Douglas B. Holt argues that the hillbilly depicted in animated Mountain Dew ads appealed to the inner "wild man" waiting to burst forth from the "buttoned-up emotions" of 1960s company men (43). In *Hillbillyland*, J. W. Williamson contends that it is "stuck-working people" who buy Ozark tacky souvenirs, "these icons of negative identity, these snapshots of the subconscious," because they understand that the "absurdly and delightfully free" hillbilly "gives the horse-laugh to middle-class respectability" (4).

Southern historian Charles Reagan Wilson has confessed his love for "Southern Tacky." Among the items in his legendary collection is a bag of dried beans labeled "hillbilly bubble bath" ("Whose South?"). Similar examples of "Ozark tacky" have been curated by cultural critics. Patrick Huber, for instance, ponders the dubious figure of the "Horny Hillbilly," a figurine of a randy ridge runner in a semirecumbent position with a massive erection protruding from the fly of his pants, complete with a carrying case that proclaims "The South Shall Rise Again" (69). Certainly, collectors of Ozark folklore have done their part to perpetuate the stereotype of the perennially "horny hillbilly." The sexual and scatological elements of Ozark lore are both exemplified by Vance Randolph in the title story of his *Pissing in the Snow*, a collection of the region's bawdiest humor:

> One time there was two farmers that lived out on the road to Carico. They was always good friends, and Bill's oldest boy had been a-sparking one of Sam's daughters. Everything was going fine till the morning they met down by the creek, and Sam was pretty goddam mad. "Bill," says he, "from now on I don't want that boy of yours to set foot on my place." "Why, what's he done?" asked the boy's daddy. "He pissed in the snow, that's what he done, right in front of my house!" "But surely, there ain't no great harm in that," Bill says. "No harm!" hollered Sam. "Hell's fire, he pissed so it spells Lucy's name, right there in the snow!" "The boy shouldn't have done that," says Bill. "But I don't see nothing so terrible bad about it." "Well by God, I do!" yelled Sam. "There was two sets of tracks! And besides, don't you think I know my own daughter's handwriting?" (5)

This story illustrates the ways in which sex and writing go hand in hand in Ozark literature, as do folklore and Ozark tacky. Both run toward the sexual and the scatological, revolving around what happens in the hillbilly's overalls.

The late novelist Donald Harington hardly shied away from such stereotypes in his bawdy treatment of Ozark hillbillies in the town of Stay More, Arkansas. Harington never claimed to write about actual hill folk; he insisted that Stay More existed only "in the mind of the reader . . . And that place may seem to be populated by hillbillies, but those hillbillies are actually the parts of oneself that one recognizes while in the process of encountering them and thereby laughs at them, learns from them, has some kind of interaction with one's own self" (*Guestroom Novelist* 168). This chapter does not claim to exhaustively catalog the abundant examples of Ozark tacky. Instead, I will explore a representative handful of Harington novels, checking them against the peddlers of the hillbilly image in comics and collectibles in trying to determine whether, in his attempts to elevate the tacky to the transcendent, the stereotypical to the sublime, Donald Harington falls in the privy or comes out smelling like a rose. For purposes of comparison, I will also briefly examine two TV series set in the Ozarks: HBO's *True Detective* and Netflix's *Ozark*, tracking the contours of Ozark tacky in more recent Ozark media.

At a casual glance, *Lightning Bug*, Harington's first Stay More novel, appears to recapitulate the tackiest possible hillbilly stereotypes. On a typical morning in Stay More, "Frank Murrison woke to discover he had a morning hard, but Rosie protested, 'It's Sattidy. My day off.' He waited for it to subside, and when it did not he went to the barn and used a ewe. Ella Jean Dinsmore came running into the kitchen, hollering, 'Maw! Baby Jim fell through the hole in the outhouse!' Selena Dinsmore smiled absently and said, 'Aw, just leave him go, Ella Jean. It'd be easier to have another'n than to clean that un up, even if we could git him out'" (33). A subplot of *Lightning Bug* has a federal revenuer tied up at the moonshiner Luther Chism's smokehouse. His daughter, Lucy, seduces the captive revenuer, and Luther discovers the pair "in the old act of carnal congress" and "peppers his backside" with a 12-gauge, all while the man is still tied up (192).

Such material would appear to confirm stereotypes of southern hill folk as "ignorant, backward people ridiculously out of step with emerging modern America and prone to little more than feuding, moonshining, idleness, and diddling livestock" (Huber 73). In interviews, Harington lamented the fact that his work never found a broader audience in his beloved home state of Arkansas. Perhaps Arkansans are understandably leery of Harington's rutting rustics. As Brooks Blevins explains, in the twentieth century the Arkansas image came to be conflated with the Ozarker image, which then became conflated with the hillbilly image (*Arkansas/Arkansaw*). H. L. Mencken, no friend of the

South, was particularly uncharitable to Arkansans, referring to their state as "the Apex of Moronia" (qtd. in Underwood and Underwood). Harington gave a new meaning to Mencken's turn of phrase by dubbing the citizens of Stay More "Stay Morons," clarifying that "strictly speaking a moron is in the age group between seven and twelve, a time of life which, as anyone who has lived through it can tell you, is simply wonderful" (*Architecture* 71). Though his Stay Morons may be infantilized caricatures, arrested in the age of sexual discovery, Harington argued that they are nonetheless written in good taste: "Well, I would say, first of all, be funny, and if you can't be funny, be of good spirit, or of good humor, or I think, despite of all the frequent obscenities in my work, it's in good taste. So if you can't be in good humor or good spirits, you can always be in good taste" (102). In this view, any work that takes a warm, obliging, or nonjudgmental view of its subject cannot be said to have been written in poor taste, while the mean-spirited invective of a H. L. Mencken is undertaken in the poorest possible taste.

A self-styled "highly-sexed hillbilly" (*Guestroom Novelist* 107), Harington spent his childhood summers in Drakes Creek, Arkansas, the model for Stay More and the country of his arrested adolescence. Once Harington became addicted to writing about Arkansas hill folk, he had to compete with such popular purveyors of the hillbilly image as Al Capp, whose *L'il Abner* comic strip featured characters like Abner, Daisy Mae, Ma and Pa Yokum, Moonbeam McSwine, and Confederate General Jubilation T. Cornpone. Worse, *L'il Abner*'s version of hillbilly heaven, Dogpatch, was transplanted from Kentucky to northwest Arkansas in 1968, when a Little Rock businessman persuaded Capp to build a *Dogpatch*-themed amusement park in Marble Falls, Newton County— Stay More's home county. Imagine if, around the time he determined to write about his native postage stamp of land and its people, William Faulkner had to contend not only with a long-running comic strip lampooning Mississippians but an amusement park up the road in nearby Taylor, with University of Mississippi students acting the parts of Varner and Snopes-like characters for their summer jobs, and this may provide some insight into the challenges Harington faced in making his southern highlanders more outrageous than those of his contemporaries yet faithful to his own memories and fantasies of Ozark life.

In the documentary *Dogpatch USA* (2019), Daisy Mae can be seen chasing Abner around the park like a caveman's courtship in reverse. The *L'il Abner* comic strip ritualizes this pursuit in the Sadie Hawkins Day Dance, at which a single fellow finds himself betrothed to the first fleet-footed gal who can run him down. Hill women chase their men in Harington's Stay More as well, as necessitated by the hereditary woman-shyness of the Ingledew men, which makes it nearly impossible for them to speak to, let alone court, females. It falls to the women of Stay More to beguile these backwoodsmen into the mysteries of sex, love, and family, and in Harington's *The Architecture of the Arkansas Ozarks*, six generations of Ingledews find highly creative methods of doing so. Emelda Swain lands the taciturn Bevis Ingledew by learning to communicate with him telepathically so that Bevis never actually has to speak to his wife. The couple sleep in separate bedrooms but share each other's dreams every night, enjoying "365 incidents of imaginary albeit almost exhaustingly true-to-life intercourse" (295). The Dinsmore twins, Doris and Jelena, share their husband, Billy Bob Ingledew, so that not even Billy Bob is sure which of the two women gave birth to the threesome's daughter, Jelena Jr. Sonora Twichell corresponds with Hank Ingledew from her aunt's house in Little Rock, describing the dates they will have when she returns to Stay More. In letter after letter, Sonora describes how they will hold hands at a romantic picture show, then find themselves kissing on the porch swing, then sneak off to the barn together. After reading this last letter, Hank goes out to the barn, finds the spot they will most likely choose for this rendezvous, and then Hank Ingledew effectively "loses his virginity by mail" (338).

Gerhart Saenger writes that men in the *L'il Abner* comics "can preserve their strength only by running away from women, who interfere with their real tasks in life, the seeking and pursuing of adventure" (qtd. in Berger 99). The inverse is true of Stay More men: the lack of female companionship spurs them into action. After Arkansas secedes from the Union, Confederate agent Virdie Boatwright comes into town in a Conestoga "catwagon" to seduce Ozark men into joining up with the secessionists. The skilled Virdie "recruits" some men "three or four times," (*Architecture* 130) and leaves a small army of sexually frustrated men in her wake who go about "kicking posts and dogs and an occasional child" (134). Noah Ingledew becomes so frustrated that he signs up with the Confederacy, prompting his unionist brother Jacob to join up in turn.

Nor are Stay More men lazy, though the idleness of mountain menfolk is a prominent stereotype of upland southerners. Milton Rafferty relates a joke that Ozark men are real "go-getters": they "take her to work in the morning and 'go get her' in the afternoon'" (248). Williamson's *Hillbillyland* displays a metal trivet with this piece of wisdom: "If more husbands were self-starters the wife wouldn't have to be a crank" (4). Paul Webb's comic strip *The Mountain Boys* (1934–1958) depicted overalled hill men leaning on trees or lying prone on the ground, watching their womenfolk pull weeds in the garden, chaps at their heels. Conversely, Harington's male Morons are capable of great feats of ingenuity. They clear hundreds of acres of land with broadaxes and build cabins, houses, and barns. They must be careful not to expend too much effort, however, lest they contract the "frakes," an enigmatic illness that only dogs Stay More men. Frakes symptoms include extreme lassitude, apathy, and a sense of the futility of life after any prolonged bout of hard labor. After weeks helping build Jacob Ingledew's cabin, Murray Swain contracts such a bad case of the frakes that he is driven to suicide by jumping off a bluff, known thereafter as Leapin Rock. Stay More women are somehow immune to the frakes, leaving them free to spend their energy cooking, sewing, quilting, gardening, keeping house, and "climbing" their men. Unlike most dealers in hillbilly humor, Harington at least offers an explanatory motif that accounts for his hill men's legendary lethargy, as well as a potential antidote: Isaac Ingledew "worked hard, but not hard enough to get the frakes, or if he did work enough to get the frakes, Salina's hearty, refreshing sensuality gave him immunity" (*Architecture* 178). If, as Anthony Harkins argues, Al Capp and other artists depicted "mountain life and culture as a site of comedic excess," Harington's hillbillies strive to achieve a balance in labor and in love (152).

The intimacy of Ozark architecture can lead to some awkward situations, however, as when one night John Ingledew sees his mother "climbing" his exceptionally tall father, Isaac, and thinking this looks like great fun, cries out, "Do me! Do me!" (188). The incident earns

John the nickname "Doomy," and causes Salina such embarrassment that she leaves off climbing Isaac, driving him to drink Chism's Dew until the town's supply of whale oil runs out and ushers in a "Spell of Darkness" that enables the happily benighted Salina to climb her man without interruption. Sex and love in *Architecture* are likened unto a childish game of hiding-and-seeking, in which lovers attempt to "get their things together" under the right circumstances. Embarrassment constitutes a major obstacle to that aim. As Harington explains, embarrassment "simply means the breakdown of this pair bonding or the attempt to reach the other, the attempt to believe in the other, the attempt to have a perfect union. Embarrassment is an impediment to true love" (129). To avoid such embarrassment, Stay More couples seek out privacy on mountain bluffs, secluded glens, and in outhouses.

The outhouse is a ubiquitous image in Ozark tacky, as a quick eBay search will reveal. Williamson offers the example of a particleboard sign, to be placed outside one's bathroom, with a spinning arrow to indicate how long the occupant will remain occupied. Options include "readin'," "doin' my chores," "washin' my feet," "trimmin' my toenails," "takin' a nap," "jist restin'," or "none uf yer bizness" (8). Stay Morons, however, are willing to share their precious alone time in the backhouse with one another, and for more than furtive lovemaking: the Dinsmore twins visit the privy together, and Dawny in *When Angels Rest* consoles his schoolmate Gypsy Dingletoon in the girls' outhouse after her lover, Gerald Coe, is killed in Iwo Jima. Harington's hillbillies may be "Morons," but they are no idiots—from "the Greek *idios*, meaning private" (*Architecture* 224). In *Some Other Place. The Right Place*, the philosopher Henry Fox explains that the structure that best expresses the bond between self and other is the two-hole privy, or two-seater outhouse: "People aspire to love . . . Few people can achieve it. To put it crudely, the two-hole privy is man's aspiration to love. As few people ever use two holes together as ever really achieve love together" (324). So prevalent is this theme in Harington that he considered writing a sequel to *Architecture* titled *Outbuildings and Others* (Chambers 138).

Harington's fiction often falls within the same romantic, Arcadian tradition as Harold Bell Wright's *Shepherd of the Hills*; he even created his own shepherd of the hills in a Stay Moron named Nail Chism in

JOSEPH A. FARMER

The Choiring of the Trees. In this novel, the "peculiar" Nail keeps a pasture of sheep and a kitchen garden, which as Linda K. Hughes observes, is considered a feminine pastime in the Ozarks. Nail is falsely convicted of raping a thirteen-year-old girl, a death sentence in Arkansas in 1914, and is put on death row in The Walls, a notorious Arkansas prison. The prosecutor asks Nail at trial if he has obtained "carnal gratification" from his sheep, to which Nail's lawyer, Jim Tom Duckworth, retorts "that "maybe those folks over around Mt. Judea got their jollies screwing ewes, but Stay More people had better sense, not to mention taste" (*Choiring* 39). Worse, Jim Tom's defense hinges on the notion that Dorinda could hardly be a virgin at thirteen, "and her with six brothers" (37).

From such inauspicious beginnings develops a novel that seeks to rehabilitate the hillbilly image while engaging many of its stereotypes—a staple, according to Blevins, of Ozark chroniclers prior to World War II, the era in which *Choiring* is set (*Hill Folks* 134). For this task, Harington enlisted a real-life defender of Arkansas's image: Julia Burnelle Smade "Bernie" Babcock, a novelist and writer for the *Arkansas Gazette* who founded the Arkansas Museum of Natural History and Antiquities in order to counter H. L. Mencken's comments regarding Arkansas's supposed lack of culture (Teske 124). Harington "converts" Babcock into an artist named Viridis Monday, who attends the first of Nail's three commuted executions and sketches his likeness for the *Gazette*. Viridis's portrait of Nail is sympathetic and ennobling—unlike hillbilly portrayals in scads of cartoons, comic strips, and pieces of Ozark Tacky—emphasizing his "splendid physique" and eyes "pale, gentle, comical, inquisitive, and brighter-than you'd like to think: certainly not the eyes of a man on his way to the electric chair" (*Choiring* 15). The novel's narrator asserts that "Nail Chism was nobody's fool. And yet there those who liked to think that he was everybody's fool" (15).

Strong but gentle, Nail protects his cellmate, Timbo Red, from the cellblock's resident rapist because he reminds him of Dorinda. Then, when Timbo grows almost "itchy and pruny" enough to allow the rapist to have his way with him, Nail relieves him with his hand (138). Convinced of Nail's innocence, Viridis travels to Stay More on

182

horseback to investigate the case, mounting an ultimately successful campaign to have Nail pardoned by the governor. Viridis and Nail's ensuing relationship reconciles the dual sides of the Arkansas image as conceived by Brooks Blevins in *Arkansas/Arkansaw*, as a progressive, image-conscious "Arkansan" falls in love with a romantic, hillbilly "Arkansawyer."

If *Choiring* offers Harington's most sympathetic treatment of Ozarkers, his funniest, folksiest defense of his countrymen occurs in a novel that likens them to cockroaches. *The Cockroaches of Stay More* presents a microcosm of Stay More, a near-ghost town that has lost most of its human inhabitants and is now replete with "roosterroaches" (the word "cock" is considered in poor taste among Ozarkers). Named for their human counterparts, Squire John Ingledew and his son, Gregor Samsa "Sam" Ingledew, dwell in Parthenon, the home of "the Woman," Sharon Ingledew. Across the abandoned town is an old hotel known as Holy House, inhabited by the Woman's estranged lover, the Man, Larry Brace. The Ingledews' country cousins, the Dingletoons, inhabit a fallen log out in the Man's yard. The novel's heroine, Tish Dingletoon, has forty-six brothers and is thus, according to the back cover, "in a fair way of losing her virginity." A cockroach Tess Durbeyfield, Tish travels to Parthenon to "claim kin" with the Ingledews and winds up mating with Sam. The roosterroaches of each house subsist off the gracious bounty of crumbs provided by Man and Woman. Followers of Joshua Crust, or "Crustians," worship the alcoholic Man, who in the depths of his drunkenness sometimes "raptures" these fortunate Crustians with his revolver, blowing holes in the walls of the old hotel in the process—thus, "Holy House." The Reverend Tichbourne leads the invasion of the temple of Parthenon, then hatches a conspiracy to kill or displace the squires Ingledew from their proximity to the divine Woman. As a political or religious allegory, the novel may indeed be "half-baked," but it works fine as a vehicle for countering some of the most negative stereotypes about hill people. The narrator explains why roaches offer the perfect microcosm for human Ozarkers:

> The roosterroach, once he has found his nightly share of morsels, crust or crumb, does nothing, knocks off, loiters about,

putters, piddles, takes his ease without any responsibility other than the heavy chore of finding ways to fill up the time between dusk breakfast and dawn supper . . . No wonder roosterroaches are fond of gossip, philosophy, kidding and kibitzing, jokes, stories, tall tales, legends, superstitions, and half-baked religion. In this natural inclination, roosterroaches are ideally suited to imitate the Man of the Ozarks, or at least the Ozark Man as He used to be, in the legendary days of Stay More's past, when Man, although a farmer, and a capable one, devoted only enough labor to His farm to provide food for His family and His devoted roosterroaches, and then spend the major portion of his life in unhurried idleness. (47)

Ironically, most of the Stay More roaches are perfectly wholesome—in the dictionary sense of "conducive to or suggestive of good health and physical well-being," while the Man (a "furriner" from Chicago) is a drunken, gun-wielding sot who shoots himself in the leg. Fortunately for the Man however, the roosterroach Ingledews contrive a way to send an S.O.S. to the Woman, effecting the couple's reconciliation. The roosterroaches celebrate the interdependence of roach and Man, and Man (or Woman at least) learns to tolerate the presence of their six-legged counterparts. *The Cockroaches of Stay More* is concerned with the acceptance of otherness, whether in the human or natural world. Again, this message seems (literally) to revolve around a toilet when Sharon rescues the lovers Tish and Sam Ingledew from a watery death in Parthenon's porcelain fountain—an act of unaccountable compassion.

Harington pushes the boundaries of taste still further in his late career novel, *With*. In *With*, pedophile Sugrue "Sog" Alan is a retired state policeman who kidnaps seven-year-old Robin Kerr from a skating rink in Harrison and removes to an abandoned homestead on Madewell Mountain. Sog's strenuous labors to outfit this child-bridal chamber, however, end with a case of the frakes so debilitating that he finally instructs Robin to shoot him, which she does, leaving him entombed in the Madewell's old outhouse. Left alone, Robin survives a decade-long sequestration on Madewell Mountain with the help of an invisible boy named Adam Madewell. Adam is the "living ghost" of a Stay

THE OZARK TACKY NOVELS OF DONALD HARINGTON

More man whose family moved to California when he was a child but whose "in-habit" still haunts Madewell land. Harington explains that an "in-habit" is "something you leave behind in a place you love very much and cannot bear to part with . . . Your in-habit will remain there long after you're gone" (*With* 257). The adult Adam returns from California, and the moment he sets foot on the Madewell homestead he is reunited with his in-habit, taking on his memories of Robin. Now complete with her Adam, the naked, long-haired Robin is an unembarrassed Eve. The couple settle down to happy life in mountain obscurity, and, at the novel's end, Robin even thanks the entombed Sog Allen for providing the circumstances for this blissful union. Such fairy tale endings are typical of Harington, for whom the Ozarks always offer the "right place" for a relationship between a woman and the right man. This tendency toward happy endings may indeed constitute the tackiest element of Harington's work, though it also speaks to his continuation of the Ozark Märchen tradition, with its common use of the Rapunzel theme.

Of the recent spate of television series set in the Ozarks, the third season of the HBO anthology series *True Detective* cleaves most closely to what I might call "traditional" Ozark tacky. *True Detective* season three was filmed in Fayetteville, which Detective Hays refers to as a "nice place," and the Arkansas Ozarks setting occasions an unlikely mellowing of Pizzolotto's macho brand of southern gothic into a *With*-like fairy tale. The mystery at the heart of that season concerns the Purcell children, Julie and Will, who went missing in 1980. Will's body is recovered in a cave in Devil's Den, but Julie's whereabouts remain a mystery for thirty-five years. By the season finale it is revealed that a recently bereaved mother, Isabelle Hoyt, the wife of a local poultry magnate, purchased Julie from her heroin-addicted mother and kept her in a secret pink room in the Hoyt mansion. The teenaged Julie escaped into the night and sought the protection of nuns at a convent until she was rescued by her childhood friend, Mike Ardoin, then a landscaper who tended the convent grounds. In the end Detective Hays finds Julie living with Mike in a beautifully manicured home in the hills. Here again the marriage of crime writing and Ozark pastoral offers a female character a fairy tale ending, complete with the right place and the right man. *True Detective* bridges the gap between Ozark Märchen and Ozark noir, as its investigators exhaust a series of red herrings corresponding to sinister stereotypes of a southern and specifically Arkansas imaginary, including long-haired teens in metal band t-shirts (*à la* the West Memphis Three), before fingering a white belle/ Dame Gothel for the crime.

Since Harington's death in 2009, most Ozark writing has pivoted harder than *True Detective* toward a different set of stereotypes: from hillbillies to "pillbillies" and from moonshiners to meth-heads. Recent fiction seems less interested in recovering the Ozarks as a "nice place" than in utilizing the region's beautiful, mysterious landscapes as a cover for criminal enterprises. Its characters are more likely to use a cave, glen, or lake to hide a body than for having sex. More pointedly, Philip Howerton suggests that the Ozarks may be "becoming like all other places as the leveling forces of capitalism and mobility absorb it" (189). Likewise, Milton Rafferty observes that the abundance of drugs like meth indicates mobility and connection, not rural, holler-bound isolation (96). Netflix's *Ozark* resembles no Ozark tradition, tacky or not, so much as *Breaking Bad*. In this series Marty Byrde, a Chicago accountant turned money-launderer for a Mexican drug cartel, relocates to the lakefront town of Osage Beach, Missouri, to evade the authorities. This is the same Lake of the Ozarks where Bill Geist, self-styled "connoisseur of the tacky and outrageous," spent his teenage summers working for the kitschy Arrowhead resort. *Ozark*, however, lifts the fog of postcard nostalgia from the Missouri resort town. The Byrdes' suburban blandness quickly "absorbs" what local culture there is, setting up a strip club and a casino, fronts for the cartel that supplant "traditional" Ozark tacky with a generic, American tacky. In these endeavors the Byrdes show as little regard for native Ozarkers as the engineers of the Bagnell Dam that impounded the Osage River in the early 1930s, displacing living and buried residents alike (Geist 3). *Ozark*'s hill folk are not trapped in amber or by history so much as by the show's relentlessly blue color palette. The heroin-producing Snells, for instance, are cussed and recalcitrant but lack an attendant self-deprecating sense of humor—Darlene Snell shoots a man in the head for calling her a redneck—perhaps the most endearing feature of traditional Ozark tacky. *True Detective* and *Ozark* both subordinate their hillbilly characters to the needs of genre, with the notable exception of comedy: their brand of Ozarksploitation rarely allows them to crack a smile, let alone a belly laugh.

The happy, horny hillbillies of Stay More were displaced by nothing but time and what Harington calls "PROG RESS." Their regional, cultural (and racial) distinctiveness exists, again, only in the memory and imagination of a happy postmodernist. Aficionados of Ozark literature continue to admire Harington and ask not if his work should but if it ever could be duplicated. Devotees of Donald Harington should not expect, however, to dodge questions of representation, historical verisimilitude, or cultural politics in a writer who traded so joyfully in tacky representations of the mountain South. As film and television producers continue to explore the Ozarks afresh, the time is also right for critics and champions alike to (if I may be allowed the requisite joke) "stay more" in Harington's world and engage in more "serious" explorations of his work.

WORKS CITED

Berger, Arthur Asa. *L'il Abner: A Study in American Satire*. UP of Mississippi, 1994.

Blevins, Brooks. *Arkansas/Arkansaw: How Bear Hunters, Hillbillies, and Good Ol' Boys Defined a State*. U of Arkansas P, 2010.

———. *Hill Folks: A History of Arkansas Ozarkers and Their Image*. U of North Carolina P, 2003.

Chambers, Douglas, ed. *Personal Souths: Interviews from the Southern Quarterly*. UP of Mississippi, 2012.

Geist, Bill. *Lake of the Ozarks: My Surreal Summers in a Vanishing America*. Grand Central Publishing, 2019.

Harington, Donald. *The Architecture of the Arkansas Ozarks*. Toby Press, 2004.

———. *The Choiring of the Trees*. Toby Press, 2005.

———. *The Cockroaches of Stay More*. Toby Press, 2004.

———. *Lightning Bug*. Toby Press, 2005.

———. *Some Other Place. The Right Place*. Toby Press, 2004.

———. *When Angels Rest*. Counterpoint, 1998.

———. *With*. Toby Press, 2004.

———. *The Guestroom Novelist*. Edited by Brian Walter, U of Arkansas P, 2019.

Harkins, Anthony. *Hillbilly: A Cultural History of an American Icon.* Oxford UP, 2004.

Holt, Douglas B. *How Brand Become Icons: The Principles of Cultural Branding.* Harvard Business School Publishing, 2004.

Huber, Patrick. "The Riddle of the Horny Hillbilly." *Dixie Emporium: Tourism, Foodways, and Consumer Culture in the American South,* edited by Anthony J. Stanonis, U of Georgia P, 2008, pp. 69–86.

Hughes, Linda K. "Knowing Women and the Fiction of Donald Harington." *Chicago Review,* vol. 38, no. 4, 1991, pp. 100–109.

Howerton, Phillip Douglas, ed. *The Literature of the Ozarks: An Anthology.* U of Arkansas P, 2019.

Rafferty, Milton. *Ozarks: Land and Life.* U of Arkansas P, 2001.

Randolph, Vance. *Pissing in the Snow.* U of Chicago P, 1976.

Teske, Steven. *Unvarnished Arkansas: The Naked Truth About Nine Famous Arkansans.* Butler Center Books, 2012.

Underwood, Edward L, and Karen Underwood. *Forgotten Tales of Arkansas.* History Press, 2012.

Williamson, J. W. *Hillbillyland: What the Movies Did to the Mountains and What the Mountains Did to the Movies.* U of North Carolina P, 2004.

Wilson, Charles Reagan. "Whose South? Lessons from Studying the South at the University of Mississippi." The Southern Documentary Project, 29 June 2014, southernstudies.olemiss.edu/watch-charles-reagan-wilsons-last-lecture/.

Wright, Harold Bell. *The Shepherd of the Hills.* Crossett and Dunlap, 1907.

THE CULTURAL PARADOXES OF RED VELVET CAKE

MARSHALL NEEDLEMAN ARMINTOR

"You ever eat any Red Velvet Cake?" I licked my lips and shifted my weight so that I wasn't leaning to the side. I looked into her eyes.

"Red Velvet Cake?" Her eyes were friendly, soft, and black as the deepest part of the night.

"It's a dessert my sister and I used to bake, unhealthy as sin and twice as delicious. Made up with chocolate, buttermilk, vinegar, and baking soda, and a little bottle of that poisonous red dye number two. Tastes like nothing you've ever had."

—from *Trash*, Dorothy Allison

A clue to the cultural status of red velvet cake can be found in the well-traveled quip of food writer Angie Mosier: "It's the Dolly Parton of cakes: a little bit tacky, but you love her" (Fabricant). The question of red velvet cake's universal appeal and unquestioned ubiquity notwithstanding, it's a cake that presents so many riddles, with the answers hopelessly wrapped up in endless layers of lore, haughty turf wars, and southern pride, three things that seem to accompany every southern regional dish. One thing missing in the cultural discussion of red velvet cake is its distinct centering as a southern dessert. The *Food History Almanac*'s entry for red velvet cake notes quite prudently that on June 16, 1960, the earliest "well-known red velvet cake" recipe appeared as the recipe of the week in the *Denton* (Texas) *Record-Chronicle* (Clarkson 576);

this buttermilk-based recipe, strikingly, restores the historical ermine icing with flour, but without boiling the milk. Stella Parks locates the first instance of a proper "red velvet" cake also in a Texas newspaper, the *San Antonio Light*, in March 1951, amid many other recipes to celebrate the Easter season (128).

The number of variations is also staggering, each betraying the idea that there is no fixed recipe for red velvet cake. Kim Nelson's *Daisy Cakes Bakes* claims (as do other cookbooks) the key to the reddish color of the cake is the reaction of the chocolate with the vinegar, which a (modest) amount of food coloring should only highlight. And as usual, there are other variations noted in the aforementioned work, including different ideas for red velvet sheet cake, recommending the latter be festooned with red and green cherries at Christmastime (30). In general, the persistent thing about this spectacle of a cake is that it's for special occasions, a festive centerpiece bespeaking comfort and hominess, despite its definitely "unserious" nature. And of course, there are famous naysayers, including James Beard, who dismiss the whole idea of red velvet cake and are baffled by its popularity (Fabricant).

Among the outstanding conundrums are the problem of its origin (where does it come from?), the problem of the recipe itself (what is it supposed to taste like?), and the problem of the right frosting (does it have cream cheese frosting, whipped-cream frosting, or butter-cream frosting?). And there are the sometimes divisive feelings that the cake itself engenders: some love it, some hate it, and some don't know what they are eating when they are eating it. The modern ambiguity and ubiquity of red velvet cake, morphing into cookies, ice cream, and scented candles, revels in the very chameleonic and familiar essence that red velvet cake embodies. But the iconographic presence of red velvet cake and its tenacity in American culture are the only true constants. Whether acknowledged by knowing asides like "you know, they used to put beets to get the red color in these things," or "you know this recipe comes from the Waldorf Astoria," the mythology of red velvet cake bespeaks a legacy of utter inauthenticity and ingenious invention, always performative in the extreme, never mistaken for high culture, and forever a centerpiece of southern hospitality.

THE ORIGINS OF RED VELVET CAKE, OR NOT

In telling the story of red velvet cake, one has to consider its purported origins at the Waldorf Astoria. This tale is itself a famous urban legend that's traveled outside its southern context; Brunvand locates a version of this narrative as far afield as Idaho in the early 1960s (156). The basic version of the myth goes something like this, found in Mary Leigh Furrh and Jo Barksdale's *Great Desserts of the South:* "During the late 1920s or early 1930s a Southern lady is said to have eaten at the Waldorf Astoria. She especially enjoyed this cake and requested the recipe. At the end of the meal she was presented with the recipe and a bill for a large sum of money. She paid it and graciously shared the recipe along with a joke on herself with friends. Now it is one of the South's favorite desserts" (13). The story is, naturally, not true: the Waldorf-Astoria hotel itself has explained many times over the decades that it can find no record of their ever having charged anyone for any of their recipes. A similar tale was told in the 1990s about the "Neiman-Marcus cookie recipe," where the author enacts revenge on those snooty rich people who think so much of their desserts. This echo of the Waldorf legend also further illustrates some of the paradoxical discourse surrounding red velvet cake itself: a signature dessert of the South whose origin story is a swashbuckling exploit to plunder the lap of Yankee luxury. Perhaps it doesn't need that much explanation, but nevertheless, layers of misapprehension and class-aspiration continue to cloud the idea of red velvet cake, as indeed they do with many of the stories behind southern cuisine. The roots of red velvet cake's tackiness are bound up with the ceremonial and aspirational nature of the lust for fancy things, authenticity be damned; the many different strains of the story of red velvet cake touch all of these rails sooner or later. The legend betrays the gaudy idea that the secret "rich" recipe of red velvet cake is something that connotes wealth, status, and overall good taste, despite the sometimes garish hues of food coloring.

A starting point for the recent popularization of red velvet cake is very often traced to the 1989 Herbert Ross film *Steel Magnolias*, itself a celebration and ruthless dissection of southern tackiness, but which

FIG. 4. Red velvet armadillo cake. Still from *Steel Magnolias*, TriStar, 1989.

nevertheless remains a touchstone for the current idea of southern culture. No one can say that it's not accurate, even down to the hair-dos, and with the inclusion in the cast of southern actors Dolly Parton (Tennessee), Julia Roberts (Georgia), and Shirley MacLaine (Virginia), the film nevertheless embraces every single extant and imagined regional trope.

In the film as well as the stage play, the appearance of the red velvet cake in the shape of an armadillo rolls in on a tidal wave of tackiness with the intrafamilial wrangling over the details of Shelby Eatenon's (Roberts) wedding to Jackson Latcherie (Dylan McDermott). At the beauty shop, after Shelby and her mother M'Lynn (Sally Field) bicker over her monochromatic wedding colors ("Pink is my signature color," which her mother characterizes as "Pepto-Bismol"), Shelby complains that she has been forced to include nine bridesmaids, and, worrying that some will accuse her of "pretension," she declares, "It will be pretentious. And daddy always says an ounce of pretension's worth a pound of manure." This war over "pretension" comes to a peaceful conclusion when talking about the groom's armadillo cake. Mother and daughter smirk ruefully about the situation, as M'Lynn drawls, "It's repulsive. It's got gray icing . . . I can't begin to think how you'd make gray icing." Shelby replies: "Worse, the cake part is red velvet cake. Blood-red. People are gonna be hackin' into this poor animal that looks like it's bleedin' to death." The actual cake itself served at the reception is indeed terrible, looking like a deflated balloon. Drum (Tom Skerrit), the father of the bride, delivers the best cake-related punchline in the film as Ouiser (MacLaine), still miffed at him, sourly chops off the tail (see Fig. 4) and serves it to him, prompting him to say, "Thanks, Ouiser. Nothin' like a good piece uh ass."

Rather than being the height of elegance and exclusivity, the cake instead appears in the guise of the gimmicky and ground-dwelling cultural symbol of the armadillo, one that most often shows up on southern highways as roadkill. The tackiness of *Steel Magnolias* is not merely limited to the trappings that subsume the entire film; one could say the disease-of-the-week melodrama is perhaps the hokiest of Hollywood genres. At the same time, the film's enduring popularity is abetted by an embarrassment of riches in a cast filled with well-liked actors (in Fields's case, really, *really* liked) who sell the story nonetheless—and, apparently, that disgusting bloody cake with the gray icing.

THE VARIOUS TRADITIONS OF RED VELVET CAKE: THE REAL, THE IMAGINARY, AND ALL THOSE BOTTLES OF FOOD COLORING

The subsequent evolution of red velvet cake is a fascinating tour into the tension between the authenticity and the endurance of a cultural idea, very often tailored to fit one's conception of what it means. Red velvet cake is itself a chimera; it is a form into which one can pour anything, literally or figuratively, so long as appearances are met. Any discussion about there being some kind of "authentic tradition" of red velvet cake is profoundly irrelevant, but one can see it as a metaphor for all of southern tradition, whether culinary or otherwise—a gesture toward the sacred idea that a tradition, a history, a story with real cultural stakes must exist in order for one to take ownership, a tradition to defend no matter how superficial or slight.

If asked, people eating red velvet cake usually cannot readily identify where the flavor comes from. Cued by the cake's color, some say strawberry (patently false, because there's no way it should come into contact with anything as organic as a piece of fruit), some say vanilla (very certainly vanilla is present), and some correctly say chocolate, but, most of all, people have no idea: it just tastes like red velvet. Even though some theorize that the original color of red velvet cake comes from beets, nobody ever says that red velvet cake tastes like a beet, a vegetable that surely divides opinion in a way that red velvet cake usually doesn't. Most agree that the coloring is intended to enhance the reddish appearance of the chocolate, which reacts with the vinegar. Beyond that, some opine that the actual cake doesn't matter, it's simply an efficient delivery system for the tasty icing. In the battle over the soul of red velvet cake, perhaps we should try to locate the idea of red velvet cake in southern culture to find out why it's there at all.

The concept of the velvet cake has its origins in the late nineteenth century. The name "velvet cake" first appears in print in the US in the 1870s (Parks 128). In *Housekeeping in Old Virginia*, printed in 1878, the recipe reads as follows: "Half a pound of butter, one pound of sugar . . . one teacup of cold water with a level teaspoonful dissolved in it . . . two teaspoonfuls cream of tartar, sifted in one pound of flour," with five eggs later beaten into it (Tyree 347). The tartar, in this instance, serves to lift the beaten eggs, as it does in meringue. By contrast, Lafcadio Hearn's 1885 *La Cuisine Creole* lists "velvet cake" as a defiantly yeasted cake, with one entire cup of yeast (!), three eggs, one quart of warm milk, a quart of sifted flour, and salt, with one lone spoonful of butter beaten in and then allowed to rise (162). In all instances, the "luxury" connoted by the mouthfeel and richness of a velvet cake is supported by two characteristics. On the one hand, the cake should have a "tender crumb" softened through leavening, and on the other, the mixing in of egg yolks to lend a silky, heavy feeling of moistness, echoing the strains of richness and decadence later in the emergence of "devil's food cake" (Parks 122). The necessary design of red velvet cake as such piggybacks on the concept of the devil's food cake, emphasizing yolks instead of the whites of a cake in order to provide a richer kind of dessert. The Famous Loveless Cafe recipe also drops a stupendous four eggs into their red velvet cake (Huntsman 76). Sometimes coffee finds its way into red velvet cakes, and indeed a variant sometimes known as "Red Earth Cake" is known to have existed, at least in Texas community-printed cookbooks in the early 1950s. The hybrid characteristics of red velvet cake are evident in the varying ways that its recipes have appeared in print over time. One paradox of the cake as we know it is that it has both characteristics of angel food cake and devil's food cake, those of leavening versus richness, respectively. The application of vinegar, sour cream, buttermilk, or some other kind of curdled agent in order to render the cake "more" tender is always present, and southern recipes usually feature both, as Parks notes, along with baking powder or soda (which excitingly fizzes in reaction with vinegar) (128). The "traditional" frosting of a red velvet cake is often identified as an ermine frosting, made by making a roux with butter and flour, another leftover from Victorian-style decadence.

Stories about red velvet cake sometimes feature deprivation, making the addition of red food coloring necessary; instead of approximating luxurious foodstuffs, the cake becomes patently, explicitly ersatz. Claire Clark notes, as does Parks, that the vibrant color "came from the acidity of vinegar reacting with a buttermilk and the anthocyanins of the cocoa powder" (128). Noting that today's cocoa powders are alkalized, this necessitated the red food coloring found in red velvet cake through the 1930s; she also claims that the Adams Extract company, hailing from Gonzales, Texas, developed a version of the cake that depended on the red food coloring in order to make it during the Great Depression, given the relative lack of cocoa powder or any other fine chocolate (128). This last point is not strictly true, given that the Adams Extract Company's red food coloring and its associated recipe began to develop during the war, and the red velvet cake with its bright coloring became popular afterward, whether out of the scarcity of postwar rationing or just the 1950s mindset of "better living through chemistry" (Severson). The estimable *Encyclopedia of Southern Culture* features a note that asserts the convention of a cake colored by beets due to the privations of the Civil War and Reconstruction, in much the same way as chicory coffee outlived that period (Edge 136). Whatever the purpose or origin of food coloring, *Cake Boss* star Buddy Valastro recalls that in his attempt to construct a red velvet cake recipe for his restaurant, he built it on a vanilla cake, thinking that red velvet cake could be made from an existing recipe with just cocoa added: "truth be told, one of the secrets it took me a while to unlock was that you really need to use a lot of food coloring" (124). As ever with the paradoxes of red velvet cake (not to mention one baked in New Jersey), this thinking flies in the face of common baking wisdom.

The origin of red velvet cake is not necessarily located in convenience food of the 1950s but nevertheless found a willing partner in the convenience-food ethos of that era. In *American Cake*, Ann Byrn conjectures that the long-lived interest in red velvet cake has had as much to do with the Adams Extract coloring as any other factor, though she also notes that John Egerton, the vaunted southern food scholar, once said of this notorious ingredient, "to me there seems no culinary reason why someone would dump that much food coloring into a cake" (206). Chefs all over are still squabbling over the unappetizing idea of a cake based on any kind of food coloring: in a 2007 *New York Times* article, Florence Fabricant documents the battle over food coloring in New York City's red velvet cakes. The Harlem restaurant Amy Ruth's version includes cocoa, yet Fabricant also notes that Mississippian Craig Claiborne does not include cocoa in his version from his own southern cookbook (Fabricant). Other Manhattan-based pastry chefs, including the one at the Waldorf Astoria itself, categorically refuse to add food coloring, but another, after trying and failing with cherries and beets, gave in to his Mississippi grandmother's recipe and went ahead with food coloring anyway (Fabricant).

But what to make of a cake whose primary identification in the southern imagination is variously through a New York hotel or a Texan seasonings company? Villas, after all, excludes Texas from the idea of southern cuisine (ix). Should Texas even be considered as part of the South, as it ambiguously spans many different regions, styles, and subcultures? Why does red velvet cake seem to spring from the outlands of southern cuisine to become an indelible marker of the dubious southern palate, an (alleged) affront to "good taste" at least, by Irma Rombauer's estimable lights?

WHOSE PIECE OF CAKE IS THIS?: THE IDEA OF SOUTHERN FOOD AND THE OWNERSHIP OF DESSERT

The idea of southern cuisine rests on two fraught concepts about historical origins. The first is the issue of determining a set of accepted traditions for southern food itself; the second is defining the constitutive members of the community that celebrates it. Red velvet cake's apparitional existence and ubiquity, as well as its lore, allow it to be seated practically at any point in the mythological southern past. The question of red velvet cake's tackiness is also bound up with the idea that it participates in both a pretension to elitism and ownership of a tradition, grounded in that famous southern hospitality. In other words, just as red velvet cake maintains an appearance that belies its taste, its origin stories are similarly bedizened parodies of upper-class intrigue and privilege. My intention in investigating the performance at the heart of southern hospitality, epitomized by the excessive spectacle of red velvet cake, is to draw parallels between the imposture and mythology of the cake itself and those of southern culture and social performance. Yet even at that, red velvet cake's distributed symbolism has also extended beyond any origins it may have had in southern cuisine, even to the celebration of Juneteenth, providing a reciprocal gesture showing its power to overcome any feeling of provinciality. Ultimately, red velvet cake as southern-culture avatar pulls off the double trick of maintaining an indelibly firm identification with southern culture and transcending it at the same time.

"Southern cuisine" is a cultural category fraught with expected pretensions and sometimes real-life stakes, and any inquiry into its history is complicated by issues of prejudicial gatekeeping. Carrie Helms Tippen observes that James Villas's complicated, ultimately diffident approach to establishing the authenticity of such dishes as Brunswick stew self-consciously recalls the tenor of courtly, gentlemanly disagreement and stubbornness characteristic of southern culture (59). This sense of ownership betrays the patriarchal character of southern food discourse, and no southern cookbook is complete without it; this results in the subsequent problems of both selectively acknowledging and ignoring swaths of history. Anthony Szczesiul notes that

John Egerton's work with the Southern Foodways Alliance refuses to acknowledge the grounding of southern hospitality with regard to antebellum slavery and unremunerated labor, without which such hospitality would have been impossible to perform (208–9). By contrast, although Villas addresses the "ignominy of slavery" in his celebratory foreword to *The Glory of Southern Cooking*, he also proudly announces that southern cooking "has blessedly undergone the fewest changes and suffered the least damage from certain pretentious culinary trends and reforms that have managed to stifle most regional traditions in this country almost into oblivion" (x). Once Villas establishes the inherently conservative nature of Southern cooking traditions, he also praises the steadfastness of southern cuisine despite the ravages of the Civil War and the Great Depression (xi). In the same vein, Furrh and Barksdale lament that, after the Civil War, the South performed hospitality on a "less elaborate scale" than in the plantation era: "The glory years of the antebellum South were gone forever" (5).

This "distinctive tradition" of southern cuisine necessitates the erasure of Black culture. The myths deployed to explain the common well of food traditions in the South engage in a familiar set of tropes. Southern cookbooks that try to excuse or explain away slavery, or appropriate wholesale the heritage of African ingredients (such as okra) in the southern diet, often dramatize, as do Villas, Furrh, and Barksdale, the act of cooking for the plantation house as a harmonious domestic collaboration between the white mistress of the property and her "head cook," a neatly euphemistic phrase eliding the real nature of their respective roles. The "southern" vision of life and food, centered around the festive table, perpetually leads back to the romance of the plantation. In his study of South Carolinian author and slavery advocate William Gilmore Simms, the late-nineteenth-century southern historian William Trent observes: "In manners and customs, in education and religion, [southern gentlemen] represented that survival of feudalism, the English squire, and they prided themselves on the resemblance" (32). Trent asserts that the southern gentleman maintained "[a belief] in social distinctions and in the respect due to himself from his inferiors" and this social role also demanded that the hospitality of the southern gentleman would in turn extend to every poor relation (33).

In a sense, the southern gentleman held the status of a duke among his similarly positioned peers, and was bound by his position to a certain noblesse oblige. Southern hospitality, as with Victorian middle-class striving, embodies a pretension to the idea of elegance but, in doing so, demands fealty to an irreducibly hierarchical fantasy.

This performance through hospitality is yet another version of the impulse to keep up appearances, endemic to southern culture and thriving from the nineteenth century to the present day. A parodic version of this kind of southern manners is found in the multivalenced phenomenon of the cakewalk, a kind of mock wedding dance, which gained in popularity through the end of the nineteenth century and was an outgrowth of the minstrel shows from the earlier part of the century (Sundquist 262). Eric Lott's seminal *Love and Theft* evaluates the minstrel show as a mediation of the conflict between Black culture and the white working classes of both the North and the South; most crucially, Lott speaks about the "embourgeoisement" provided by the spectacle of white performers embodying but also claiming the Black persona wholesale (163). This racial othering and appropriation did a great deal to establish the myth of the plantation in 1840s popular culture, for the North as well as the South. In his assessment of racial "feeling" in the antebellum era, Lott reserves special consideration for the figure of the Black dandy, a character type singled out as a pretender to whiteness and used as a foil to foster white solidarity (139). This persona of the dandy appears in Charles Chesnutt's *The Marrow of Tradition* in the guise of Sandy Campbell, a family servant falsely accused of murdering a white woman, an event that triggers an apocalyptic race riot. Early in the novel, there is a performance of a cakewalk put on for a delegation of wealthy northerners in town to inspect the new cotton factory. During the performance, Sandy is spotted by Ellis, an editor for the local paper:

> . . . [his] choice of diversion . . . seemed out of keeping with his employment as attendant upon an invalid old gentleman, and strangely inconsistent with the gravity and decorum which had been so noticeable when this agile cakewalker had served as butler at Major Carteret's table. . . . the conspicuous features of his attire being a long blue coat with brass buttons and a pair of

plaid trousers . . . [presenting a cake to his partner] with a gran-
diloquent flourish, [he] returned thanks in a speech which sent
the Northern visitors into spasms of delight at the quaintness of
the darky dialect and the darky wit. (118)

Sandy is later banished from his church for engaging in such an unbe-
fitting display, a signal that his community rejects this pastime as
less than innocent (120). As Eric Sundquist notes, Chesnutt chooses
the metaphor of the cakewalk to invoke the resurrection of white
supremacy and the cultural transmission of plantation ideology (276).
However, Sandy himself feels there was no harm in it, and though he
sees the foolishness and dissipation of Mr. Delamere's son, Sandy lends
him his hard-earned money to cover the younger Delamere's gambling
debts. Later, finding himself torn by nostalgia for the old world that
no longer exists, he nevertheless resolves that he will not betray the
younger Delamere's confidence, resolving instead to die, if necessary,
"like a gent'emen" (171). Although spared in the end by the older Delamere, Chesnutt effaces this chivalric ideal through this ironic character;
though he is censured for his pretensions to upper-class behavior, he
aspires only to be dutiful and trustworthy.

My intention in this detour through an anatomy of southern
manners is to underline its roots in the Victorian-adjacent culture
of southern gentility. Both cultural milieus are equally vulnerable
to charges of heightened pretension, feigning, and elaborated ritual
at their cores; for both, this sensibility extends to food as well. The
fundamental tackiness of red velvet cake stems from the familiar mix
of lore surrounding it. As much as red velvet cake is embraced and
loved, there is always something awkward about it; never as neat or
refined as crème brûlée or mousse, there is a kind of democratization
in its elegance. It arrives like an apparition that resembles nothing but
itself. It is inexplicable comfort food that can nevertheless be presented
accompanied by fanfare, with all that clean white icing; in the decep-
tive conceit of the pristine exterior giving way to the ruby-red layers,
it awes the viewer even through its gaudiness.

But because red velvet cake is so excessive, it can overcome any
pompous mythology or cheeky insolence. One happy result of the

expansive reach of red velvet cake involves another cultural mainstay associated with Texas, that of Juneteenth and its central focus on red desserts and drinks. Wherever Juneteenth was celebrated in the post-war twentieth century, red velvet cake was known to pop up, even as far north as Harlem: Wimp's Southern-Style Bakery, on West 125th Street, was known for its homemade desserts, specifically red velvet cake (Kinloch 27). Juneteenth often features the color red in its celebratory foods, especially the idea of the red drink—circus lemonade, "red whiskey," and the like—and the substance is not nearly so important as is the purely symbolic quality of the color itself. Food colorings were certainly not unknown. The idea of "red lemonade" and other sorts of beverages after emancipation are well-documented in the late nine-teenth century and persists at soul food establishments. Drinks menus also commonly include sassafras tea, a drink borne of the deprivations of the Civil War (Miller 230).

The tackiness of red velvet cake lies in the pretension that it even has something like a "tradition," the product of an unbroken lineage from the echo of Victorian-era southern performance. This idea is also present in the aspirational legends about its origins in New York and its fierce appropriation by scorned southerners. However, in its present mode, as the idea of red velvet cake continues to replicate and reinvent itself, the prospects of looking for its "true" origins or claiming owner-ship recedes further from view. And much like Dolly Parton (herself a product of Sevierville, Tennessee), red velvet cake has transcended every possible boundary to embody a relatable ideal most everyone can relate to. The perpetual liminal nature of red velvet cake may leave it unsettled among all other American cakes. However, ultimately, the story of red velvet cake is one of undecidability that scoffs at the very idea of tradition and even good taste, disarming us and signaling that it's time to shove our preconceptions aside and just dig in.

WORKS CITED

Allison, Dorothy. *Trash*. Penguin, 2002.
Brunvand, Jan Harold. *The Vanishing Hitchhiker: American Urban Legends and Their Meanings*. W. W. Norton, 1981.

Byrn, Anne. *American Cake: From Colonial Gingerbread to Classic Layer, the Stories and Recipes Behind More Than 125 of Our Best-Loved Cakes.* Rodale, 2016.

Chesnutt, Charles. *The Marrow of Tradition.* 1901. Edited by Nancy Bentley and Sandra Gunning, Bedford St. Martin's, 2002.

Clark, Claire. *80 Cakes From Around the World.* Bloomsbury Publishing, 2014.

Clarkson, Janet. *Food History Almanac: Over 1,300 Years of World Culinary History, Culture, and Social Influence.* Rowman and Littlefield, 2013.

Edge, John T. *The New Encyclopedia of Southern Culture: Volume 7: Foodways.* U of North Carolina Press, 2014.

Fabricant, Florence. "So Naughty, So Nice." *New York Times*, 14 Feb. 2007, www.nytimes.com/2007/02/14/dining/14velv.html.

Furrh, Mary Leigh, and Jo Barksdale. *Great Desserts of the South.* Illustrated edition, Pelican, 1988.

Hearn, Lafcadio. *La Cuisine Creole: A Collection of Culinary Recipes from Leading Chefs and Noted Creole Housewives, Who Have Made New Orleans Famous for Its Cuisine.* F. F. Hansell and Bro., 1885.

Huntsman, Alisa. *Desserts from the Famous Loveless Cafe: Simple Southern Pies, Puddings, Cakes, and Cobblers from Nashville's Landmark Restaurant.* Artisan Books, 2011.

Kinloch, Valerie. *Harlem on Our Minds: Place, Race, and the Literacies of Urban Youth.* Teachers College Press, 2015.

Lott, Eric. *Love and Theft: Blackface Minstrelsy and the American Working Class.* Oxford UP, 2013.

Miller, Adrian. *Soul Food: The Surprising Story of an American Cuisine, One Plate at a Time.* U of North Carolina P, 2013.

Nelson, Kim. *Daisy Cakes Bakes: Keepsake Recipes for Southern Layer Cakes, Pies, Cookies, and More.* Clarkson Potter/Publishers, 2018.

Parks, Stella. *BraveTart: Iconic American Desserts.* Foreword by J. Kenji López-Alt. Norton, 2017.

Severson, Kim. "Red Velvet Cake: A Classic, Not a Gimmick," *New York Times*, 14 May 2014, www.nytimes.com/2014/05/14/dining/red-velvet-cake-from-gimmick-to-american-classic.html.

Steel Magnolias. Directed by Herbert Ross, TriStar, 1989.

Sundquist, Eric J. *To Wake the Nations: Race in the Making of American Literature.* Harvard U P, 1994.

Szczesiul, Anthony. *The Southern Hospitality Myth: Ethics, Politics, Race, and American Memory.* U of Georgia P, 2017.

Tippen, Carrie Helms. *Inventing Authenticity: How Cookbook Writers Redefine Southern Identity.* U of Arkansas P, 2018.

Trent, William P. *William Gilmore Simms.* Houghton and Mifflin, 1892.

Tyree, Marion Cabell. *Housekeeping in Old Virginia.* John P. Morton and Co., 1878.

Valastro, Buddy. *Cake Boss: Stories and Recipes from Mia Famiglia.* Simon and Schuster, 2020.

Villas, James. *The Glory of Southern Cooking.* Houghton Mifflin Harcourt, 2012.

PERFECT REFLECTIONS OF HUMAN IMPERFECTIONS

GRITTY, QUEER TACKINESS IN THE MUSIC OF ROBERT EARL KEEN

TRAVIS A. ROUNTREE

*T*here are stories about country music icon Hank Williams: his drinking, his womanizing, and even one where Waylon Jennings used to put on Hank's boots to feel the muse of him to write songs. However, no songwriter has ever put Ol' Hank in drag until Texas singer-songwriter Robert Earl Keen, Jr. In his 2005 song "The Great Hank," Hank sadly sings on stage in a Philly bar in full drag, drinking out of a "brown paper bag" while a ballgame plays. Keen's gender-bending with one of country music's most sacred icons demonstrates his music's engagement with both camp and tackiness. Leigh H. Edwards connects the performance of camp to tackiness, stating, "Camp can be defined as a style and performance mode in which a performer presents exaggerated, over-the-top, ostentatious, theatrical artifice meant to be amusing to a sophisticated in-the-know audiences precisely because it is framed as tacky, trashy, or outlandish" (31). Drag Hank highlights Keen's penchant for the tacky by transforming one of country music's foremost masculine icons into a campy drag queen.

However, before Keen was able to transform Hank, he first had to engage with working-class tackiness to establish a fan base. Looking at his discography, the first few albums certainly coincide with the Grit Lit genre with such classics as "The Road Goes On Forever," appearing on *West Textures* in 1989 (also covered by The Highwaymen); "Feels So Good Feelin' Good Again" on *Walking Distance* in 1998; and "Merry Christmas from the Family" on *Gringo Honeymoon* in 1994, as well as a host of others that are covered by both mainstream country musicians as well as other Texas and Americana musicians. These songs then make room for Keen to expand his songwriting to include interspecies love among animals, gender-nonconforming songs, and even putting Hank up on stage in drag on his 2005 album *What I Really Mean*. By expanding from working-class tackiness to his more eccentric, gender-bending songs, Keen critiques country music for its overtly masculine, heteronormalized characters.

Robert Earl Keen, Jr.'s songs depict situations that not only apply to his home in Texas but address working-class folks nationally in ordinary, everyday situations. The basic definitions of tacky derived from the term's *OED* entry as "shabby, vulgar, or in poor taste" are a critical part of Keen's oeuvre of songwriting and storytelling. The songs sometimes drip with sentimentality but convey a sense of realism combined with camp in their over-the-top self-awareness. He and his friend Lyle Lovett helped to set the stage (both literally and metaphorically) for college-based Texas singer-songwriters like Cory Morrow, Pat Green, and many others who produce a similar kind of Texas tacky music.

Keen's songwriting began around the same time as the development of the "Grit Lit" genre of southern literature featuring Harry Crews, Tim McLaurin, and Dorothy Allison, authors whose characters are just trying to survive in their everyday lives, who also rely on trashy, campy characters to carry their narratives. It's worth noting as well that Grit Lit was a mainly male-dominated genre until Dorothy Allison's texts *Trash* (2002), *Bastard Out of Carolina* (1992), and *Two or Three Things I Know for Sure* (1996) were published. Robert Gingher defines "Grit Lit" as "a facetious shorthand for fiction devoted to the rough edges ('grit') of life, or to the regionally commonplace or comic ('grits'), or to both. Such homespun stories grounded in the grime or 'grit' of reality typically deploy stark, sometimes violent narratives of poor white southerners"

(319). Like Keen's music, much of Grit Lit focuses on poor white southerners and depictions of the working-class South. Keen's connection to the genre was further solidified when one of the foremost Grit Lit authors, Larry Brown, traveled off and on with Keen from the spring of 1999 to the spring of 2001 for an article he wrote in *No Depression*. Brown describes Keen as

> a big guy and there seem to be no large signs of the sensitive wordsmith or poet about him, but all you have to do is watch him set the microphone and start playing and begin to pull his voice up out of himself and listen to the songs he's written to find out that isn't true. Somewhere deep inside him he must have a secret cave where he keeps care and love and heartbreak and loneliness and the joy of life and irony and even humor stashed away, and he lets pieces of them out when he's writing about the people in his songs. (100)

Music writer and scholar Jan Reid agrees, noting that "the songs work because they are filled with emotion and tell terrific stories. Free verse is hard to find in songwriting. Keen achieves some measure of that with his talking blues, but songwriters have to deal with rhyme" (171). Keen cut his teeth on songwriting going back to the mid-1980s. Most of these early songs teem with a masculine, western cowboy motif that served Keen's earlier Texan audiences.

Musicians and scholars alike agree that Keen's strongest songs are his story songs. One of his most well-known, "Merry Christmas from the Family" on the 1994 album *Gringo Honeymoon*, demonstrates Keen's perception of a working-class Christmas. Reid writes that "he hit a masterfully droll key with a song about a dysfunctional Sunbelt family's lame attempts to celebrate Christmas" (171). The song was further made popular when the country duo Montgomery Gentry recorded it on their 2000 album *All Night Long*. The stream-of-consciousness storytelling in the song depicts a realistic Christmas day with a working-class, more than likely white, family. Country music scholar Nadine Hubbs describes the importance of Keen's emphasis on the working middle class:

In short, middle-class power and privilege stand upon the continual, daily deprecation of working-class existence. Country music is an audible emblem of that existence and is instrumental in the self-valuing, other devaluing contests of class formation. This is true from both sides: just as middle-class-identified subjects devalue country and the working-class people, style, and lifeways it represents, working-class-identified country creators and audiences use the music to criticize middle-class people, values, and dominance, particularly in the hard-country genre of the anti-bourgeois song. (19)

Instead of belittling working-class life, Keen is able to present this socioeconomic status with honesty and truth in "Merry Christmas from the Family." These characters are not judged but are presented as realistic, for Keen chooses certain aspects of the family to dwell upon while also invoking a departure from the normal, nuclear working-class family.

The song begins with the speaker's parents getting drunk at the family Christmas party. Keen then gives more information about the family: "Little sister brought her new boyfriend / He was a Mexican / We didn't know what to think of him 'til he sang / Feliz Navidad, Feliz Navidad." The song was released long before Trump's wall and immigration concerns but still demonstrates the hesitancy of the family to accept Latinx culture, a culture outside of their own, presumably working-class white culture. While short, this line does demonstrate the family's willingness to embrace the newcomer to the party because of his Christian beliefs.

The second and subsequent verses vacillate from describing family members to listing items needed at the grocery store. We get another glimpse of the extended family as Keen sings: "Brother Ken brought his kids with him / The three from his first wife Lynn / And the two identical twins / From his second wife, Mary Nell / Of course he brought his new wife Kay/ Who talks all about AA." Then the fourth stanza talks of Fred and Rita, who blew out the family's Christmas lights when they plugged their motor home into the house. These descriptions of family members demonstrate that this is not the traditional nuclear family.

This extended, and what some would call broken, family overcomes bigger difficulties like divorce and smaller inconveniences like a busted fuse to come together to sing and celebrate Christmas.

The listing of objects at the store is another feature that designates the song as tacky. The narrator asks for specific items at the store that could be designated as taboo or "cheap," including bean dip, Diet Rite, tampons, Marlboro Lights, and a can of fake snow. The store that the narrator is going to is referenced as the "Quickpak Store" or "Stop 'N Go." Most grocery stores would be closed at Christmas, so any family would be forced to go to a convenience store. However, because of the nature of the song, listeners get the feeling that shopping at these places is a common occurrence for this family. These convenience stores are not places where they would buy fine cheese or fancy wine (nor would this family be concerned about those types of products). These characters want Bloody Marys or margaritas. While some could designate these items and drinks as tacky, the stories and items in the song clearly show that, despite their troubles, this family shares good memories, food, and drink during the holiday.

Despite being one of Keen's most popular mainstream songs, "Merry Christmas from the Family" nonetheless expresses some aspects of queerness that are more apparent in his later work. Varying definitions of queer, from Butler (1993), Warner (1993), Halperin (1995), Duggan and Hunter (1995), Dean and Lane (2001) among others, are useful and provide the groundwork for queer theory, but the current definitions given by Charles E. Morris III and K. J. Rawson (2013) argue that "'queer' does not simply signify a nonheterosexual identity" (75). This definition of queer focuses on its capacity to "challenge[s] the normalizing mechanisms of state power to name its sexual subjects: male or female, married or single, heterosexual or homosexual, natural or perverse" (Eng et al. qtd. in Morris and Rawson 75). Noting queer's "commitment to interrogating the social processes that not only produced and recognized but also normalized and sustained identity," Eng et al. continue to argue that "the political promise of the term reside[s] specifically in its broad critique of multiple social antagonisms, including race, gender, class, nationality, and religion, in addition to sexuality" (ibid.). They elaborate that "queer is not interchangeable with lesbian, gay, or homosexual; instead, queer implies a broad critique of normativity along many different axes of identity, community and power" (ibid.). These definitions demonstrate that queer not only questions heteronormativity but also acts as an umbrella term for multiple identities. In applying this to "Merry Christmas from the Family," we see that there is heteronormativity at play here; however, the scene that Keen sets can indeed be labeled queer to a certain extent. In the nontraditional parts of the family, as well as the listing of the items, Keen writes about how this family lives on the boundaries of the traditional heteronormative family life. The power in this song relies on how Keen disrupts a traditional Christmas family. Instead of a glowing Norman Rockwell painting, we get a messy, drunken, but truthful depiction of this working-class family, warts and all. Queerness here resides not in the homosexual behavior but in the absurd, nonconforming nature of the family.

The scholarship of Nadine Hubbs on the Foo Fighters' 2011 song "Keep It Clean (Hot Buns)" demonstrates joining middle-class working groups and queerness in popular music as we will see in "The Great Hank":[1]

> Against prevailing assumptions of perennially homophobic working class, I propose an alternative reading. It regards sex-gender deviance as moving recently from a hundred years' primary residence in the realm of the working class, where the two overlapping disreputable groups shared conceptual and often physical space while enduring abjection from middle-class moralism, social norms, and institutions. Since the 1970s, especially, sexual and gender queerness has been recast, domesticated and moved upmarket, brought from working-class disrepute into the respectable realm of the middle class, in a shift I call the middle-classing of queerness. (856)

Despite this essay coming out several years after *What I Really Mean* was released, Hubbs's ideas are still applicable to Keen's work. While "Merry Christmas from the Family" has aspects that steer away from a nuclear family, its center still resides in heteronormativity and middle-class socioeconomic conditions. However, Hubbs's "middle-classing of queerness" explains how the evocation of queer identity shifts into the exposure and uplifting of the middle/working class. It now allows for a sense of queerness to become a main component of the songs. Keen's "The Great Hank" is a song about the middle class that includes these aspects of queerness in it. We see with this song that Keen is branching out and doing as Hubbs describes above. In his writing career, he has already found his audience and can now expand outward to criticize the country music genre. He could not have recorded "The Great Hank" without establishing this base with "Merry Christmas from the Family" and other working-class tacky songs.

After establishing a base of fans, Keen started to experiment with the country music genre; in fact, now he tends to be grouped with Americana instead of country music because of his nontraditional and eccentric approaches. Such new approaches can be seen in the 2005 album, *What I Really Mean*. The album starts with "For Love," one of Keen's cowboy songs; however, the next song "Mr. Wolf and Mamabear" contains a Bonnie and Clyde meets *Wind in the Willows* theme. The song starts with Mr. Wolf and Mamabear breaking into the hen house and killing chickens and ends with the two of them eating a dead raccoon among a slew of other animal antics that happen in the song. The next song on the album song is "What I Really Mean," which does not mention gender, but listeners can assume it's Keen writing to his wife, recounting how he misses her on the road. However, it's the song "The Great Hank" that stands out on the album because of the overt queer nature of Hank Williams in drag.

"The Great Hank" is another song that demonstrates Keen's eye for bar culture (and, in this case, couture in drag) but is also the only song that I know of that has Hank Williams in drag. The tone of the song drips with melancholy, and Keen's voice places the listener at the bar, drinking with the narrator and Hank round-for-round. The song starts in medias res, as the bar patron is watching Drag Hank perform in a bar in Philadelphia, Pennsylvania. Keen provides a vivid description next: "From his rose red lips to his rhinestone hips he belted / Out song after song as he drank from a brown paper bag / And the songs he sang of love and pain, / So pure perfect reflections of human imperfections, / It damn near choked me up." From these lines, Keen not only provides a description of Drag Hank but also falls within the theme of Hank Williams's dark, lonesome songs. The line "perfect reflections of human imperfections" works incredibly well here because it demonstrates that Drag Hank isn't perfect and that in that imperfection is beauty. This definition could be applied to the tacky in most of Keen's songs as these moments reveal instances of beauty in the day-to-day.

Keen evokes a sense of love lost here, but his most important move is to place Hank in drag. Hank is a cultural icon for not only country music but also masculinity in country. However, as Isabel Duarte-Gray notes in this collection ("Rhinestone Cowgirls"), Hank, known for his Nudie suits, also represents camp and tackiness. Putting him in drag evokes not only a sense of tackiness but also gender-bending in a male-dominated field. Keen is clearly making a jab at country music but also at his own music for being so male-dominated.[2] Judith Butler's idea of performativity fits well with Drag Hank's position as tacky at the bar and occurrence in a country music song:

> [Norms] can also be exposed as non-natural and nonnecessary when they take place in a context and through a form of embodying that defies normative expectation. What this means is that through the practice of gender performativity, we not only see how the norms that govern reality are cited but grasp one of the mechanisms by which reality is reproduced *and* altered in the course of that reproduction. The point about drag is to not simply produce a pleasurable and subversive spectacle but to allegorize the spectacular and consequential ways in which reality is both reproduced and contested. (218)

Hank's performance in drag embodies this defiance toward the masculine in country music. To use Butler's words, his drag allegorizes the absurdity of the lack of recognition in country music, but it also connects drag to camp and tackiness. By exaggerating gender in country music, Keen creates depictions that are "Dowdy, shabby; in poor taste, cheap, vulgar" ("Tacky"). To the conservative country music fan, putting Hank in drag would very much be "in poor taste" or "vulgar"; to the more progressive, it's exciting and makes room for more opportunity.

In the lines that follow, "Mascara streaked his cheeks" as Drag Hank tells his story that connects camp with the loss of traditional country music, explaining, "how he had been a big star but now / country music was full of freaks." The irony here is too delicious. Drag Hank noting that "country music is full of freaks" is Keen's own statement toward the development of country music in 2005 but also evokes Susan Sontag's position on camp: "the whole point of Camp is to dethrone the serious. Camp is playful, anti-serious. More precisely, Camp involves a new, more complex relation to 'the serious.' One can be serious about the frivolous, frivolous about the serious" (288). What we see with Drag Hank is a falling to the morose from something that was fun at first. The "frivolous" nature and play of drag takes a turn to something serious. Keen's turn here is to expose the truth of the gendering of country music.

Much like George Strait and Alan Jackson in the song "Murder on Music Row," Keen sings about the changing of the music from traditional to progressive. While putting Hank in drag is revolutionary, Keen is also demonstrating the change that country music needs to go through and what it will take to make that happen for both women and LGBTQ+ artists. At the 2020 Grammys, Lil Nas X, an openly gay, African American singer-songwriter, wore a pink cowboy suit to represent his and Billy Ray Cyrus's top country song, "Old Town Road." The same year, Country Music Television (CMT) agreed to play female artists' videos in 50 percent of the programming on their station (Willman). Both are small steps, but we can see the shift from straight, cisgendered, white men to a more inclusive genre that allows for all voices to be not only heard but celebrated. While tacky, the representation of Drag Hank here has a powerful significance to represent Keen's progressive songwriting and his approach to the widening of the country music genre. Not surprisingly, Keen is seldom played on mainstream pop country radio stations outside of his home state of Texas.

In 2020, for the *Americana Podcast*, Robert Earl Keen interviewed Waylon Payne, the son of Jody Payne (who played in Willie Nelson's band) and Sammi Smith (who is famous for writing "Help Me Make It

Through The Night"). Payne's album is called *Blue Eyes, The Harlot, The Queer, The Pusher, & Me*. During the podcast, Keen asks Payne several questions that demonstrate his (Keen's) knowledge of LGBTQ+ issues in country and Americana music. When Keen observes, "In 1990, that was a relatively conservative and constrictive time and that was the time you came out as gay," Payne responds by talking about his coming out at a Baptist college in Oklahoma. He says that his father supported his coming out, but he had a falling out with his mother. This exchange is interesting because it is during this time that Keen's own music was still being developed. Although Keen didn't include overtly queer aspects until the early 2000s, his comments about this time show that he did, indeed, know that he had to establish his conservative fan base to be able to write and perform songs that are more progressive.

Keen's "Merry Christmas from the Family" demonstrates the nontraditional family that exists in the chaos of the holiday. It shows a family who, while splintered in many ways, still comes together to celebrate. It invokes camp and absurdity, but most of all, it is a way that Keen could connect with his conservative audience members. The song allowed his name to be known and became an anthem at most of his shows. Meanwhile, "The Great Hank" represents a new side of Keen's songwriting that includes the fabulous, campy but sad performance of Drag Hank. But even more, this performance indicates how Keen uses tackiness to represent how his own songwriting is forcing country music to grow. While he keeps the western cowboy songs that are on *What I Really Mean*, he also makes room for queer characters like Drag Hank to comment on the gender-bending qualities of the genre. Keen's work demonstrates that the future of country music relies on the "perfect reflections of human imperfections" that exist and will continue to appear in his tacky, queer characters.

NOTES

1. For more on queerness in country music, see Erich Nunn's "'He Ain't Wrong, He's Just Different': Willie Nelson's Queer Outlaws," *Studies in American Culture*, vol. 34, no. 1, Fall 2011, pp. 87–102.

2. Country music is still a male-dominated genre, and it's only been since the release

of The Highwomen that there has been real movement in the genre to not only acknowledge women but give them real playtime on country music radio.

WORKS CITED

Bessette, Jean. *Retroactivism in the Lesbian Archive: Composing Pasts and Futures.*
Southern Illinois UP, 2018.

Brown, Larry. "The Whole World's Out There to Write About: Filling in the
Pictures with Robert Earl Keen and His Band." *No Depression*, July–Aug.
2001, pp. 95–105.

Butler, Judith. *Bodies that Matter: On the Discoursive Limits of "Sex."* New York:
Routledge, 1993.

———. *Undoing Gender.* Routledge, 2004.

Dean, Tim and Christopher Lane. *Homosexuality and Psychoanalysis.* Chicago: U
of Chicago P, 2001.

Duggan, Lisa, and Nan D. Hunter. *Sex Wars: Sexual Dissent and Political Culture.*
New York: Routledge, 1995.

Edwards, Leigh H. Dolly Parton, Gender and Country Music. Indiana UP, 2018.

Eng, David L., et al. "What's Queer about Queer Studies Now?" Introduction.
Social Text (Fall/Winter 2005): 1–17.

Gingher, Robert. "Grit Lit." *The Companion to Southern Literature*, edited by
Joseph M. Flora et al., Louisiana State UP, 2002, pp. 319–20.

Halperin, David M. *Saint Foucault: Towards a Gay Hagiography.* New York: Oxford
UP, 1995.

Hubbs, Nadine. "Country, Music, the Queer, and the Redneck." *Journal of the
American Musicological Society*, vol. 66, no. 3, 2013, pp. 852–56.

Keen, Robert Earl. "The Great Hank." *What I Really Mean*, Koch Records, 2005.

———. "Merry Christmas from the Family." *Gringo Honeymoon*, Sugar Hill, 1994.

———. *The Road Goes On Forever and the Music Never Ends.* U of Texas P, 2009.

Morris, Charles E., III, and K.J. Rawson. "Queer Archives/Archival Queers."
Theorizing Histories of Rhetoric. Ed. Michelle Ballif. Carbondale: Southern Illinois UP, 2013. 74-89.

Reid, Jan. "Lyle Lovett and Robert Earl Keen: Cosmic Aggies." *Pickers and Poets:
The Ruthlessly Poetic Singer-Songwriters of Texas*, edited by Craig E. Clifford and
Craig Hillis, Texas A&M UP, 2016, pp. 66–173.

Sontag, Susan. "Notes on 'Camp.'" *Against Interpretation and Other Essays.* Farrar,
Straus and Giroux, 1966, pp. 275–92.

"Tacky." OED Online. July 2020. Oxford UP, www-oed-com.proxy195.nclive.
org/view/Entry/196947?rskey=WujpES&result=1&isAdvanced=false#eid.

Warner, Michael. *Fear of a Queer Planet: Queer Politics and Social Theory*. Minneapolis: U of Minnesota P, 1993.

Willman, Chris. "CMT Pledges to Air 50% Female Artists in Music Video Programming From Now On." *Variety*, 21 Jan. 2020, variety.com/2020/music/
news/cmt-announces-50-percent-female-artists-music-videos-1203474234/.

THAT TACKY LITTLE DANCE BAND FROM ATHENS, GEORGIA

ON SEAMS, ASSEMBLAGES, AND THE DEMOCRATIC BEAT OF THE B-52S

MICHAEL P. BIBLER

Fred bought his hairpiece at the thrift store, you know why?
Why?
'Cause he didn't want *toupee*.
—The B-52s, "Wig"

What could be tackier than a thrift-store wig, except maybe a pun so obvious you almost don't see it coming? In theory, a hairpiece should fit the wearer so well that the line between natural hair and wig should be as invisible as possible. But a hairpiece meant to fit one person cannot look natural on whoever buys it secondhand. The toupee will be just the wrong color or shape, and the artifice of the wig cannot be hidden. Its secondhand commodity status will be so obvious that, like the pun, some observers will be almost in denial about seeing it at all, looking away to hide their uncomfortable laughter or shock, if not also distaste. This combination of obviousness and cheapness is part of what makes both the hairpiece and its wearer tacky. The wig is discarded trash, an unwanted commodity that never loses the stigma of being trash even though it is now wanted again. Recycling puts it back in use, but the toupee chafes against current expectations of style and consumerism as much as it probably chafes the wearer's scalp. And it marks the wearer as tacky by making him look unable or unwilling to follow those expectations because of bad taste, poverty, apathy, or cluelessness. Or maybe the Fred in this joke never intends the wig to blend. Maybe he wants a hairpiece that deliberately clashes in order to present a hip and ironic sartorial style that openly rejects bourgeois norms of consumerism, gender, and/or sexuality. In this case, the toupee is a freedom and celebration, as the song drives home. But nonconformity does not make the wig any less tacky. Like the obvious line between hairpiece and hair, tackiness is the opposite of seamless sophistication, no matter what the intention might be.

Although the B-52s[1] never use the word "tacky" to describe the hairpiece, the song evokes the word through the jokiness of the pun, the reference to the thrift store, and the association with the band itself. For more than forty years, the B-52s have been tagged as the "tacky little dance band from Athens, Georgia," and this up-tempo song about wigs by a band famous for wearing them appears to epitomize that ethos. Thinking about what the label "tacky" says about the B-52s can help us better understand the word's power and meaning in broader contexts, particularly in relation to the idea of a tacky South referenced through their hometown of Athens. To be clear, I reject any narrow application of the term to the band and their music, because their creative output is far too varied in terms of style, genre, tempo, and topic to reduce to any single category. Nevertheless, a more critical understanding of tackiness still enables a productive analysis of the band's complex aesthetics, especially in the body of work after their first two albums, which has received almost no scholarly attention. My aim is not necessarily to reclaim tacky from its pejorative uses. Rather, studying the B-52s' complicated association with the word shows how tackiness, like the wig, exposes the seams where competing hierarchies of taste and value intersect. These seams, I argue, reveal a uniquely democratic aspect of tackiness that foregrounds multiplicity and difference in opposition not only to conformity but also to *any* unifying system of aesthetics.

The tagline began appearing in the press as early as 1978 in *The Village Voice* (Christagau), and it quickly became ubiquitous when they released their first album in 1979.[2] Although subsequent mentions might simply be citing earlier ones, it seems equally plausible that the band's label, Warner Bros., pushed the tagline to capitalize on the band's reputation for quirkiness and the cachet of the Athens music scene that the B-52s helped pioneer. In an email interview, band member Fred Schneider explained that "a friend came up with it," adding: "I don't know about the others [in the band] but I never liked or used it. Seems the media chose to repeat a stupid sound bite" (Miller). In an interview from 2015, Kate Pierson admits that there is "something tacky about the band," but her explanation ultimately reveals the same skepticism as her band-mate, for she describes the band's tackiness not as intentional but as something fans misunderstand: "at first [tacky] seemed to overshadow the band. It seemed to be like the wigs, the outfits and the hairdos and our lyrics, we felt, were misunderstood. And we felt like everyone [was] just calling us whacky, whacky, whacky and they didn't understand the incredible seriousness of the band" (May). Probably the band was not *entirely* innocent about using and promoting the tagline in their early days, but it makes sense that Schneider and Pierson would want to create some distance from it now. Nevertheless, the tagline endures.

But what does it do? In the 1980s, the mention of Athens added enormous prestige, but for *this* band it also marked them as regional, even provincial. The B-52s played their first professional show in Max's Kansas City in New York City on December 12, 1978 (before that they had played at house parties in Athens), and they played the majority of their early gigs there and at CBGB's before the success of their first album launched them on a world tour in the second half of 1979. It is impossible to overstate the importance of Athens's unique culture to the band's distinctive combination of styles, especially in their formative years, as Rodger Lyle Brown and Grace Elizabeth Hale have documented in glittering detail; and the band continued to write about Athens in songs on *Whammy!* and the quadruple-platinum *Cosmic Thing*. Yet, even with their massive international success, the constant reminder in the 1980s that they were from Athens implicitly divided them from other bands with whom they shared a stage, including Talking Heads and

Blondie. The word "little" underscores this regional designation through its implicit nod to the phrase "little ole" in stereotypes of white southern dialects; and it marks the band as both small and minor, despite their initial five-member lineup and their global stardom. "Dance band" further pigeonholes the group by implying that their music doesn't make a more thoughtful intervention in or commentary on the larger cultural scene beyond giving you a lively beat to dance to.

Finally, although this is not all it does, "tacky" oversimplifies their style in ways similar to the terms "kitsch," "camp," and "trash." From the moment the B-52s splashed onto the scene, critics focused on how they incorporate a stunning range of musical and cultural influences from the past, including Motown, lounge music, art rock, Dada, pop art, science fiction, monster movies, teenage beach movies, and so much more. As music scholar Theo Cateforis summarizes, critics invoked the trinity of kitsch, camp, and trash to argue that "the B-52's had forged a distanced, critical relationship with the frivolities and trivialities of the lower rungs of the cultural hierarchy" (97). In these accounts, trash signifies "the discarded remnants" of culture "that were now completely without value"; kitsch describes their use of works from mass culture and "low" art to create "an aesthetic of bad taste"; and camp refers to "a more knowing and theatrical inversion of pop's extravagance, artifice, and inevitable obsolescence, and one that was often coded to be read by an appreciative, queer audience" (Cateforis 97). Cateforis adds that this "trash aesthetic," as so many critics and reviewers called it, "amplified" the supposedly cheap and disposable culture "of the lower classes" and created a "garish, gaudy, and tacky" "look and manner" that "is marked by an unaffected obliviousness" (107). Although Cateforis does not elaborate on the word "tacky," his comment points to the word's similarity to trash, kitsch, and camp—as well as a crucial difference. Like those other words, tacky describes cheap, usually mass-produced commodities that bourgeois culture treats as disposable objects of "bad taste." Like camp and kitsch, one can be ironically tacky: intentionally wearing a cheap toupee, for example. However, tacky can also suggest an unironic, sincere embrace of those trashy objects with "an unaffected obliviousness." Here, tacky strays from kitsch and camp by suggesting that the tacky love of tacky objects *might really be* a matter of bad taste.

Thus, as a term that threatens to squeeze this "tacky little dance band" into a narrow classification, "tacky" undermines the band's savvy use of cultural influences and paints the B-52s either as something close to a novelty act or as "oblivious" consumers of the cheap, tawdry, and outmoded.

Early discussions of the band's use of camp, kitsch, and trash were so common that by 1982 reviewer Betty Page called them clichés: "It's bloody hard to find bold new exciting statements to make about the B-52s, the hippy-hippy shakedown/pap pop pastiche/kitsch clichés all having been well exhausted" (Page). Yet, saying that it's hard to find something new to say about the band also suggests that those clichés are *all there is* to say about the band. Some recent scholarship, as good as it is, seems to back that that up. Cateforis offers an excellent study of these aspects of the band's aesthetic and usefully pushes past cliché affirmation of those labels, arguing that "these supposed musical and cultural kitsch items served as loci for new, creative ideas" that placed the B-52s "among the most modern bands at the turn of the 1980s" (114, 122). Jennifer Le Zotte similarly addresses the limitations of these labels by showing how the band's use of retro styles and fragments inspired the gender-bending, "anticonsumer consumerism" of the thrift-store-based grunge style of the 1990s (215).[3] Nevertheless, these scholars continue to put these terms at the center of their analyses, implicitly reaffirming the importance of those classifications for understanding the band despite their limitations. Focusing on tacky risks the same effect. However, paying attention to the cultural and aesthetic *seams* that tackiness makes visible can also shift our attention from recursive questions about tacky objects or attitudes to larger questions about how tackiness foregrounds competing aesthetic systems at the same time. Sometimes these seams are sites of contestation, but sometimes they establish something more like a democratic plurality of styles such as we see and hear in the irreducible multiplicity of the band's influences and references, as well as the decentralized structure of the band itself.

While irony is a key factor in how we judge tackiness, unlike with camp and kitsch it is not necessarily a constitutive factor. The B-52s constantly balked at reviewers and critics who claimed the band was being ironic. In a 1979 interview, Schneider protests, "We're not trying to be camp or trashy. I'm not interested in wallowing in that stuff" (Wuefling). In 1981, Pierson added, "people are always hitting us with this 'American trash aesthetic' [label]—and *we won't take it*. I mean, we don't use that term and the supposed 'trash' that we're interested in is good trash!" (Rose). At one point or another, all the band members have stressed that the cultural elements they use and adopt are things they actually like and appreciate—"that the objects themselves [are] to be enjoyed for their own inherent worth and value" (Cateforis 122).[4] The band has further challenged claims about their use of irony when speaking about their famous interest in thrift stores. In 1981, Schneider complained, "We said it a million times. . . . But we have always dressed this way. We don't try to capitalize on our clothes any more than on some sort of '60s thing" (Rose). He repeated this point in his email interview: "We bought thrift store clothes because we didn't have money. It had no bearing on our music. Sci-fi, Dada & Surrealism, & all kinds of humor influenced me. And I still like going to thrift stores and yard sales" (Miller). In the capitalist system of the music industry, such denials of irony make sense. A "thrift store rock" that is intentionally ironic can be sold to fans as countercultural (Hale 34)—a trendy alternative to trendiness that's so tacky it's cool—but only for so long until the band starts to sound redundant. If the band is not being ironic, as they claim, they can still be marketed as a "tacky band" as long as fans see their *own* enjoyment of the band as ironic. Otherwise, the band's tackiness will appear too far removed from current trends and consign the B-52s to the same thrift-store record bins that they mined for inspiration. When it is understood ironically, "tacky" can be a lucrative label, if still a constraining one. But irony is better understood as part of the external frame we use to interpret and regulate the seams of tackiness whenever we encounter them.

The band confronted this emphasis on irony and "trash aesthetics" on the EP *Mesopotamia*. If their first two albums mined cultural artifacts of the mid-twentieth century, the song "Mesopotamia" reaches back much farther. Pierson casts her voice back in time and sings, "I'll meet you by the third pyramid / oh come on, that's what I want," while Schneider speaks from the present. He admits, "I am no student of ancient culture. / Before I talk, I should read a book," but then shares his knowledge anyway: "But there's one thing that I do know: / There's a lotta ruins in Mesopotamia." Schneider mocks the idea of the band's "distanced, critical relationship" with the past by stressing his ignorance about Mesopotamia even as he sings about it, thus striking a deeply ironic pose about being ironic. The song implicitly plays with the question about whether trashy "ruins" from "six or eight thousand years ago," or even "a hundred thousand years ago," could count as retro or kitsch, while it also collapses the difference between past and present by stressing the universality of desire across human history. In the same way it is hard to tell whether the band is parodying their thrift-store finds or simply honoring what they love, "Mesopotamia" plays havoc with the idea that such distinctions even matter. Similarly, "Throw That Beat in the Garbage Can" confounds the expectation that a B-52s song *must* be built out of "trash" culture. In part, the song is about the band's neighbors in Mahopac, New York, where the B-52s had moved in 1979, who constantly complained about noise at the band's house.[5] But Schneider also mocks critics' obsessions with the band's love of thrift stores when he shouts/sings, "Stop that beat, it makes me apprehensive. / Sweat ruins my clothes, they are very expensive." If Schneider's clothes are truly expensive, they signal to his listeners that he and the band are interested in far more than novelty thrift-store finds. If Schneider is being sarcastic and actually wearing cheap clothes, then the sarcasm is directed at critics' assumptions that thrift-store clothes must carry some greater significance beyond simply being affordable and comfortable. The song dwells in the indeterminacy of being *pulled* toward what they like in the vast flea market of culture and resenting being *pushed* toward what others call "trash" in that marketplace, where throwing the beat in the garbage is supposedly a way to salvage the beat rather than dispose of it. Instead of adopting one aesthetic principle over the other—garbage or nongarbage—the song positions itself at the seam between those aesthetics.

The southern associations of tackiness create the same kind of friction. Especially in the early years, the band's southernness profitably distinguished them from others in the New Wave scene. Their music clearly references southern dance and soul music, and often the band "played to and with their New York audiences' expectations about southerners" and "seemed to ham it up with journalists, laying their regional identity on thick," even though Schneider and Pierson were not originally from the South (Hale 37). However, calling them the "tacky little dance band from Athens, Georgia" also threatened to exoticize them as narrowly and exclusively southern—as tacky *because* they are southern. In his email interview Schneider wrote, "the band's influences and inspirations were wide ranging; we never thought of ourselves as just 'southern'" (Miller). But sometimes journalists seemed content to treat the band's moments of "hamming it up" as representative of the Athens scene and, implicitly, of the entire South, as in 1980 when the *New York Rocker* wrongly reminded readers to "wear a beehive in your hair" if they visited or moved to Athens (quoted in Brown 156). As Brown writes, "no one would wear a beehive in their hair in Athens in the summer of 1980. That was The B-52's style, and . . . their wigs [were] already sanctified and quickly becoming clichéd themselves" (157). Conflating regional difference with tackiness through the wigs reduces the B-52s and every other Athens band to a one-dimensional style that must be interpreted as *either* ironic *or* cliché, thus obscuring the complexity and diversity of both the band and the scene.

When the band incorporates southern elements in their songs, they often play on tensions between regional and nonregional reference points rather than taking one side or another. Sometimes their songs convey a comic image of the South reminiscent of Flannery O'Connor, especially "Devil in My Car" (*Wild Planet*), which was inspired by a southern evangelical preacher they heard on the radio while driving to a Captain Beefheart concert (Sexton 161). "Dry County" (*Cosmic Thing*) lists southern tropes of "lazy days," summer heat, and a "porch swing" as antidotes to "when the blues kick you in the head"—until the very end of the song, when what looks like southern leisure turns out to be simply the boredom of living in a dry county, where the girls "can't do" "what they wanna do" because they can't get alcohol. The band's visual style also plays with these tensions, especially in their use of wigs. In 1981, Cindy Wilson explained that they were "inspired by wigs in Fellini movies and from when Diana Vreeland was editor of *Vogue*," but then Pierson quickly added that wigs were also ordinary features of the Georgia landscape, where "there's lots of waitresses. And don't forget the trailer-park gang" (Goldstein). And in "Wig," when Pierson says, "I bought my wig at the Diana Shop with a purse to match," she is being literal. For their very first gig in Athens, Cindy Wilson and Pierson bought fake-fur purses at a local boutique called the Diana Shop and turned them into wigs (Sexton 35). The tackiness of the wigs does not exactly mock the South so much as it plays with the contrast—the seams—between the working-class glamour of southern waitresses and the urbane sophistication of Fellini and *Vogue*.

It is possible to read this wiggy, southern playfulness as camp, especially in the way that camp emphasizes style, theatricality, and artifice over content and celebrates "Being-as-Playing-a-Role" over notions of authenticity, as Susan Sontag has famously theorized (Sontag 56). Although the band claimed to resist camp as a label, there's no denying the campy subversiveness of their look and lyrics. Thrift stores inevitably gave the band some of this subversive edge by making it possible for Keith Strickland and Ricky Wilson, like so many others, to buy dresses and other outfits for drag when they were young (Hale 21).[6] As Le Zotte argues, wearing secondhand clothes in the 1970s and 1980s was often considered a "radical" and "dissident" act that rejected mainstream consumerism and conformity (219, 223). This sartorial dissidence shocked the band's early audiences in New York, not least because some mistook Cindy Wilson and Pierson for men in drag (Gaar 257), but also because the band's entire ethos diverged from the largely masculine seriousness of punk: "Where punk was serious, rude, macho, and violent, the B's were polite, nonthreatening, feminine. The punks wore black; the B's wore thrift" (Brown 51).[7] However, while there is a lot more to say about the irrepressible queerness of the band, reading them strictly as camp oversimplifies their style to a *single* characteristic rooted in their (and our) ironic relation to their material. Indeed, for all its undeniable campiness, "Wig" is only partially interested in ironic subversion. Instead, the song dwells in the positivity of putting on a wig for fun and going out "on the neon, neon side of town." It doesn't matter whether that side of town is the unfashionable red-light district or the fashionable zone of high-end nightclubs, because the goal is to come together in the pleasure of being who you want to be and occupying both contradictory spaces equally—not striking an ironic pose that distances you from one side or the other. Hence the song's recurring cheer: "We all got wigs, so / let's go!"

If there is a single, unifying principle that defines the entire aesthetic project of the B-52s, it is their commitment to the kind of positive affect we see in "Wig." But there is a certain truth to calling the band "tacky" *as long as* we accept a fairly neutral definition of it as meaning something like antiseamlessness, where the joining of different styles, forms, and references always makes itself felt as it creates something new. Cateforis calls the "unusual stylistic assemblages" of their songs a form of bricolage—"a combination of appropriated commodities whose connotations were now thrown into question" and thus enabled audiences "to see the familiar objects of our world in new and startling ways" (105). I want to build on that notion by thinking about how tackiness, understood as a form of juxtaposition, produces something even more democratic. The band's emphasis on "positive thinking" certainly stresses the notion that the music is meant for everyone. But the B-52s also hit an unusually democratic beat in their approach to writing and performing. The band has always composed songs by jamming spontaneously and seeing what comes out. Sometimes the bricolage of the final song preserves this sense of spontaneity, especially in songs like "Rock Lobster" (*The B-52's*) or "Love Shack" (*Cosmic Thing*) that break away from conventional repetitions of verse, chorus, bridge. The band is also democratic in the sense that no one acts as the lead figure, whether one person contributes most of the vocals or sits out entirely, or whether the song is an instrumental. As when Schneider holds back from speaking for his bandmates in the email interview, no one in the B-52s has ever stepped forward to take the role of "an obvious leader," as *New Musical Express* observed in 1979 (Rambali). Even their presence onstage maintains a decentralized and multifaceted structure, as Schneider described elsewhere: "The visual part is real important. It's so busy. There's so much going on it's hard to focus on any one thing, which is good" (Cohen). As Scott Creney and Brigette Adair Herron write, "the B-52s function more like an anarchic collective." Whereas bricolage suggests a certain auteurship, where all the parts add up to showcase the artistry of the creator, a theory of tackiness allows us to acknowledge the messier, more obviously collaborative and "anarchic" assemblages of individual parts as they work with and in contrast to each other to create something new.

Other songs explicitly imagine this new, queer futurity made possible by these clashing cultural seams. "Song for a Future Generation" (*Whammy!*) lists several pairings of male- and female-identified figures taken from pop culture, including the "Daughter of Dracula" and the "Son of Frankenstein," followed by the call, "let's meet and have a baby now." A focus on kitsch would emphasize the retro stylings of the figures themselves, but the song pulls our attention to the infinite possibilities of a "future generation" produced at the tacky seams where those figures "meet." The "Captain of the Enterprise" and the "King of the Zulus" are not half as interesting as the baby they'd produce together. Similarly, "Funplex" (*Funplex*) puts seemingly incommensurable references next to each other in the hyperconsumerism of the shopping mall, as in the tacky combination of Mexican and Polynesian signifiers in the "Taco Tiki Hut." But, by repeatedly emphasizing how "you broke my heart in the Funplex," the song calls our attention to the alternative possibility of finding the "real thing" of love and authenticity "on the escalator" *between* levels of commodified culture.

The word "tacky" will likely never lose its negative associations with cheap, outmoded, and/or aesthetically displeasing objects and styles. Moreover, while ironic or dissident reclamations of tackiness can be empowering, they equally become constraining by locking what they name in a narrow framework of meaning and purpose. We see this narrowness in the tagline used to describe the B-52s as the "tacky little dance band from Athens, Georgia." By contrasting the cool chic of Athens with larger stereotypes of southern backwardness and bad taste, and contrasting the seeming thoughtlessness of a "dance band" with an alternative music scene dubbed "college rock" in the 1980s, the tagline has no doubt restricted the band as much as it helped promote them. The B-52s are woefully underappreciated in the larger narratives of both pop and avant-garde music and art from 1977 to the present. My aim in this essay has been to build a better appreciation of the band by also showing what they can teach us about the democratic possibilities of tacky assemblages. But I am not interested in trying to rehabilitate the label "tacky" for more radical, critical purposes. Rather, a more open inquiry into what the word can tell us about the B-52s—and what the B-52s can tell us about tackiness—reveals what an emphasis on irony can sometimes miss: the obvious seams between unlikely or clashing styles, references, and cultural systems. With their wide-ranging influences and references in their songs and visual style, the B-52s resist efforts to categorize them within a single, unifying system of aesthetics. Thus, if we call the band "tacky," their tackiness lies not so much in their focus on "trash" and retro elements of culture but in the way that the seams between past and present create something decidedly new and democratically future-oriented. Tackiness is not the cheap toupee joked about in "Wig," in other words, but the seamy hairline that the toupee draws between artificial and natural, cheap and valuable, trash and commodity, obvious and subtle, old and new. And when we, like Fred, don this secondhand hairpiece, it allows us to navigate those seams and recreate our identities however we want. We might be the tackiest people on the neon side of town, but our tackiness can help us use those wigs to meet and have a baby now.

NOTES

1. I follow the band's practice since 2008 of omitting the apostrophe from their name, even when discussing earlier work. When quoting others who include it, I leave the apostrophe.

2. I am grateful to Scott Creney and Brigette Adair Herron for pointing me to this early reference, as well as their help and comments on the essay as a whole.

3. Her discussion repeats much of Cateforis's argument (see Le Zotte 224–27).

4. See also Cateforis 97–98; Le Zotte 226.

5. See Sexton 41, 67.

6. For a discussion of thrift shops and drag, see La Zotte 183–213.

7. Strickland, Schneider, and Ricky Wilson (who died of AIDS-related complications in 1985) are gay but were not publicly out in the 1980s. Pierson was married to a man when the band formed and is now married to a woman. I revel in the band's playful and transgressive queerness and regret that I don't have room to say more about it in this essay; nevertheless, like all other labels, narrowly categorizing them as "gay" obscures their complexity.

WORKS CITED

B-52s, The. *The B-52's*. Warner Bros., 1979

———. *Bouncing Off the Satellites*. Warner Bros., 1986.

———. *Cosmic Thing*. Reprise, 1989.

———. *Funplex*. Astralwerks, 2008.

———. *Mesopotamia*. Warner Bros., 1982.

———. *Whammy!* Warner Bros., 1983.

———. *Wild Planet*. Warner Bros., 1980.

Brown, Rodger Lyle. *Party Out of Bounds: The B-52's, R.E.M., and the Kids Who Rocked Athens, Georgia*. Everthemore Books, 1991.

Cateforis, Theo. *Are We Not New Wave? Modern Pop at the Turn of the 1980s*. U of Michigan P, 2011.

Christgau, Robert. "A Little Night Music II: Ain't Got No Home." *The Village Voice*, 23 Oct. 1978, www.robertchristgau.com/xg/music/home-78.php.

Cohen, Mitchell. "The B-52s: Climate Control in the Land of 16 Dances." *Creem*, Dec. 1979, www.rocksbackpages.com/Library/Article/the-b-52s-climate-control-in-the-land-of-16-dances.

Creney, Scott, and Brigette Adair Herron. *Neon Side of Town: The Story of the B-52s*. U of Georgia P, forthcoming.

Gaar, Gillian G. *She's a Rebel: The History of Women in Rock and Roll*. Seal Press, 1992.

Goldstein, Toby. "Do You Dig the B-52s?" *Creem*, Jul. 1982, www.rocksbackpages.com/Library/Article/do-you-dig-the-b-52s.

Hale, Grace Elizabeth. *Cool Town: How Athens, Georgia, Launched Alternative Music and Changed American Culture*. U of North Carolina P, 2020.

Le Zotte, Jennifer. *From Goodwill to Grunge: A History of Secondhand Styles and Alternative Economics*. U of North Carolina P, 2017.

May, Adam. "Kate Pierson Talks to Adam May." *Al Jazeera*, 30 Apr. 2015, america.aljazeera.com/watch/shows/talk-to-al-jazeera/articles/2015/4/30/kate-pierson-talks-to-adam-may.html.

Miller, Kevin. "Re: Interview with Fred Schneider Followup." Received by Michael Bibler, 4 May 2020.

Page, Betty. "The B-52s: Mesopotamia (Island) ****1/2." *Sounds*, 13 Feb. 1982, www.rocksbackpages.com/Library/Article/the-b-52s-imesopotamiai-island12.

Rambali, Paul. "The B-52s: Hot Pants, Cold Sweat and a Brand New Beehive Hair Do." *New Musical Express*, 9 June 1979, www.rocksbackpages.com/Library/Article/the-b-52s-hot-pants-cold-sweat-and-a-brand-new-beehive-hair-do.

Rose, Cynthia. "The B-52's: Hair Today Gone Tomorrow?" *New Musical Express*, 3 Jan. 1981, www.rocksbackpages.com/Library/Article/the-b-52s-hair-today-gone-tomorrow.

Sexton, Mats. *The B-52's Universe: The Essential Guide to the World's Greatest Party Band.* Plan-B Books, 2002.

Sontag, Susan. "Notes on Camp." 1964. *Camp: Queer Aesthetics and the Performing Subject: A Reader,* edited by Fabio Cleto, U of Michigan P, 1999, pp. 53–65.

Wuelfing, Howard. "On Target with the B-52s." *Unicorn Times*, Dec. 1979, www.rocksbackpages.com/Library/Article/on-target-with-the-b-52s.

III.

Dolly as Common Ground

TACKY-LACHIAN DOLLY

DOUBLE-D FEMME IN THE DOUBLE-WIDE MOUNTAIN SOUTH

ANNA CREADICK

ISLANDS IN THE STREAM: DOLLY'S BODY

You can set and talk with me for five minutes and know that there's a little more to me than tits.
—Dolly Parton, *Washington Post*, 17 Nov. 1989 (Kempley)

*I*f you're going to talk tacky, you're going to have to talk about Dolly Parton, and if you're going to talk about Dolly, you're going to have to talk about boobs, so let's just put them out there, because lord knows, they're the first thing you'll notice.[1]

This essay loiters at the intersection of tackiness, Appalachia, and the body to consider that particular variety of mountain mama who expresses her excesses with glee. What I am calling "tacky-lachian femme" rests at that intersection, upon the irrepressible chest of the "hillbilly gal." From Dolly's double D's, propped up and bedazzled, we could go to Daisy Mae's spilling over her off-the-shoulder in Dogpatch, or Daisy Duke of Hazzard, whose tied-up crop top barely holds them down. For the tacky-femme record, we might even consider the string of man-eating hussies of mid-1960s hixploitation films. Figures like Dolly's raise delicious questions: Is the bodacious body in its garish garb the source of her oppression or her strength? Is it armor, is it drag, or is it a kind of burlesque, satirizing the respectability of the southern belle? What is this tacky femme form's relationship to race, to class? And what does any of this have to do with the mountains? What I find is that Dolly's powerfully out-of-bounds taste rattles some of our most entrenched social hierarchies, as it also bends the boundaries of gender.

Normally, we can see an inverse relationship between pneumatic chests and class-crossing success. Take, for example, a brilliant, buxom friend of mine who climbed from a poor/working-class background into academia, only to receive this comment on a student course evaluation: "If you have to pin your blouse closed in front, it doesn't fit." This surveillance of her body, specifically her breasts, is of course about whether *she* does or doesn't "fit" at the powerful space behind the lectern. The reality that chestiness can impede successfulness is one reason breast reduction surgery is big business, seeing an estimated ninety thousand procedures annually, with such high-profile figures as Drew Barrymore, Roseanne Barr, Jeanine Garofalo, and Queen Latifah having had the surgery (Grant). Tackiness and embodiment threaten to converge in the large-breasted person because the figure itself is always-already figured as low-class. But when it comes to being stacked and tacky, Dolly seems a special case. "Have you ever thought about [breast] reduction?" one interviewer asked. "Oh no!" Dolly laughed. "I worked too hard to get them this big!" ("Straight Talk").

Parton's tacky-lachian femme aesthetic is all about excess: too much hair, too much cleavage, leaving "no rhinestone unturned" (Petridis). Her style invites celebration, an excess of pleasure. Dolly's body plays a central role in that pleasure in part because of its *unreality*, which operates in such high contrast to the apparent honesty and unpretentiousness of her personality (Scofield). Her body is part of her brand of tacky because it is such a put-on: DP's DD's are always, at least to some degree, *plastic*.

The body itself is a burlesque with Parton, a joke waiting to happen: "I've had nips and tucks and trims and sucks, boobs and waist and butt and such, eyes and chin and back again, and I'll never graduate from collagen" ("Morley Safer"; see also Scofield). By keeping her body unfixed, uncontained, and changeable, Dolly transgresses the limits of embodiment in general: "I wasn't naturally pretty, so I make the most of what I've got . . . whatever it takes, I do. I try to make the most of everything" ("Dolly Parton, the legend"). The "most" in this case means going over the top on every front. Dolly's body is central to her spectacle; bedazzled and teased into further excesses, it does all the things middle-class femininity forbids. Let's break it down.

The makeup is no accent, it's painted-on-thick. The hair is too blonde to believe, too big to tame, adding inches to her height or curling like a boa about her shoulders. It's hyperreal: we sense there is no *there* there, and of course there is not. "How long does it take to do your hair?" asks Morley Safer on *60 Minutes*. "I don't know, I'm never there," Dolly says, slyly referring to her preference for elaborate wigs. "I've been set up," the interviewer replies. Yeah, you have. We all have.

Dolly's costumes always appear to have been built around her cleavage, with plunging necklines or peek-a-boo cutouts. This is not a game chesty girls are supposed to play. We (yes, we) are told to minimize, draw the eye away. High neck, full coverage, monochrome, maybe. Don't make people *look*. Meanwhile, Dolly's increasingly tiny waist produces an hourglass figure too ka-blam to believe, all wrapped in clothes fashioned to rivet the gaze: ruffles! colors! sequins and fringe! The fabrics scream with wild, unhinged, outrageous, made-you-look patterns and are cut to fit tighter than any Spanx. Pockets appear where no pocket should be (made you look!), as she drips with rhinestones, tinsel, even chains. Her hands spellbind us with bejeweled fingerless gloves, then rings, then long, bright acrylic nails (which, it turns out, provided all the between-takes typewriter-percussion she needed to write that multi-platinum title song "9 to 5"). And all of this is piled atop a pair of tiny, too-high mules. No sensible shoes, these are high-anxiety heels. But they add another five inches, and she stomps around the stage in them like they are the comfiest of brogans.

Dolly Parton's body blends two of the most iconic stereotypes of Appalachian women: her demeanor echoes the slapstick foolishness of the granny/ma figure, while her style promises the uncontained eroticism of the hillbilly vixen (McCarroll; Williamson). These fantasies of Appalachian femininity form two edges of the same weapon, one built to hew women back into the roles of mother or lover. "Mannish" granny-women are made to seem "out of step" in a world made for men, while the buxom vixen reduces women to easy-access sexual receptacles, offering an uninhibited, uncomplicated roll in the hay.

Thinking about tackiness as embodiment may seem like anatomy-as-destiny. But Dolly Parton's radical self-possession conveys pleasure, enjoyment, and power in the manufactured and uncontainable body, as well as in the unabashedly gaudy. "It is true that I look artificial, but I believe that I'm totally real," Parton explains ("Dolly Parton, the legend"). Tellingly, one of the only times I found her use the actual word *tacky* was when she described to Roger Ebert how someone *else* might respond badly to her body:

Q, "Do you get bothered by constant references to your bust size?"

A. "Well, it is sorta obvious, ain't it? No, I don't. It don't bother me so much unless people dwell on it. Get *tacky* and all. It's part of the act. If someone gets really carried away, well, I sort of pity him. Cause it's his problem, not mine. Other than that, I'm a good sport. I know some of the best Dolly Parton jokes. I made 'em up myself." (Ebert, emphasis added)

The irreverence of Dolly's tacky-lachian femme form, as the opening "more to me than tits" quote suggests, is pointed directly at any "tacky" people who aim to diminish her worth. And it is for this, as much as anything else, that she is revered.

COAT OF MANY COLORS: LOOKIN' CHEAP

I don't feel cheap, but I don't mind lookin' cheap, you know? I don't.
—Dolly Parton, television interview, 1986 (Ganick)

That Dolly doesn't mind "lookin' cheap" is subversive stuff. The higher the paycheck, the higher the hair: her style asserts a pride in her past of poverty, a freedom to mock middle-class aesthetics with a look that is flossy, femme, and fiercely regional in its country kitschiness. She has found a way to own, possess, or repossess tacky in a way that upends its usual consequences.

Parton loves to tell the story of how she got her look by emulating the most beautiful woman she ever saw as a child, "she had big yella hair, heavy makeup, red lipstick, tight clothes." Only later did Dolly learn that this woman was the "town tramp." Over and over she tells this tale, even while doing makeup tutorials with talk show hosts: "Burn a match to darken your beauty mark . . . I used poke berries and mercurochrome [as makeup]." Her father tried to wipe the makeup off. "Daddy! That's my *natural color!*" she protested ("Dolly Parton Shares"). And in a sense, it was. With this story, Parton shows Hallmark Channel viewers how her tacky aesthetic has "natural" roots in rural, mountain poverty and deprivation, as well as in an early lesson she apparently absorbed with a wink: this is how women need to look if they want to be somebody, to make a name for themselves, and to make money.

"Well if she's trash, that's what I'm gonna be. I want to be 'trash' when I grow up," the young Dolly reportedly announced. This story recirculates disarmingly right alongside the line, "Mama always said, 'Be yourself.'" Parton grew up one of twelve in a Smoky Mountain cabin, and only got attention when she wrote and sang songs. Was she trash *then?* Is she trash *now?* And why are we laughing? At the story of a woman who sold sex appeal in a Tennessee mountain town to survive? Or at the irony of self-possession that precedes possession by a crowd? Like the "town tramp," Dolly's look is a smart business decision, and she suggests that maybe *we* are the ones being taken for a ride: "I look like a woman but I think like a man. I've done business with men who think I'm as silly as I look. By the time they realize I'm not, I've got the money and gone" (Alexander; Wilson). Making up, putting on a painted face, is part of the process Dolly follows in order to be seen. But it also allows her to escape *unseen.*

Lord knows Dolly isn't the tackiest thing in country music. Next to Porter Wagoner, especially early on, she looked downright dowdy in her high-necked dresses and pale pink lip gloss. But you can tell she was struggling to emerge. The hair is a telltale sign: it just gets higher and higher until, *pow,* she breaks free and goes solo: No, *I* am the star here! To be a star, you have to shine. Parton took that challenge literally.

What is so astonishing is that the arc of Dolly Parton's career has seen her move not away from tackiness but toward it. For Parton, greater success has translated into greater freedom to mock middle-class aesthetics with her own tacky taste. And here I am reminded that it's impossible to describe her style as "tacky" without reinforcing the power of that word to condemn. When I call Dolly "tacky" I position myself as middle-class/tasteful because "[t]aste classifies, and it classifies the classifier" (Bordieu 6). Perhaps Parton tarts up to such a degree in part to help her fans feel muted, respectable, or middle-class-by-comparison. Or perhaps she does it to help them feel bold, irreverent, and tacky-lachian by association.

Either way, "lookin' cheap" is a deliberate strategy for Dolly. To manufacture the "country girl's idea of glam," Dolly and her "creative director and wardrobe designer" Steve Summers have collaborated to create "as many as 300 outfits each year, down to every shoe and accessory" (Freitelberg). The deck is as stacked as she is, since everyone who interviews her wants to talk first about appearances, her fashion, her looks. Parton then parlays that attention to her surfaces into an invitation to consider her depths. In her inimitable squeaky-toy voice, she lets viewers in every time: married fifty-three years, a writer of forty-seven hit songs, a pro-LGBT Christian. We learn about her lived feminism, her entrepreneurship, her humanitarianism, ethics, and activism: through Dolly's Imagination Library, she has donated over 130 million books worldwide. We get her views on the election: "We could use more boobs in the race," she quipped in 2016 (Guarino). As the flesh becomes word, we begin to understand her cultural work as a kind of Appalachian American ambassador. "God Bless Dolly Parton," reads a bumper sticker somewhere in Arizona.

Dolly Parton is on to us. We look at Dolly, but then we *listen* to Dolly. And she had this planned all along. She calls her 2008 album, for example, *Backwoods Barbie:* an insult that can't stick to her, because she thought of it first. The debut release on her own Dolly Records imprint, the title single is both autobiography and artist's statement, laying out the story of her look with a series of one-two punch couplets that deliberately contrast her surfaces with her depths: "I've always been misunderstood because of how I look. / Don't judge me by the cover 'cause I'm a real good book." In the music video for the song, Dolly, plays again with the hooker trope, literally walking the city streets at night, sporting leopard print minidress, stiletto heels, and gauzy hot pink floor-length lingerie jacket, in a move the *Telegraph UK* says just "elevat[es] her tacky reputation higher and higher" ("'It costs a lot'"). But the song itself resists the look: "I'm just a backwoods Barbie, too much makeup, too much hair," Parton warbles to the camera, but "Don't be fooled by thinkin' that the goods are not all there."[2] When Dolly controls the means of production, her tackiness is her brand, and she leverages it as a site of power.

The *femme* part of tacky-lachian is so inherent to "lookin' cheap" that the binary logic is worth unpacking. Is tacky-butch even possible, or would it just be femininity expressed on male-identified bodies? Whither Porter Wagoner, Lil Nas X, even Elvis? Jo Weldon proposes that "tacky is likely to be feminine, ethnic, queer, deviant; not manly, not practical, not businesslike, not serious. Tacky, like hell, is always other people." Country music's sequined Nudie Cohn suits might be called "flashy," not "tacky," when men wear them. Elvis's early style statements were, like his music, lifted from African American culture, which gave him much of his edge and appeal. True, Dolly's high falsetto seems put-on femme in much the same way Elvis's hunka-hunka sneer was put-on butch. Yet Parton's voice reverberates through gender to class and region. Consider Dolly's Appalachian cackle and spangle against that maven of the New England upper middle class Martha Stewart, whose voice stays at an impossibly deep timbre, subdued, understated, just like her makeup, highlights, flavors, and interiors. Tacky inevitably signals class. But how does Dolly's brand of tacky connect to the South?

Even her mountains have a certain reputation. On a national level, if the South is already our scapegoat, Appalachia is America's most embarrassing country cousin. And Pigeon Forge was tacky long before Dollywood got there, even *within* Appalachia. In popular culture, "poverty with a white face," as bell hooks terms it in the documentary *hillbilly*, is either the site of ridicule (*The Simpsons'* Cletus the slack-jawed yokel), horror (*Deliverance*, for example), or pity (documentary film and photography examples abound). Dolly Parton should be triply mistrusted as the daughter of a maligned community within a stereotyped region within the scapegoated South. And yet she is beloved. Why? Because she flaunts it.

Dolly's "Tennessee Mountain Home"-cooked representation of Appalachia bears a truthfulness. Dolly doesn't just look tacky or, in her choice of words, "cheap," she *means* to. With her endless one-liners, like a collection of Zen koans from the Dolly Lama, she spits a philosophy of self-possession and empowerment that rehumanizes the pathologized rural poor. In this way, Dolly Parton's brand of tacky is both gender warfare and class warfare, with more than a wink toward sexual liberation.

(TWERKIN') 9 TO 5: DOLLY'S QUEER CRED

> I have a huge gay following, and I'm proud of them. Sometimes some of them look more like me than I do.
> —Dolly Parton, *New York Times*, 2016 (Ryzik)

In the spring of 2020, celebrity contestant Vanessa Williams (of first-African-American-Miss-America-resigns-in-*Penthouse*-scandal fame) dressed up as Dolly Parton and performed on *RuPaul's Drag Race*. Lip-synching a remix called "Twerkin' 5 to 9," Williams punctuated the tune with quotations from interviews with Parton that telegraphed Dolly's queer sensibility to fans: "It's a good thing I was born a girl, otherwise I'd be a drag queen"; "I'm not so sure I'm *not* a drag queen"; "If I hadn't been a singer, I'd have been a beautician!" Teetering in tall heels, tight red-fringed dress, and push-up bra, Williams said the performance pushed her out of her "comfort zone." In taking on Dolly's image, she had indeed crossed multiple boundaries: racial cross-dressing in the whiteface of blond wig and brightly powdered face; regional crossing by portraying a country star in a cartoonish Appalachian accent; and the queer triple-dip of being a woman in drag,[3] surrounded by men in drag, playing Dolly, who always-already appears to be in drag. The twisting of Parton's song "9 to 5" into the cheeky "5 to 9" inverts daytime respectable "work" into a night shift of sexually-charged "twerk," a move that returns us to that Tennessee "town tramp" whose look, if not labor, inspired Dolly's tacky-lachian look from the beginning. Williams won the *Drag Race* competition and donated her thirty-thousand-dollar prize to The Trevor Project, an LGBTQ youth suicide prevention charity (Newcomb).

Let's be clear: Dolly's tacky-lachian femme, whether it's the original or a copy, is decidedly queer. This quality is why I use the term tacky-lachian *femme*, despite the fact that Dolly ostensibly identifies as straight.[4] Femme is a particular category of queer identity, but I propose that the plastic embodiment that Dolly achieves makes this quality so malleable as to be highly transferrable. As gay Kentucky author Silas House testified, "For me, growing up, two of the main people that I was really proud of were Loretta Lynn and Dolly Parton. . . . For me, they were real heroes growing up. And they had enough clout that they could control their image" (*hillbilly*). Dolly's femme form makes the region itself more plastic, allowing Appalachia to function as a kind of queer prosthesis, a national instrument that might (could) just restore the broken body politic.

Dolly's tacky style is the exaggerated, manufactured look of someone looking at wealth from the outside. She ties her bedazzled fashion sense not just to the sexuality of the "town tramp" but also to what she thought *wealth* meant, when she was young and poor: "A lot of people get all turned off by the wig, the heels, the fingernails, the whole artificial bit. I do dress kinda pretty but old-fashioned. I think maybe I dress this way partly because of the image, you know, and partly because when I was a little girl growing up in a big old poor family, this was the way that the rich folks' wives dressed, when we'd see them drivin' through in their big old cars" (Ebert). Similarly, drag can appear to be the manufacture of exaggerated gender by someone looking at it from the outside. Drag, like Dolly, has its roots in poverty, as one performer explains: "Drag is about creating eleganza, extravaganza—from *nothing*" ("Trixie Mattel Crashes").

Both drag and Dolly also rely on the power of comedy. As she has aged, Dolly's body has diminished: fragile, thin arms and legs, angular face, but still the enormous breasts intact, making her look more and more like the impossible physiology of Barbie (Scofield). With her stiletto slides, cinched waist, and flossy blonde hair, she is now a caricature of her caricature. And she has admitted as much. Dolly calls herself "a cartoon character that I created," a character that uses humor to charm and disarm. Of her comic timing, Parton says, "A good sense of humor comes from both sides of my family. I think that's how country people—poor people—get by. It's either laugh or cry, and I'd prefer to laugh" ("Morley Safer"). In this way, Dolly offers a wide target for drag appropriation. She is always-already a get-up, a put-on, a send-up, a take-off. She is living proof of gender as manufactured, as fun, funny, fantasy, and as work (werk).

At this point, the line between Dolly and Dolly's drag devotees has all but collapsed. Parton has declared herself a drag queen. She has performed as herself and lost in Dolly Parton look-alike competitions: "They had these big drag queens—I mean they looked great too, they were prettier than I could ever dream of being" (Koniki). Of perhaps her best-known hit, "Jolene," she says: "I see so many drag queens at my concerts I sometimes think I should sing: 'Drag queen, drag queen, drag queen'" (Phibbs). Drag artist Trixie Mattel, scheduled to perform at the Austin Paramount Theater, was relieved to learn it was the same place Dolly's *The Best Little Whorehouse in Texas* premiered in 1982: "That comforts me," Mattel said in an interview, "because that means I'm not going to be the first drag queen at the venue" (Webb).

How does "drag Dolly" (and yes, that feels redundant) deconstruct sex and gender, as well as class and region? One of her most famous contemporary drag homages comes from Mattel, who describes herself as "indisputably the most successful drag queen country singer in the world," and who, in addition to a successful YouTube series and documentary, also won *Rupaul's Drag Race: All-Stars* [season] 3 and hosts a meta-series called *I Like to Watch* in which we watch while Trixie and her drag coconspirator Katya watch Dolly Parton's new Netflix series *Heartstrings* while providing comic commentary. Mattel has pushed the surreality of drag Dolly into new dimensions, with unsettling makeup techniques that give her face a hyperexaggerated look that reads like a startling combination of Barbie and Dolly but with Tammy Faye Bakker-meets-My Little Pony eyes (Salandra). "I love Dolly Parton, who to me represents the marriage and the intersection between storytelling and music," Mattel says. "She makes people laugh as much as she

FIG. 5. Thrift store fan portrait featuring Dolly in pink ruffles, 1979. Author's collection.

makes people sing along, and that's obviously the direction I like to go in. She's an icon" (Webb).

While Parton's love for the LGBT community is part of her Christianity and her humanism, tackiness is also an important part of Dolly's appeal to the queer community, especially in Appalachia and the South. Her country pride, when combined with a loving acceptance of queer lives and LGBT rights, slides into a pride of a more rainbow variety. Her fearlessly over-the-top-style glamour, glitter, glitz, and schmaltz make her an "icon" on a par with Elton or Liberace, whose rhinestone courage also telegraphed love and understanding. Parton explains her queer appeal: "They know I'm a little different myself. I've fought for the right to be myself, so that is one of the reasons that the gays and lesbians relate to me. They know that I appreciate everybody for who they are. We are who we are, so why can't we be allowed to be that? I ain't out to preach no sermons, I'm just out to do my work, sing my songs and write them, and love people, and share them" (qtd. in Guarino).

Also important to her queer cred is the unusual fact that Dolly Parton is childless. "Nurturing motherhood and well-balanced heteronormativity have never managed to co-exist with great camp," argues Bruce LaBruce. Her childlessness opens up the possibility that her fans are her children—and/or her lovers, thanks in part to her utterly invisible husband. Being thus unencumbered, Dolly can appear to be ours alone. Her name—Dolly—also matters here. She is our plaything.

Two sorts of consumer culture cohere around Dolly. One is the formidable swag she generates, from her music to her theme park to her new line of greeting cards for WalMart. But the other is the swag that honors her, generated by fans and admirers. If the former is tacky, the latter is camp. "To be campy" writes Jo Weldon, "is, among other things, to be tacky on purpose. Campiness is . . . a self-aware version of tackiness. Campy is smart tacky, glamour with an ironic twist. Campy is always too much, whereas tacky is somehow not enough." My personal collection of Dolly swag includes a lovingly rendered 1979 fan oil portrait, with Dolly's piercing gaze in tight focus above her poorly proportioned, supersized, pink-ruffled chest. The "too much" in this case is the formal oil portraiture, the ruffles atop the overabundance of already-abundant breasts (see Fig. 5).

More contemporary queer homages to Dolly's tacky-lachian femme include T-shirts featuring Dolly cuddling a possom above the slogan "Rhinestones and Trash Forever" (see Fig. 6), or special Trixie Mattel limited edition bedazzled rhinestone autoharp lapel pins, or phone cases in which disembodied Dolly-faces float like planets across a blue-and-purple galaxy. Such productions are powerfully important to queer Appalachians' sense of place, but the products can also seem unstuck in time, channeling a high-retro rhinestone '80s throwback aesthetic even as they spin us toward an interplanetary moment where everything and nothing is Appalachia anymore (*Queer Appalachia*; see also Heath). Importantly, this consumer culture—like Vanessa Williams's prize money—has an ethics: organizers put the merch to work for urgent queer Appalachia causes, including homelessness relief, sex ed, and community health programs (Nichols). The playful drag and swag appropriations of Dolly Parton's tacky-lachian style become a return on her public investment in queer survival.

FIG. 6. Queer Appalachia
merch, "Rhinestones and
Trash Forever" T-shirt/sticker
design, 2020.

[DOLLY] WILL ALWAYS LOVE YOU

Dolly, if you hadn't noticed, is having a moment. By 2019, a feature
titled "We need to talk about Dolly" notes the singer had 1.8 million
Instagram followers, had sold over 100 million records, and had won
eight Grammys, and the production *9 to 5: The Musical* was still playing
the West End. Just as I was trying to nail down my own thoughts, Ken
Burns documented the whole of country music, including Dolly; the
BBC dropped a feature-length Dolly-documentary *Here I Am*, and the
Netflix series *Dolly Parton's Heartstrings* premiered, with every episode
based on an "iconic Dolly Parton Song." By early 2020, a made-for-Net-
flix feature film *Dumplin'* (based on a popular young adult novel) told of
a curvy, Dolly-loving country-girl who has her heart and self-esteem
saved by a cadre of drag performers, all to a Dolly soundtrack. Parton
partnered with IMG to produce a "lifestyle brand" of licensed fashion,

jewelry, accessories, and home goods, and was doing a line of greeting cards for WalMart. Dollywood—which one journalist called Dolly's own Appalachian "Economic Stimulus Package" ("Morley Safer")—was in its thirty-third year with two million visitors annually, a resort and spa, and a newly completed $37 million amusement park expansion called "Wildwood" (Feitelberg). And damn if Jad Abumrad didn't have to go and drop a nine-part, twelve-hour, Peabody-Award-winning podcast, the product of three years of research: *Dolly Parton's America.*

Why Dolly now? Why is she taking center stage in this moment, even in this here essay? One explanation is that, at a time characterized by anxiety and civic division, Dolly is a mediating force, drawing fans from across the political spectrum. "She's become a kind of national monument," right at a time when national monuments are being torn down ("Morley Safer"; Abumrad). But Dolly offers something more dangerous than that.

Dolly Parton's tacky-lachian femme figure offers tantalizing possibilities for transformation. She pairs the rural with the glamorous; she pairs power with the pleasures of what my friend Wendy calls the "feminine arts": hair, heels, nails, jewels, and cleavage. She pairs buxom with bold; candor with camp. She manages to build wealth without tearing down poverty. And she proffers a powerful antidote to the fear and loathing of our time: love.

When she finally got shed of Porter Wagoner in 1976, Parton headlined her own prime time variety show, *Dolly.* At close of every episode, she would speak, sotto voce, that recited portion of her song, "I Will Always Love You": "And I hope life treats you kind, and I hope that you have all you ever dream of. I wish you joy and lots and lots of happiness, but above all this, I wish you love. I love you." And then she says, "Goodnight," and sings the rest of the tune, as the closing credits roll.

NOTES

1. Gratitude to J. W. Williamson for the quote in the above part epigraph and for launching this and so many other worthwhile investigations. Thanks also to Rebecca Burditt for the steadfastness, Susan Pliner for the structure, and Kevin Dunn for the time.

2. While I don't discuss music here as much as I might, the language with which

her music is described, especially in the UK, often drips with the classism that adheres to "tacky." For example, "from flinty and sparse to syrupy and sentimental . . . if Dolly would just dial down the kitsch a bit more. . . . sea of slush . . . mawkish filler . . . sharp realism . . . submerged beneath corn and goo" (Petridis). See also Christensen's reading of the feminism in Parton's lyrics.

3. Of course drag is, especially now, an activity that people of many genders and sexualities participate in. In December 2019 the *OED* definitions were changed so that a "drag queen" is now defined as: "A person, usually male, who dresses up as a woman and performs as an entertainer." See www.itv.com/news/central/2020-03-04/misogy-ny-in-the-drag-queen-community-how-lacey-lou-from-birmingham-is-tearing-down-gender-stereotypes.

4. Fans have long harbored theories that Dolly's lifelong friend Judy Ogle is secretly her lesbian lover. See Nelson.

WORKS CITED

Abumrad, Jad, and Shima Oliae. *Dolly Parton's America*. WNYC Studios, Oct.–Dec. 2019, www.wnycstudios.org/podcasts/dolly-partons-america.

Alexander, Ella. "Life Lessons from Dolly Parton: What Would Dolly Do?" *Harpers Bazaar*, 19 Jan. 2021, www.harpersbazaar.com/uk/people-parties/people-and-parties/news/a26180/dolly-parton-quotes/.

Bordieu, Pierre. *Distinction: A Social Critique of the Judgment of Taste*. Translated by Richard Nice, Harvard UP, 1984. p. 6.

Christensen, Samantha. "'Where It Counts I'm Real': The Complexities of Dolly Parton's Feminist Voice." *Walking the Line: Country Music Lyricists and American Culture*, Edited by Thomas Alan Holmes and Roxanne Harde, Lexington Books, 2013. pp. 163–74.

"*Dolly* (1976 series)." *Wikipedia.com*, en.wikipedia.org/wiki/Dolly_(1976_series).

"Dolly Parton Shares Her Beauty Secrets." Hallmark Channel, *YouTube*, posted by Beautyworkout, 12 May 2016, www.youtube.com/watch?v=csGlCmvXz7g.

"Dolly Parton, the legend." *YouTube*, uploaded by *CBS Sunday Morning*, 10 Feb. 2019, www.youtube.com/watch?v=g1m_nof-X2g.

"Drag Queens Trixie Mattel and Katya React to Dolly Parton's Heartstrings." *I Like to Watch*. Season 1, Episode 3, Netflix, 2019, *YouTube*, uploaded by haran, 19 Dec. 2020, www.youtube.com/watch?v=YLy3F5odM_w.

Ebert, Roger. "Dolly Parton: Gee, She's Really Nice." *RogerEbert.com*, 7 Dec. 1980, rogerebert.com/interviews/dolly-parton-gee-shes-really-nice.

Feitelberg, Rosemary. "Dolly Parton Signs Global Licensing Deal with IMG to Develop Fashion, Accessories and Home." *WWD*, 3 May 2019, wwd.com/

fashion-news/fashion-scoops/dolly-parton-signs-global-licensing-deal-with-img-to-develop-fashion-accessories-and-home-1203123160/.

Ganick, Elaine. "Dolly Parton RARE 1986 TV Interview 'Changing Record Labels?'" *YouTube*, uploaded by USAHEARTBEAT, 15 Sept. 2011, www.youtube.com/watch?v=mB-UioI_an8.

Grant, Eva Taylor. "14 Fascinating Facts about Getting a Breast Reduction." *Bustle*, 10 July 2018, www.bustle.com/p/14-fascinating-facts-about-getting-a-breast-reduction-9702106.

Guarino, Mark. "Dolly Parton on the Election: 'We Could Use More Boobs in the Race." *The Guardian* [UK], 12 July 2016, www.theguardian.com/music/2016/jul/12/dolly-parton-tour-hillary-clinton-lgbt-community.

Heath, Scott. "The Other Side of Time: Theorizing the Interplanetary South." *PMLA*, vol. 131, no. 6, 2016, pp. 170–73.

hillbilly. Directed by Sally Rubin and Ashley York, The Orchard, 2018, hillbillymovie.com.

"'It costs a lot of money to look this cheap': As Dolly Parton Releases Her 43rd Album, Look Back at her Greatest Fashion Hits." *The Telegraph* [UK], 19 Aug. 2016, www.telegraph.co.uk/fashion/people/dolly-partons-greatest-fashion-hits/parton-elevating-her-tacky-reputation-higher-and-higher-on-the-v/.

Kempley, Rita. "Dolly Parton Going for Glitter." *Washington Post*, 17 Nov. 1989.

Koniki, Lisa. "Dolly Parton Recalls The Time She Lost A Dolly Parton Look-Alike Contest." *OneCountry*, 2 Nov. 2017, www.onecountry.com/country-music/dolly-parton-harry-connick-jr/.

LaBruce, Bruce. "Notes on Camp—and Anti-Camp." 2012–13. Rpt. in *Gay and Lesbian Review*, Mar. –Apr. 2014, glreview.org/article/notes-on-camp-and-anti-camp-2/.

McCarroll, Meredith. *Unwhite: Appalachia, Race, and Film.* U of Georgia P, 2019.

"Morley Safer interviews Dolly Parton." *60 Minutes*. CBS, 5 Apr. 2009, www.cbsnews.com/news/dolly-parton-the-real-queen-of-all-media.

Nelson, Jeff. "Dolly Parton Brushes off Rumors about her Sexuality Again: 'I'm Not Gay.'" *People*, 19 Feb. 2019, people.com/country/dolly-parton-not-gay-accepts-everybody/

Newcomb, Alyssa. "Vanessa Williams transforms into Dolly Parton on 'Celebrity Drag Race.'" *Today*, 2 May 2020, www.today.com/popculture/vanessa-williams-transforms-dolly-parton-rupaul-s-drag-race-t180623.

Nichols, James Michael. "Grassroots groups help LGBTQ people survive—and thrive—in Appalachia." *NBC News*, 6 Mar. 2020, www.nbcnews.com/feature/nbc-out/grassroots-groups-help-lgbtq-people-survive-thrive-appalachia-n1144881.

Parton, Dolly. "Backwoods Barbie." *Backwoods Barbie*. Sony, 2016.

———. "I Will Always Love You." Record single. RCA, 1974.

Petridis, Alexis. "Dolly Parton Pure and Simple Review—toning down the schmaltz . . . a bit." *The Guardian* [UK], 18 Aug. 2016, www.theguardian.com/music/2016/aug/18/dolly-parton-pure-and-simple-review-toning-down-the-schmaltz-a-bit.

Phibbs, Harry. "Dolly Parton: feminist icon?" *The Guardian* [UK], 9 July 2008, www.theguardian.com/commentisfree/2008/jul/09/1.

Queer Appalachia. Produced by the Electric Dirt Collective. www.queerappalachia.com/qa-merch. Accessed 7 Oct. 2019.

Ryzik, Melena. "Dolly Parton Is Proud of Her Gay Fans and Hillary Clinton." *New York Times*, 24 June 2016, www.nytimes.com/2016/07/03/arts/music/dolly-parton-is-proud-of-her-gay-fans-and-hillary-clinton.html.

Salandra, Adam. "Drag Race: Why Does Trixie Mattel Look So Different From Other Drag Queens?" *Fandom*, 8 Mar.h 2018, www.fandom.com/articles/drag-race-why-does-trixie-mattels-makeup-look-so-different.

Scofield, Rebecca. "'Nipped, Tucked, or Sucked': Dolly Parton and the Construction of the Authentic Body." *Journal of Popular Culture*, vol. 49, no. 3, 13 June 2016, pp. 660–677.

"Straight Talk with Dolly Parton." *The Wendy Williams Show*. 15 Mar. 2014, www.youtube.com/watch?v=iMsq1Qo2Z9s.

"Trixie Mattel Crashes the Set of #AllStars5" *YouTube*, uploaded by RuPaul's Drag Race, 12 July 2020, www.youtube.com/watch?v=LaFR_BAm4jo.

Webb, Eric. "Trixie Mattel in Austin: 'Drag Race' star talks Dolly Parton and doubts." *Austin360*, 5 Mar. 2020, www.austin360.com/entertainment/20200305/trixie-mattel-in-austin-lsquodrag-racersquo-star-talks-dolly-parton-and-doubts.

Weldon, Jo. "Who Decides What's Tacky, Anyway?" *LITHUB*, 2 Aug. 2018, lithub.com/who-decides-whats-tacky-anyway/.

Williamson, J. W. *Hillbillyland: What the Movies Did to the Mountains and What the Mountains Did to the Movies*. U of North Carolina P, 1995.

Wilson, Pamela. "Mountains of Contradictions: Gender, Class, and Region in the Star Image of Dolly Parton." *South Atlantic Quarterly*, vol. 94, no. 1, 1995, pp. 109–35.

RHINESTONE COWGIRLS

REIFICATION AND THE ART
OF SOUTHERN DRAG

ISABEL DUARTE-GRAY

J want to begin by quoting a 1969 *Rolling Stone* description of country western aesthetics as epitomized by "rodeo tailor" Nudie Cohn: "Nudie somehow has managed to convince nearly 25 years of rough and rugged cowboy types they should buy blue boots studded with costume jewelry and suits of magenta elastique dripping with rhinestoned fringe" (Hopkins). This statement is singular in that it belies one cultural misapprehension by revealing another. Author Jerry Hopkins believes the famous Nudie suit has accidentally subverted an apparent incommensurability of cowboy masculinity with the joys of feminine folderol. He does this by savoring the high camp of Nudie Cohn's tackiness, his ecstasies of "dripping" fringe, kitsch embroideries ranging from the iconic to the arcane, ersatz stone, and synthetic fiber. Hopkins creates a startling juxtaposition of taste, and implicitly of *class*, when he highlights what he believes to be unconscious irony in the "synthetic" gender construction of a cultural niche that otherwise rigidly polices such gender and other boundaries. *Rolling Stone*'s class and gender juxtapositions here bring me to the basic question of this essay: Is tackiness expressive of failure, like Sianne Ngai's theory of cuteness? Does it uncover the artistic aspirations of a performer who has missed his mark in the eyes of the onlooker? Or is tackiness an aesthetic subversion, a critique of class-based aesthetic

250

hierarchy itself? I argue the latter. The work of Nudie Cohn—so institutionally bound to Nashville's cultural production that the Country Music Hall of Fame houses his original 1947 display sign—began as one of post-45, post-Fordist class critique, now long forgotten.

To highlight this latent critique, I will first turn to the work of Nudie Cohn, then to these characteristic misprisions of the Grand Ole Opry from *without*, and finally, to drag appropriations of this aesthetic by Dolly Parton and Trixie Mattel. I will argue that drag's rhinestone cowgirls defamiliarize the country western aesthetic sensibility to draw its class struggles to the fore, while also underscoring the limits of southern gender representation. In so doing, I will consider "tackiness" as an aesthetic in the same hierarchy-bending traditions as Walter Benjamin's allegory, the carnivalesque, and camp. By reading the class-conscious camp of the Tacky South reparatively, I hope to suggest that southern aesthetics have made tangible contributions to Marxist, queer, and feminist logics. We may find in the study of tackiness not only homologies between southern class struggle, gender struggle, and queer rebellion, but something new, terrifying, and joyful, something like hope.

ON TAILORS AND TAYLORIZATION

Though Nudie Cohn—born Nuta Kotlyarenko in Kiev—was not the first tailor to design country western suits, he is synonymous with the rhinestone cowboy. Cohn popularized the use of contemporary, synthetic materials, memorably rhinestones, in the tailoring of custom gabardine suits for country western performers. The legend Cohn circulated about the rise of his suits begins with Roy Rogers, who needed a costume to play Madison Square Gardens in the early 1950s and asked Cohn to design one that would render him visible to the "nosebleed" section of the audience (Murguia). Cohn, who had tailored G-strings and feather costumes for burlesque dancers as a teenager in New York, applied rhinestones to every inch of Rogers' classic western fringe. Cohn effectively combined the raw material of burlesque with the romanticized costumes he had seen in Western films he had devoured as a child, which descended in turn from Buffalo Bill's Wild West shows and other vaudeville performances (La Chappelle 8).

Cohn believed that entertainers should wear "flashy outfits to be fair to the public" (Hopkins). The cultural historian Peter La Chapelle argues this issue of "fairness" is political, insisting that Cohn's transformative country western suits rebelled against 1950s workplace conformity: "If the man in the gray flannel suit represented conformity, the man in rhinestone and gabardine represented a sort of working man's antihero, a blue-collar renegade who was bold enough to challenge the reigning orthodoxy" (La Chappelle 8). The suits' custom embroidery was key: Cohn decorated Porter Wagoner's brightly colored suits with his namesake frontier wagons and bejeweled wagon wheels, Ferlin Husky's featured an embroidered husky, and Dale Evans enjoyed a fringe dress with a single, embroidered bull's head stitched from shoulder to shoulder (La Chappelle 7–8).

The "personality" stitched in each suit deliberately contrasted with the emergence of the work uniform—be it the ubiquitous gray flannel suit of the rising service industry or the blue-collar factory uniform. While the standard-issue uniform as we know it is synonymous with industrial labor, its precursors, aristocratic livery and officer's uniforms, developed concurrently with the Early Modern period, as a means of identifying otherwise unknown members of specific professions, or servants of particular houses. American economist Thorstein Veblen—most famous for coining the term "conspicuous consumption"—identified livery as a belittling symbol of the working class's (ironic) dependence on the aristocracy for wages:

> In a heightened degree . . . livery comes to be a badge of servitude, or rather servility . . . The livery becomes obnoxious to nearly all who are required to wear it. We are yet so little removed from a state of effective slavery as still to be fully sensitive to the sting of any imputation of servility. This antipathy asserts itself even in the case of the liveries or uniforms which some corporations prescribe as the distinctive dress of their employees. In this country the aversion even goes the length of discrediting—in a mild and uncertain way—those government employments, military and civil, which require the wearing of a livery or uniform. (Veblen 79–80)

For blue-collar workers laboring in increasingly Taylorized factories, the standard-issue uniform anonymized the experience of alienated labor, eliding the machine and the laborer as equally replaceable bodies, or means of production.

Both the suit-and-tie and the blue-collar jumpsuit evoked the alienations of the post-45 American economy as it shifted indoors and away from its agrarian roots. The Grand Ole Opry, the Western film, and similar sites of self-conscious Americana swelled with nostalgia for the freedom of agrarian life, or the self-fashioning promise of the bygone frontier.[1] Or, to quote Cohn, "You don't have to have cows to be a cowboy" (Hopkins). The role of the country star, then, was not simply to rebel against anomie and confinement but to do so by flaunting a parodic image of conspicuous consumption, the ersatz diamond. The tackiness of the rhinestone performed a specific function: capturing the eye with gimcrack excess. Country music performers dressed ecstatically precisely because to do so was to offend "good taste," as defined and policed by the leisure class. In their Nudie suits, Roy Rogers, Porter Wagoner, and even Elvis Presley rebelled on behalf of uniformed laborers in what Sontag might call an act of "wholly conscious" camp: a joyful, exaggerated inversion of taste hierarchy and a "glorification of character" (Sontag 285).

IN PRAISE OF THE GARISH, GAUDY AND GAUCHE

The carnivalesque atmosphere of the Grand Ole Opry did not translate, however, beyond the still-vaudevillian world of country western performance. Jerry Hopkins's profile of Cohn defined his vocation as "turning grown men into neon peacocks" of the "garish-gaudy-and-gauche" variety, suggesting that mainstream culture recirculated Cohn's class rebellion as "naïve" camp (Hopkins). In other words, Hopkins and his contemporaries misapprehended the carnivalesque class inversions of the Grand Ole Opry as sincere, magpie-like admiration for all things shiny. Such misapprehension, while condescending, is necessary to the in-group sensibility of camp. Camp distinguishes between those who are sensible to its critical faculties and those who are insensible, the vast majority of consumers who will read a costume or performance according to larger cultural norms. Hopkins applies, as it were, the wrong criteria to his readings of the rhinestone cowboy, which is what allows the inherent transgression of rhinestone cowboy to perpetuate itself.

Rock legend Gram Parsons cemented this "naïve" interpretation of country western aesthetics when he commissioned Cohn to construct a kitschified Nudie suit that would invoke the cultural turn of the 1960s. Parsons replaced the wagon wheels and roses of the Nudie tradition with marijuana leaves, opium poppies, and pharmaceuticals. Soon, globally popular rock musicians, such as Keith Richards and Elton John, followed "suit." Parsons publicly described Cohn's aesthetic as "cosmic Americana," donning the rhinestone in a winking, postmodern parody of Porter Wagoner's folk sincerity (Diamond). This resulted in a kind of double-inversion of the carnivalesque, or an elaboration upon an elaboration: Parsons' tongue-in-cheek appropriation assumed "tackiness" arose from a failure of high aesthetic hopes, rather than a burlesque of American conformity and Veblerian conspicuous consumption. Wittingly or unwittingly, Parsons's counterculture developed a critical homology between folk nostalgia and the forward-looking utopianism of the hippie generation. Like the stars of midcentury country music before them, Parsons and the 1960s counterculture rejected conformist American values, from the confinement of post-GI Bill respectability politics to the paranoia of the Cold War to the anomie of the corporate workplace. The impulses of the country western musician and the flower child, however disparate, are utopian in that they are critical, or critical in that they are utopian. Both single out the reification of American laborers in search of a more dignified, whole means of living.

I invoke Bakhtin's carnivalesque here as a paradigm for reading the Nudie suit—as worn by country western stars and 1960s rock stars— because the carnivalesque refers not to a specific aesthetic signature so much as to a mode of reading power differentials. In his work on camp, David Bergman has attended to the significant parallels between the carnivalesque and camp as ways of seeing. He writes that "classic camping" has four hallmarks, all shared with Bakhtin's hermeneutic tool, the carnivalesque: first, both author and consumer wear disguises; second, the masquerade produces intimacy among "the initiated" who share this special mode of seeing, while holding the uninitiated at a distance; third, it is maintained by a spirit of comedy and joy; and finally, all performances are circumscribed by "an elaborate style which while seemingly superficial, reveals to the initiated an unspoken subtext" (Bergman 99).

This style, to be found in the sensibilities of queer readers and rhinestone cowboys alike, operates by questioning what is organic to a given cultural context. Like the carnivalesque, camp denaturalizes dualisms we take for granted—male/female, inside/outside, wealthy/poor—and introduces a utopian sense of possibility to entrenched social hierarchies. Both camp and the carnivalesque view the marginalization and suffering of persons within a broader allegory of value as fundamentally *unnecessary*. To suffer alienated labor, or forced reproductivity of any kind, is to suffer for the sake of a material surplus we cannot enjoy. Per Walter Benjamin, an allegorical method of reading observes how modernity has drained the world of objects and actions of their metaphysical meaning. What remains, after the disenchantment of the world, is exchange value. Howard Caygill writes that Benjamin identified the fetish commodity as a translation of "all values and meanings into its own terms—exchange value—and destabilizes them in the process. The condition of 'petrified unrest' thus comes to stand for the stabilized instability of the capitalist economy in which values are perpetually being assigned and devalued" (Caygill 251). Eve Kosofsky Sedgwick has similarly framed camp, to which we will add the country western carnivalesque, as a form of reparative reading, which rejects rigid social determinism and troubles the social order: "Hope, often a fracturing, even a traumatic thing to experience, is among the energies by which the reparatively positioned reader tries to organize the fragments and part-objects she encounters or creates. Because the reader has room to realize that the future may be different from the present, it is also possible for her to entertain such profoundly painful, profoundly relieving, ethically crucial possibilities as that the past, in turn, could have happened differently from the way it actually did" (Sedgwick 146). Camp, in other words, reveals shimmering, joyful, even terrifying cracks in our inherited structures of order—cracks desperately in need of repair.

IMITATING DOLLY: THE ERSATZ ERSATZ

Enter the drag queen. The drag rhinestone cowgirl strikes me as peculiarly salient to discussions of the Tacky South for two reasons. The
first is historicity; while modern country western fashion has largely
pared down the self-conscious camp of the post-45 era in favor of mainstream styles, drag appropriations of country western style still celebrate the extravagance and specificity of the rhinestone, fringe, and
other accoutrements of the Nudie suit. This is not surprising. American drag performance and honky-tonk both originated in marginal
spaces—the bar, the front porch, the ball—and consistently mock the
conspicuous consumption of luxury goods for their very unattainabil-
ity (La Chappelle 4). As such, the second reason becomes clear. The
self-conscious theatricality of drag performance is perfectly "suited" to
highlight the latent camp and concomitant social critique of the Grand
Ole Opry, even as it reveals the rigid gender and sexual boundaries also
to be found there.

Consider the drag queen Trixie Mattel, or performer Brian Firkus,
who in 2017 released her country album *Two Birds*, which debuted at
No. 2 on the overall iTunes sales chart. The cover of this album highlights the dialogism of drag performance: Trixie and Brian *both* appear
in costume as a country family act reminiscent of Johnny and June
Carter Cash or Roy Rogers and Dale Evans. Trixie wears a fitted dress
printed with cowgirls, not unlike the topless pinup printed on Cohn's
original clothing label. This accompanies the classic Trixie beat, or
look, in which Mattel paints herself to resemble a clownish Barbie
doll (as manufactured by toy giant Mattel) with eyeliner reaching to
her forehead and lips overdrawn nearly to her nose. Like Dolly Parton
and June Carter Cash, Trixie carries an autoharp, an instrument rarely
featured in contemporary pop music. Brian, meanwhile, wears the
classic embroidered Nudie shirt, matching cowboy hat, and bolo tie.
In the music video for the album's first single, "Mama Don't Make
Me Put on the Dress Again," Brian performs in front of a Grand Ole
Opry sign, while Trixie, in a platinum blond wig nearly a foot high,
watches transfixed. In interviews surrounding *Two Birds*, Trixie cites
the doll-like, flamboyantly ersatz Dolly Parton, former singing part-

ner of Porter Wagoner and regular wearer of Nudie originals, and a key influence (Büscher). Trixie began her public transition from drag comedian to country/folk artist by performing Parton's "Coat of Many Colors" during a touring drag show, to which I'll turn shortly. When I spoke with Mattel at RuPaul's Drag Con 2018, she explained that she draws inspiration from Parton because "Dolly is a drag queen" already,[2] and because she, like Mattel, transforms the raw material of her rural and socioeconomically disadvantaged background into imminently consumable art (Mattel). Both artists exaggerate their feminine qualities, from their extensive wig collections to their matte pink costumes to their exaggerations of the feminine silhouette. In short, Dolly is camp. Parton has famously joked that her iconic look is modeled on the "town tramp" of her hometown in the Smoky Mountains, telling Barbara Walters in 1977 that "show business is a money-making joke, and I like telling jokes" (Episode 2.1).

Parton and Mattel share a commitment to the "money-making joke," which is why they also share a fondness for the Nudie suit. Per Cohn, performers must exceed the limits of taste out of fairness to their audience, because they are commodities soliciting consumption from that audience. By purchasing the commodity—here, a performer in the "drag" of the Nudie suit—the consumer symbolically rebels against the reification of human bodies under late capitalism, even as she knowingly participates in that same market of exchange. In her work on cuteness, Sianne Ngai has observed that Marx troublingly compared commodities to vulnerable women in his theory of commodity fetishism, including to victims of sexual violence. Marx noted that, like marginalized subjects, commodities lack the literal and political power to resist their consumers and therefore can be consumed by force. Ngai concludes that Marx's association of the consumable object with the consumable woman stems from our libidinal investments in purchasable objects. Consumers form a "phantasmic displacement of the sociality of human labor onto its products," which renders commodity fetishism "inseparable from the production of commodities" (Ngai 61–62). Kitsch, she adds, forms faux-social intimacies with consumers by cozying up to us, as though begging to be purchased. The carnival of kitsch short-circuits our capacity for contemplative distance, forcing us to "inhabit [kitsch] like an atmosphere, one enveloping [us] like a coat, or pulled over [our] head like a mask" (Ngai 75).

Dolly Parton and Trixie Mattel seize control of the "joke" that is the consumption of human beings as though they were kitsch products of factory labor. Their feminine excesses exploit consumers' inability to peel an object of consumption apart from the libidinal fantasy it conjures. By overperforming the fetishized elements of femininity, conspicuously masquerading as mass-produced dolls or "town tramps," Dolly and Trixie upend the power dynamic between consumer and consumable. Such performances draw our attention to the unending loop of consumer capitalism, in which laboring persons are reified as things and manufactured things are animated into persons. The Nudie suit is central to this performance. If the Nudie suit turns a human being into a highly visible commodity while also ridiculing the anonymous reduction of persons into things, then the suit, as a costume or an artist's "uniform," functions as an ambivalent sign of capitalist disenchantment. It is a coat of many colors first desacralized by the market, then reenchanted by its own performance of individuality, personality, and even aura. Both Dolly Parton and Trixie Mattel—musical artists and lovers of the Nudie suit—perform "Coat of Many Colors" in public venues, wearing the drag of the living commodity. The lyrics of "Coat of Many Colors" heighten this burlesque, speaking to the uncertain relationship between labor, commodities, and value: "I recall a box of rags that someone gave us / And how my mama put those rags to use / There were rags of many colors / Every piece was small." Here, Dolly and Trixie describe how the coat of many colors was constructed from the tatters of old clothing fallen into disuse. In the Book of Genesis, Joseph's father, Jacob, gifts him the coat of many colors—as Dolly's mother does in turn—as a sign of paternal love and favor. Parton implies that maternal love, expressed through labor and storytelling, has transformed a box of disused material into an object of near-spiritual value. Benjamin has written of his own method of allegorical reading that he "[constructs] constellations out of the material of the past," as though he were his own Angel of History (Caygill 245). As we've seen already, Benjamin wrote that late capitalism organizes persons and objects into a disenchanted allegory of value, which occults

the act of labor and renders the laborer into an anonymous manufac-
turer, or form of equipment. Caygill notes that "the commodity fetish
is itself allegorical, modern culture is intrinsically allegorical, with
the exchange value of the commodity devaluing all other traditional
or use values, but being itself prone to crises of inflation or deflation"
(Caygill 251).

The song then describes how the labor of a specific artist, Dolly's
mother, constellates the raw material of the past into an object of rare
value: "Mama sewed the rags together / Sewing every piece with love
/ She made my coat of many colors / That I was so proud of." The coat
has use value and sentimental value but exists entirely outside the allegory of exchange, and therefore, of fetishism. This is incomprehensi-
ble outside the framework Parton has established, however, as Parton
leaves home in the coat and enters the larger world. Her schoolmates
mock the coat of many colors for its homespun appearance even after
she explains its importance to her as a rejection of deterministic visions
of human value: "But they didn't understand it / And I tried to make
them see / That one is only poor / Only if they choose to be."

Parton and Mattel have both performed these pieces in custom
Nudie or Nudie-like suits. Parton has stated in interviews that she
wrote "Coat of Many Colors" while on tour with Porter Wagoner,
another wearer of custom embroidered suits. When the song became
a hit in 1969, Parton offered to purchase her mother a transparent or
allegorically correct object of value to signify her success, namely, a
mink coat. Her mother argued that in the rural Smoky Mountains she
had nowhere to wear such a thing and asked for money instead. Dolly
conceded the point and gave her mother the value of the coat in lieu
of the fetish object (Liptak).

The Nudie suit, like the coat of many colors, inverts what Benjamin calls "petrified unrest," or the allegory of value and its arresting
impact on class struggle. In her suit, Parton self-consciously blurs the
line between the commodity and laborer, thing and person. It is no
accident that the impish Andy Warhol included Parton among his pop
art silk screens of endlessly reified, endlessly recirculated celebrities. If
southern culture demands that women don a particular "uniform," in
the form of compulsory sexual availability, eventual reproductivity, and

domestic docility, in order to function within a market of exchange, the Nudie suit simultaneously performs and rejects that uniform. The ersatz rhinestone, which is neither stone nor diamond, unpetrifies Parton's unrest.

For Trixie Mattel, the Nudie suit assumes a new critical dimension, in that it conjures the historical nostalgia we find in Parton's deployment of the Book of Genesis and in Cohn's use of Wild West vaudeville aesthetics[3] but also reflects the role of queer aesthetics in recuperating a world outside the marketplace. If the coat of many colors refuses compulsory participation in a hierarchy of value, the rainbow—to be found in Cohn's work as well as queer iconography—rejects compulsory heterosexuality and compulsory reproduction as "uniforms" of the marketplace. Known as the "Betsy Ross" of queer liberation, artist-activist Gilbert Baker sewed the first rainbow flag, which is now synonymous with queer liberatory politics. He writes in his memoirs that Harvey Milk's protégé, Cleve Jones, asked him to produce a symbol for "the dawn of a new gay consciousness and freedom," specifically to decorate San Francisco's Civic Center Plaza for 1978 Pride, or what was then called Gay Freedom Day (Baker 42). Baker came up with the rainbow after studying the history of flags; he realized, after considering the US and French flags, that so much of our modern, even normative, national iconography originated in "a riot, a rebellion, or a revolution" and looked to the simplicity of color as a leap out of conformity, compulsory heterosexuality, and the closet (Baker 42). The rainbow flag, like the coat of many colors, performs its own liberation, by asserting joy, pleasure, and originality outside the market of exchange. By addressing the dragginess already latent in Cohn's aesthetics, Mattel draws our attention to that same joy, pleasure, and originality to be found in country western music and performance. Moreover, the proud, out queerness of Mattel's aesthetics draws our attention to its unspoken codification within existing Opry artifacts, as though asking when, and not if, the Opry will come out of its culturally rigid closet and delight fully in its own extant subtexts.

Nudie Cohn once told an interviewer that he modeled his suits after flashy female apparel, because "every man has an aspect of woman in his personality that longs to be expressed" (La Chapelle 8). Cohn intimates that the normative "uniform" of gender performance, be it heterosexuality, masculinity, or femininity, limits the range of self-expression available to everyone, if unequally. On Parton, the Nudie suit accentuates the very artificiality of the artist's gender performance, her false breasts and false hair forcing the irony of gender representation into satire: the self-commodifying woman mocks the consumer during the act of consumption. On Mattel, meanwhile, the duality of the Nudie suit reaches its logical conclusion: Mattel's costumes on the cover of *Two Birds* merge socioeconomic struggle, nostalgia for the freedom of agrarian life, and burlesque femininity into a single ironic commodity, embodied by one person in two gender performances.

RIOT, REBELLION, REVOLUTION: THE REPARATIVE DIMENSIONS OF THE NUDIE SUIT

I want to conclude by suggesting that drag appropriation of the rhinestone cowboy is, per Eve Sedgewick, a reparative act. The critical faculties, which support the high camp appreciation of tackiness and the conscious critique of income inequality to be found in Nudie Cohn's carnivalesque ur-sensibility, do not exist at a great remove. To quote the queer theorist Scott Long, "[Camp's] particular endeavor is to fix the nature of the absurd: the society that laughs at the wrong things has gone wrong . . . Behind camp is the expectation that, once the absurd is properly recognized, a sense of the serious will follow" (Long 80). Rhinestone cowgirls substantiate the economic critique of the "tacky," to which they add a gender-critical point of view. The convergence of Trixie Mattel's drag-camp sensibility with the historical origins of country western music strikes me as productive: though contemporary consumers of these cultural productions—drag performance and Grand Ole Opry—typically occupy opposite ends of the political spectrum, they share many political goals. They invert hierarchies of taste, rebel against cultural conformity (including, in some cases, gender and sexual conformity), and rail against the tangible symptoms of income inequality. Both, in short, seek to name the absurdity of late capitalism, and in the camp semiotics of tackiness, they begin to share a common language.

If the uniform is a kind of conformist mask, like the masks of gender conformity and compulsory heterosexuality, then the Nudie suit reveals the extent to which we are none of us free to navigate the world as we will. The strategic shedding of these uniforms by performers like Dolly Parton, Trixie Mattel, and even Cohn himself invites us to contemplate the extent to which that world, *too*, is manufactured. Eve Kosofsky Sedgwick describes hope—in the context of reparative reading and epistemological rebellion—as a nearly traumatic experience. The epistemology of the Nudie suit, the camp performance, and the rainbow shows us the extent to which class, race, and gender hierarchies, expressed within Benjamin's allegory of value, frame our pain as necessary to the visible, functioning world. The market requires that we suppress our least productive, least reproductive qualities—that we Taylorize our persons to fit the needs of the collective economy. To find hope through reparative practices of reading, seeing, and dressing is to discover that this pain was not necessary to keep the world turning. To don "blue boots studded with costume jewelry and suits of magenta elastique dripping with rhinestoned fringe" may not allow us wholly to escape these hierarchies, nor to evade the danger that comes from flouting their enforcement. But still, the rhinestone makes room for new expressions of value, as well as potential political alliances. If the world has been tailored to a particular shape, it can be retailored, too, with much more glitter and fringe.

NOTES

1. I would be remiss if I didn't note that much of the country western iconography we associate with frontier life is drawn from, and represents the genocide and displacement of, First Nations cultures. Buffalo Bill's Wild West Shows began in the 1880s and included Native American performers performing acts of horsemanship, marksmanship, recreations of famous battles, (often apocryphal or sensationalist) vignettes of frontier and Native American life, and other matters popularized by dime novels of the frontier. See McNenly.

2. To parse this definition of "drag queen" could be the subject of an entire paper. It is not unusual for a drag queen to label a pointedly artificial or self-fashioned, but female-assigned and identifying, performer a "drag queen." Rather than take Trixie literally, however, we might assume she is making a subtler point: Drag queens draw

inspiration from camp female performers, precisely because both draw attention to the self-fashioning and artifice, or constructed quality, of gender performance. To make the unconscious performance of gender norms, or of culturally constructed desirable traits, a theatrical act is to remark on the unmarked.

3. As I've noted before, Buffalo Bill's Wild West Show reduced Native American experience to ambient set dressing. This is operative in Trixie Mattel's own aesthetics, as she is Ojibwe, and occasionally signifies on white appropriations of Native American dress. Per an interview with *Milwaukee Magazine:* "There's something to be said that I grew up in a Native American family and poor, and I portray a character who is full-on white, Valley Girl and rich . . . If I was allowed to have girl's toys when I was little and nothing bad ever happened to me, I wouldn't look like a kid's toy now and have dark comedy." See Brooke.

WORKS CITED

Baker, Gilbert. *Rainbow Warrior: My Life in Color.* Chicago Review Press, 2019.

Bakhtin, M. M., and Hélène Iswolsky. *Rabelais and His World.* Indiana UP, 1984.

Benjamin, Walter. *Origin of the German Trauerspiel.* Translated by Howard Eiland, Harvard UP, 2019.

Bergman, David. "Strategic Camp: The Art of Gay Rhetoric." *Camp Grounds: Style and Homosexuality,* edited by David Bergman, U of Massachusetts P, 1993.

Brooke, Zach. "Q&A: Trixie Mattel." *Milwaukee,* 8 Sept. 2015, www.milwaukeemag.com/qa-trixie-mattel.

Büscher, Christopher. "Q&A: Trixie Mattel On Her Debut Album *Two Birds.*" *ArtMag.,* 11 May 2017, medium.com/artmagazine/q-a-trixie-mattel-on-her-debut-album-two-birds-c1ae15b1f84c.

Caygill, Howard. "Walter Benjamin's Concept of Allegory." *The Cambridge Companion to Walter Benjamin,* edited by David S. Ferris, Cambridge UP, 2004.

Diamond, Jason. "Country Music's Sparkle King." *Tablet Magazine,* 31 May 2012, Tabletmag.com.

Episode 2.1. *The Barbara Walters Summer Special.* ABC News, 6 Dec. 1977.

Hopkins, Jerry. "Nudie: The World's Flashiest Country and Western Stylist." *Rolling Stone,* 28 June 1969, Rollingstone.com.

La Chapelle, Peter. "All That Glitters: Country Music, Taste, and the Politics of the Rhinestone 'Nudie Suit.'" *Dress,* vol. 28, no. 1, 2001, pp. 3–12.

Liptak, Carina. "Story Behind the Song: Dolly Parton, *Coat of Many Colors.*" *The Boot,* 2019, theboot.com/dolly-parton-coat-of-many-colors-lyrics.

Long, Scott. "The Loneliness of Camp." *Camp Grounds: Style and Homosexuality,* edited by David Bergman, U of Massachusetts P, 1993.

ISABEL DUARTE-GRAY

Mattel, Trixie. Personal interview with author. 9 Sept. 2017.

McNenly, Linda Scarangella. "Foe, Friend, or Critic: Native Performers with Buffalo Bill's Wild West Show and Discourses of Conquest and Friendship in Newspaper Reports." *American Indian Quarterly*, vol. 38, no. 2, 2014, pp. 143–76.

Murguia, Adri. "Nudie Cohn." *Vice Magazine*, 19 Apr. 2012, Vice.com.

Ngai, Sianne. *Our Aesthetic Categories: Zany, Cute, Interesting*. Harvard UP, 2012.

Parton, Dolly. Lyrics to "Coat of Many Colors." *Genius*, 2020, genius.com/Dolly-parton-coat-of-many-colors-lyrics.

Sedgwick, Eve Kosofsky. *Touching Feeling: Affect, Pedagogy, Performativity*. Duke UP, 2003.

Sontag, Susan. "Notes on Camp." *Against Interpretation and Other Essays*. Picador, 2001.

Veblen, Thorstein. *The Theory of the Leisure Class: An Economic Study of Institutions*. Macmillan, 1902.

264

IN COUNTRY MUSIC, WOMEN RECLAIM, REFRAME, AND WEAPONIZE TACKY

SUSANNAH YOUNG

*L*ike getting a handful of seashells to stay put while hot-gluing them to a box that will sit atop the toilet in a beach-themed guest bathroom, "tacky" can be hard to pin down. It's easy enough to dash off a broad definition—media and objets d'art that appeal to (and, in many instances, are designed *specifically* to appeal to) "unrefined" tastes, thus defying rules of decorum—but such a definition invites two important questions: Who decides what constitutes good taste—and why? What does how we define "good taste" say about us? It's no coincidence that much of what we consider to be aesthetically refined is financially beyond the reach of many (Congdon and Blandy 198) and that much of what we consider "tacky" has been classified as such not only because it is financially accessible but because it has been created by or for people society neither values nor respects. We roll our eyes at the technicolor jungle sprawling across the cover of a Lisa Frank notebook just as we roll our eyes at preteen and adolescent girls. We ridicule velvet paintings of Elvis just like we ridicule working-class "rednecks" and "hillbillies." We roast shirts bearing script-font-inscribed, late capitalist adages like "This mom runs on true crime, wine, and Amazon Prime" and erode or erase systemic social support for overworked mothers.

Yet from acrylic nails to oversized hoop earrings, neon eyeshadow to neon signs hanging indoors, certain accessories and art objects that would historically have been considered "tacky" have become part of the twenty-first-century mainstream aesthetic, especially in womxn's fashion and decor. Some of this shift can be attributed to third-wave feminism's emphasis on racial, cultural, and class intersectionality and openness to expressions of power and beauty that are decoupled from Western, white, cis, and male expressions of the same. Indeed, one can think of kitsch, of tackiness, as a "move toward liberating pluralism, an affirmation of the possibility of creative expression in all quarters" (Congdon and Blandy 199). As the internet has made it easier to explore other perspectives and aesthetics and eliminated some of the gatekeepers that have historically denied marginalized communities a platform, we have begun to borrow from one another, and we—especially younger generations, who grew up with decentralized taste-making as the norm and who are statistically more likely to *be* members of these marginalized communities—are less likely to subscribe to the historical standard of "good taste," understanding that the line between Tasteful and Tacky was drawn by racism, homophobia, transphobia, misogyny, and classism.

Aesthetic choices immediately broadcast identity or affiliation and thus often play crucial roles in the process of defining or redefining who and what we respect: "it is through our bodies that we make visible, to ourselves and others, what we are" (Congdon and Blandy 206). The immediacy of the seen communicates a perspective faster—and in a way that's harder to ignore and more likely to pique a person's interest. Take the Nudie suit as an example, which Isabel Duarte-Gray discusses at length elsewhere in this collection. In the 1950s, a Ukrainian immigrant named Nuta Kotlyarenko (rechristened Nudie Cohn by United States immigration officials) began designing and producing expensive, intricately embroidered, rhinestone-bedazzled suits for country stars to wear while performing. "They wanted to stand out on stage and screen and make an indelible impression on their audiences," author Holly George-Warren explains. "Many of these entertainers came from impoverished backgrounds and these clothes sparkling with rhinestones turned them into our own American 'royals'" (Meares). Nudie suits were a way to flaunt success *and* shift an audience's perspective:

to emphasize that country musicians could become wealthy (and, thus, powerful), too. Country musicians have also used aesthetics to more subversive ends: especially artists whose voices deeply ingrained prejudices have conditioned us to reflexively silence or ignore. Patrick Haggerty of Lavender Country sang (and still sings) explicitly about queer sex and relationships, but in sound and structure his songs are quite traditional and, forever clad in Western shirt, cowboy hat, and boots, he looks indistinguishable from other country musicians. Charley Pride's songs also upheld the dominant sound and aesthetic of country music at the time, even if, as a Black man, his mere presence did anything but.

Adjusting one's look and sound to appeal to the broadest possible audience is both a disheartening compromise *and* a highly effective strategy for an artist. Doing so can mean denying, to a degree, who one is—but it can also make what the artist says more likely to be heard. Simply put, ideas and beliefs that might have raised hackles had the artist not presented in such an appealing package may instead find willing ears. In the right artist's hands, country music's particular brand of tacky can be weaponized: it can become a means of subversion, a roundabout way to reclaim power. Women in country music have deployed this strategy to successful ends for reasons that sit squarely at the intersection of misogyny and classism: we find women more pleasant if they look the way we expect them to, and we've been conditioned to never expect a woman with hair jacked to Jesus wearing a sparkly jumpsuit to say anything worth taking seriously.

This isn't to say that presenting the "right" way is a foolproof strategy: the ways we express ourselves—the products we make, the words we write—divulge and reinforce personal prejudices and societal inequities. Country music is especially conservative by this measure *and* when it comes to its aversion to telling new stories and embracing new sounds (although this, too, is becoming less true with time, at least for young men: cf. the spike in rap-tinged "bro country" songs courtesy of artists like Florida Georgia Line, Sam Smith, and Jason Aldean; the resounding crossover success of Lil Nas X's "Old Town Road"). Fans of The Chicks[1] turned their backs on the group after a 2003 show in London, where, in her lead-in patter to "Traveling Soldier," lead singer

Natalie Maines criticized the United States' impending invasion of Iraq and said she was embarrassed that President George W. Bush lived in Texas. Within a week, radio stations were refusing to play The Chicks, and communities were organizing get-togethers to burn the band's albums. Prior to this moment, The Chicks had made no secret of their politics in their song lyrics or in their public comments: the trio only paid the price when they didn't sugarcoat their beliefs and opinions in trappings more broadly palatable to a red-state audience.

At the time, The Chicks' songs used traditional-sounding melodies, instrumentation, and arrangements to deliver messages that were anything but, calling home and hearth to mind while simultaneously eviscerating stifling gender norms. "Goodbye Earl" deftly weaponizes familiar tropes (in the most literal sense: protagonist Wanda cooks black-eyed peas for her abusive husband, Earl, and doses them with poison before she serves him) in a frank portrayal of the way domestic abuse often doesn't manifest in its most extreme form until marriage makes a woman a man's state-sanctioned "property." The song posits a solution that is radical (Wanda and her best friend, Mary Ann, deal with the situation by killing Earl, knowing that the criminal justice system would likely not mete out true justice) but passes muster with a culturally conservative crowd: in the end, the two make a living as successful entrepreneurs cooking and selling "Tennessee ham and strawberry jam." Wanda and Mary Ann used home cooking to defy the patriarchy and then again to find a way to live under it while eking out some degree of autonomy. The message is transparently there but delivered in such an appealing package that "Goodbye Earl"—a song about killing your husband and getting away with it—became one of The Chicks' most enduring and beloved.

Of course, every woman in country music who used its tropes and its fans' biases to gain a following before paving her own path owes a debt of gratitude to Dolly Parton. Critic Pamela Fox asks, "is 'Dolly Parton' an explicit invention with subversive undercurrents?" (Fox 258)—and it's hard to not reflexively answer "yes." Parton built a career around being radically open about her roots, her beliefs, and her faith while never expressing a potentially divisive opinion about anything or anyone. She espouses kindness and inclusivity but eschews polarizing labels, doesn't openly align with any particular ideology, and stays mum about issues most celebrities are all too eager to comment upon. She played the man's game and became successful and powerful enough to no longer be fully beholden to its rules yet refuses to identify as a feminist. And she has always taken pains to present (and to preserve) a very specific, heteropatriarchal—and very tacky—idea of beauty.

By Parton's own admission in her 1994 autobiography, *Dolly: My Life and Other Unfinished Business*, as a child she thought herself ugly and saw beauty and freedom in the painted and primped pinup girls who graced the pages of magazines and the sex workers who walked the streets in town. In contrast to the mothers she saw tethered to their husbands, children, and the never-ending grind of domestic labor, these were women with agency over their images and bodies: the ones who could define their terms and tell others how to treat them. In them, tackiness represented a kind of freedom—a visible indication that you'd risen above something; exceeded expectations; defied the quiet, crushing brutality of the life you were supposed to live. Parton also saw that freedom and possibility in even more unexpected places:

> [Parton] recalls discovering her childhood cousin "Myrtle" as the "alligator girl" in a local sideshow[2] . . . : "I could understand her completely. After all, I wanted to leave the mountains too, and I wanted attention. She probably thought I was making fun or blowing her cover, but I just wanted to say, 'Hello, I understand. Be the alligator girl. Be whatever your dreams and your luck will let you be . . . Give them a quarter's worth of wonder.'"
>
> Rather than viewing her cousin's situation as a pathetic or shameful tragedy—as the exemplification of her white trash upbringing—Parton envisions it as an opportunity for escape, transformation . . . the autobiography as a whole suggests that making oneself into a spectacle, even an abject one, is better than being erased/ignored/silenced altogether. (Fox 260)

Instead of seeing her cousin's livelihood as yet another indignity foisted upon women living in poverty, Parton sees it as freedom: an opportunity to escape—for a moment, or maybe forever; to become something different, better, *more*. This anecdote speaks volumes about Parton: her tendency to gloss over the rough parts even though she sees the full picture (see: the Dollywood theme park, occasionally criticized for depicting a highly sanitized version of Appalachian poverty); her keen understanding of what you must sacrifice—and what you stand to gain—once you choose to walk a different path. Along with her talent, Parton's wigs, sequins, and figure-hugging wardrobe were her ticket out of the mountains, just like Myrtle's fake scales.

Parton's appearance and her relationship to it calls to mind another feature of tackiness: that what we characterize as such "looks both genuine and skillfully fake" (Sheldon 62). Tacky is impersonally personal; it is just enough, but *not* enough. It satisfies in the moment but still leaves you wanting—and this impersonally personal sensibility is, I think, one of the reasons *everyone* loves Dolly Parton. Her ability to achieve this seemingly impossible feat stems from the way she speaks candidly and without shame about who she is and where she comes from without disclosing information that could potentially leave her vulnerable or prove divisive (for example, the political candidates she supports, the rationale behind personal decisions she has made). We love her and find her compelling because in spite of how much we feel like we know about her, she is still an enigma: as critic Lindsay Zoladz points out, "hers has been one of the most scrutinized female bodies in the history of modern celebrity, and yet no one can tell you for certain what her forearms look like" (Zoladz).[3] Over the years, cosmetic surgery has both preserved and exaggerated all of Parton's most distinctive physical characteristics—her buxom figure, high cheekbones, wide smile. They are now easy to see for what they have always been: a mask and a suit of armor; there to protect, to help her simultaneously blend in and stand out. She is authentically herself, and wholly a construct: like each of us, a composite of where she came from, what she *had* to be, and who she *wants* to be. In Parton, teased hair, acrylic nails, and rhinestones became an expression of agency and an embedded lesson that talent and power come in packages that look like this, too. When she quips, "it costs a lot of money to look this cheap," she's reminding you in her signature pithy, unthreatening way that you can think whatever you like about the way she looks, but her artistic talent and shrewd business sense have netted her money, success, and fame beyond most artists' wildest dreams: over 100 million albums sold, more than three thousand songs published, seven Grammys, a branded theme park, a beloved literacy charity, and more.

However marginalized, "female performers . . . have existed since the inception of country music as a genre and as an industry" (Poey 4)—and not just as pretty faces singing songs written by men, but women like Parton who wrote their own songs, told their own stories. Before it happened elsewhere, it was de rigueur in country, and this historical precedent for female storytellers is now helping to move the genre forward. Today, there are so many young women imbuing country music with new life—and for two of the most successful, looking the part of Country Star helped them get the platform they are now using to redefine what country music and musicians can do and be.

Kacey Musgraves has been successful at convincing country music to meet her on her terms, launching and pursuing an extraordinary—and extraordinarily *successful*—career without ever hiding or apologizing for her progressive politics, her bluntness, or her love of *actual* blunts (as well as taking psilocybin mushrooms and microdosing LSD). Yet Musgraves' introduction to the world came in a familiar package guaranteed to earn a thumbs-up from any CMT focus group: long, wavy blowout; a wardrobe that shifted from One-of-the-Guys casual (tight jeans and a Gentleman Jack T-shirt) to Millennial Patsy Cline (fringed vests, short shorts, gingham shirts, cowboy boots), depending on the mood and venue. Looking the part of a "country star" helped Musgraves get a platform and blend in just enough to avoid being blacklisted for her beliefs—and while the industry has not endorsed (and will likely *never* endorse) her politics, its titans recognize and acknowledge her talent: in 2019 *Golden Hour* picked up Grammys for Country Album of the Year *and* Album of the Year. Musgraves' irreverence, empathy, and compassion have also made country fans of people who never dreamed they'd love a country musician, at once broadening the genre's fandom and showing the world that Texans with pageant hair can be socially progressive, too.

"Biscuits," the lead single from 2015's *Pageant Material*, demonstrates Musgraves' ability to reach across the aisle: she uses charming wordplay that leans heavily on southern tropes to coax biscuits-and-gravy-loving Bible Belters into tacitly agreeing that a person's sexuality is none of their business and has no effect on their lives, so it shouldn't be used to judge a person's character ("mind your own biscuits and life will be gravy"). "Follow Your Arrow" is more direct and explicit ("Kiss lots of boys, / or kiss lots of girls / if that's something you're into") but still makes its point in a way that brings people along rather than alienating those who do not already agree: she compares the way we condemn people for their sexuality to the way we condemn people for being "too" fat or "too" thin, remaining a virgin *until* or having sex *before* marriage, etc.—the types of shaming and discrimination that exist across race, class, gender, and political affiliation. The song lifts up the listener rather than chastising their behavior, leaving little choice but to extend empathy. It's a tidy distillation of Musgraves' ethos—all of us are special and no one is special; do your own thing, and let everyone else do their own thing, too—that resonated deeply and broadly: "'I didn't have any expectations for ['Follow Your Arrow']," she said, "but it brought so many people to the party that wouldn't have been there before. It opened some minds; it made some people walk a little bit taller that felt like they didn't really have a place in country music . . . If you look at what it did on the radio, it might not make sense matched up to what it did in different areas . . . Maybe there's different metrics of success here, and that's fine'" (Snapes). Like Parton, Musgraves nimbly walks the allyship tightrope—that is, making your stance known without making it about you—and it's one of the reasons that both have adoring queer fanbases (plus, country music and drag culture share a tacky aesthetic rooted in performative femininity—big hair, thick makeup, outré clothes, gaudy accessories—all of which Parton and Musgraves have embraced).[4] But it's also because they are gifted at writing about their own experiences in ways that empathize and overlap with aspects of the queer experience, and, indeed, the experiences of any marginalized community[5]: what it feels like to be underestimated or never taken seriously, what to do when you realize that the people you come from would change you or disown you before accepting you as you are, what it means to have to leave the place you love in order to find happiness and live honestly. Musgraves writes this story time and again—not just from the perspective of the most oppressed but from the perspective of white people in small-town, red-state America who've been convinced to uphold the toxic systems that bring them down, too. In songs like "Merry Go 'Round" she offers a nuanced, empathetic read on tacky, "redneck" behavior and the ways it is rooted in restlessness and defeat: feeling left behind and misunderstood with no way forward and no way out ("Mama's hooked on Mary Kay / Brother's hooked on Mary Jane / And daddy's hooked on Mary two doors down . . . Just like dust we settle in this town").

Reflecting on her career, Musgraves once said, "my goal for myself has always just been achieving total musical freedom, and I feel like I'm on my way to doing that" (Maicki). Paradoxically, not trying to please anyone but yourself can help you reach others: honesty invites conversation and makes space for empathy. Parton achieved crossover success and built a diverse fan base by opening up, but never completely, careful to never offend; Musgraves has achieved the same (to a lesser degree) by doing the opposite. If she feels like it, she stays seated while others stand at awards ceremonies. She spoke out against former President Donald J. Trump and speaks out on behalf of strict gun control. She deftly neutralizes Twitter trolls and is unafraid of alienating industry gatekeepers: after *Golden Hour* claimed its two Grammys, Musgraves replied "Sometimes the best songs win: Grammys" to a Tweet about a Country Radio Seminar panelist saying "sometimes the best songs win" in response to a question about why Musgraves doesn't get much airplay in spite of her popularity. Fans of Musgraves and Parton love them as people and as artists because neither lets anyone else dictate or set her boundaries—or, at least, it's easy to perceive it that way.

But initially, both had to relinquish some agency and check certain iconoclastic tendencies. It's no coincidence that Parton and Musgraves both started out making music that wouldn't sound out of place in a playlist of songs recorded decades prior, or that even though their political leanings diverge from many other country artists and fans, they speak respectfully of the places they grew up and the people they grew up with. And unsurprisingly, once secure in their success, they both began to take artistic and sartorial risks. On *Golden Hour* especially, Musgraves' music started to genre-hop, and so did her particular brand of tacky: from the cowboy boots and hot pants of 2013's *Same Trailer Different Park* to the current aesthetic she describes as "cosmic country"—a rainbow of colors, sequins and rhinestones, open-backed jumpsuits, purple fur coats, fringed jackets, and colorful nail art. This is undoubtedly linked to personal evolution; our tastes, preferences, and beliefs change with time as we encounter new ideas and learn more about ourselves. But it also speaks to the very real need to play by the rules until you're powerful enough to break them without putting your career at risk. Musgraves wanted to be a successful country artist: if she was to accomplish that goal singing songs like "Follow Your Arrow," she had to look the part until she became successful and popular enough to diverge without threatening her career. And while she may have had to appear a certain way to get in the door, once she was in the room, talent became her job security.

Miranda Lambert's career trajectory has taken a similar path: like Musgraves, she got her start on "Nashville Star," finishing third in its 2003 season, and, also like Musgraves, she *looks* like a country star (arguably to an even greater degree)—a tiny, conventionally pretty blonde favoring flowy sundresses appropriate for a pastoral album shoot at golden hour, and the flashy (and yes, tacky) fringed jackets and rhinestone-covered shirts befitting a musician who can sell out a stadium. Lambert—whose accomplishments include two No. 1 albums, a Grammy nomination, two consecutive nods for the Country Music Association's Horizon Award, stints opening for Keith Urban and Toby Keith, *and* a supergroup called The Pistol Annies (alongside Angaleena Presley and Ashley Monroe)—has never calibrated what or how she writes to her listeners' comfort levels, perhaps because she is rightfully confident in her unimpeachable talent and how much she looks the part of a country star (and perhaps because radical ideas are rarely interpreted as real threats when they come from the mouth of someone we find unthreatening). To wit, Lambert's 2005 debut, *Kerosene*—named for a song where the protagonist sets her ex's house on fire, featuring the line "You can't hate someone who's dead"—went platinum.

Throughout her career, Lambert has used her power and her platform to amplify the voices of other women: her contemporaries in the industry, as well as the women in her songs. She comes honestly by her desire to elevate the ignored and give voice to the unheard, as well as her ability to accomplish both with empathy and grace—the daughter of two private investigators who often literally brought their work home: "The Lambert family ended up taking in some of the abused women and children whose situations they had investigated. [Says Lambert,] 'I had Mom making cookies after school, and I also had moms whose partners were beating the crap out of them. [Lambert's 2008 top 10 hit] 'Gunpowder & Lead' was in my household for a long time'" (Macpherson). The songs Lambert has written with Presley and Monroe for The Pistol Annies draw on those formative experiences. She tells the stories of women like the ones who sat around the dining room table in her childhood home, expressing a desire for justice on their behalf. Lambert coined the term "housewife-scorned music" to describe her songwriting, and—in sharp contrast to many pop country songs—she has never written about her scorned housewives' tacky, "trashy" behavior (recreational drug use, wearing skimpy clothes, screaming at your husband, locking down a sugar daddy, and so forth) in ways that disparage her protagonists. In her solo career and with The Pistol Annies, Lambert offers honest, complete portrayals of these women: songs like "Cheyenne" link this "tacky" behavior to its roots in poverty and abuse, explaining how it shapes and is used to shame women while encouraging listeners to empathize with people they have been conditioned to either condemn or ignore: "She lives for the nightlife and trashy tattoos / She loves country music and broken-in boots . . . Her daddy says she was destined for sadness / And her grandmama Lily's to blame for the madness / The only forever she knew ended tragic." Lambert immerses listeners in her protagonists' worlds (like the first-person "Leavers Lullaby") and skillfully deflates any sense of superiority the listener might have felt to the subjects of her songs: the chorus of "When I Was His Wife" goes, "He'd never cheat, he'd never lie / He'll love me forever 'til the day that we die / He'll never take me for granted I / Said that too when I was his wife." Her songs are honest about the shortcomings of the women they describe but emphasize that these behaviors are coping mechanisms necessary to survive in a world that does not recognize their worth. This quality in Lambert's songwriting has always felt special and refreshing: a deeper character development rarely present in country music, where people are frequently archetypes (women who are angels, whores, or mamas who love you no matter what you've done) and world-building happens through deploying well-worn tropes: loyal dogs, cold beer, good times. It's an approach to storytelling that is conservative in the broadest sense of the word: where the goal is to remember, reinvoke, and reinforce rather than to introduce new ideas. Uncomplicated people in a familiar world, fake as rhinestones.

In an excellent 2012 *Nashville Scene* piece, critic Jewly Hight writes of Lambert, "we're hearing women working with traditional country sounds while they sing about staking claim to personal freedom and demanding equal footing in relationships, and men more frequently drawing in rock sounds while they define redneck identity and traditional masculinity in their lyrics." It's a concise characterization of the 2010s pop country dynamic: women eagerly using country music to tell new stories but presenting as familiar and nonthreatening to ensure those stories are heard (at least until they become as popular as Musgraves or Lambert); men given latitude to expand or change country music, only to repackage the same stories the genre has told for decades. Familiar frustrating gender double-standards aside, it's exciting to see artists successfully coax country music to evolve, and it has been at once encouraging and discouraging to see that artists don't necessarily have to "look" the part to get traction as long as they pay some homage to tradition (see: "Old Town Road") in the form of a fiddle or a pair of boots. Expanded representation doesn't equate to full-throated acceptance, but it is a start. May teased hair and sparkly cowboy hats become catalysts that make us kinder, more humane, willing and able to see the value and beauty in anything and everything—even a Live | Laugh | Love sign.

NOTES

1. Formerly The Dixie Chicks.

2. As the "alligator girl," Myrtle wore a swimsuit and glued cornflakes dyed green to her skin for "scales."

3. It is often speculated—but never conclusively proven—that this is because they are covered in tattoos.

4. To wit: the first time Musgraves met Elton John, he gave her a pair of oversized, sparkly Gucci sunglasses.

5. In episode six of the podcast *Dolly Parton's America*, acclaimed bluegrass musician Justin Hiltner describes listening to "Wildflowers" on a loop as he left town for good after coming out to his family (Abumrad and Oliae).

WORKS CITED

Abumrad, Jad, and Shima Oliae. *Dolly Parton's America*. WNYC Studios, Oct.–Dec. 2019, www.wnycstudios.org/podcasts/dolly-partons-america.

Congdon, Kristin G., and Doug Blandy. "What? Clotheslines and Popbeads Aren't Trashy Anymore?: Teaching about Kitsch." *Studies in Art Education*, vol. 46, no. 3, 2005, pp. 197–210, doi:10.1080/00393541.2005.11650074.

Fox, Pamela. "Recycled 'Trash': Gender and Authenticity in Country Music Autobiography." *American Quarterly*, vol. 50, no. 2, 1998, pp. 234–66, doi:10.1353/aq.1998.0016.

Hight, Jewly. "Unpacking the Audible Divide between Country's Solo Women and Men." *Nashville Scene*, 3 May 2012, www.nashvillescene.com/music/article/13043023/unpacking-the-audible-divide-between-countrys-solo-women-and-men.

Macpherson, Alex. "Miranda Lambert: 'I'm Not Just That Girl with Fire in My Head.'" *The Guardian*, 28 Mar. 2016, www.theguardian.com/music/2016/mar/28/miranda-lambert-country-renegade-interview.

Maicki, Salvatore. "Kacey Musgraves' Golden Hour Is Here." *The FADER*, 30 Mar. 2018, www.thefader.com/2018/03/30/kacey-musgraves-golden-hour-is-here.

Meares, Hadley. "Giddying-up in Glitz: The Blinged-Out Western Wear of Nathan Turk and Nudie Cohn." *PBS SoCal*, 19 Sept. 2019, www.pbssocal.org/country-music/giddying-glitz-blinged-western-wear-nathan-turk-nudie-cohn/.

Poey, Delia. "Striking Back without Missing a Beat: Radical Responses to Domestic Violence in Country Music's The Dixie Chicks and Salsa's Celia Cruz." *Studies in Popular Culture*, vol. 32, no. 2, 2010, pp. 1–15.

Sheldon, Glenn. "Crimes and Punishments: Class and Connotations of Kitschy American Food and Drink." *Studies in Popular Culture*, vol. 27, no. 1, 2004, pp. 61–72.

Snapes, Laura. *Kacey Musgraves: 'I'd Sound Country Even If I Didn't Want to.'* The *Guardian*, 6 Aug. 2015, www.theguardian.com/music/2015/aug/06/kacey-musgraves-sound-country-even-if-didnt-want-to.

Zoladz, Lindsay. *Is There Anything We Can All Agree On? Yes: Dolly Parton. New York Times*, 21 Nov. 2019, www.nytimes.com/2019/11/21/arts/music/dolly-parton.html.

Contributors

ELISABETH AIKEN is associate professor of English at Saint Leo University in Saint Leo, Florida, where she currently serves as the associate chair of the Department of Interdisciplinary Studies and Experiential Learning. In her research she is interested in southern and Appalachian literature through ecocritical, postcolonial, and cultural studies lenses; she is also committed to furthering both the academic and social connections between interdisciplinary humanities and community activism.

JILL E. ANDERSON is associate professor of English at Tennessee State University, where she teaches women's studies, American literature, and media literacy. She is not a southernist but an enthusiast of all things *Murder, She Wrote* and *The Golden Girls*. Her book, *Homemaking for the Apocalypse: Domestic Horror in the Atomic Age*, was published in 2021.

MARSHALL NEEDLEMAN ARMINTOR is principal lecturer in English at the University of North Texas. He has published articles on neo-Victorian literature and *MAD Magazine*. His book, *Lacan and the Ghosts of Modernity: Masculinity, Tradition, and the Anxiety of Influence* was published in 2004. He maintains a blog on theory, neo-Marxism, and art in the age of late capital at posthegel.com.

MICHAEL P. BIBLER is Robert Penn Warren Associate Professor of English at Louisiana State University. He is author of *Cotton's Queer Relations: Same-Sex Intimacy and the Literature of the Southern Plantation, 1936–1986* (2009), and he has contributed essays to the *Oxford Handbook of the Literature of the U.S. South; Keywords for Southern Studies;* and the *Cambridge Companion to American Gay and Lesbian Literature.* His current book project, "Literally, Queerly: The Silly Pleasures of Silly Pleasures," includes a chapter on the B-52s.

KATHARINE A. BURNETT is associate professor of English and the coordinator of the English and Gender Studies programs at Fisk University in Nashville, Tennessee. She is the author of *Cavaliers and Economists: Global Capitalism and the Development of Southern Literature, 1820–1860* (2019), and her work has appeared in the *Cambridge History of the Literature of the U.S. South*, the essay collection *Southern Comforts*, *PMLA*, *College Literature*, and the *Southern Literary Journal* (later *south*).

JOE T. CARSON is an independent scholar and farmer in Central Virginia. His current book project, "American Anthropocenes: Race and Deforestation in the Novel," develops a literary history of climate change and details the importance of deforestation and timbering in shaping the politics of race and labor in the American South. His peer-reviewed work has appeared in *South: A Scholarly Journal* and *Green Theory & Praxis* and is forthcoming in *Studies in the Novel*.

ANNA CREADICK is professor of English and American Studies at Hobart and William Smith Colleges. Author of the book *Perfectly Average: The Pursuit of Normality in Postwar America* (2010), she has also written about Appalachia, popular fiction, Carson McCullers, disability, whiteness, Faulkner, teaching, reading, Willa Cather, and other topics in *Southern Cultures*, *Post-45 Peer Reviewed*, *Appalachian Journal*, *Mosaic*, *Transformations*, and other venues.

ISABEL DUARTE-GRAY is a PhD candidate at Harvard University and Instructor at Emerson College, specializing in Latinx literature and Ecostudies. Her first poetry collection, *Even Shorn*, debuted in 2021.

AARON DUPLANTIER is assistant teaching professor in Syracuse University's Writing Studies Department, where he researches New Media and Pop Culture. He is the author of the book *Authenticity and How We Fake It: Belief and Subjectivity in Reality TV, Facebook, and YouTube* (2016).

JOSEPH A. FARMER is associate professor at Northeastern State University in Tahlequah, Oklahoma, in the foothills of the Ozarks. He teaches courses on Faulkner, Poe, African American literature, southern women's literature, and writers of the Ozarks. He is currently preparing a book on southern women's life writing.

JARROD HAYES is professor of French Studies at Monash University. He is the author of *Queer Nations: Marginal Sexualities in the Maghreb* (2000) and *Queer Roots for the Diaspora, Ghosts in the Family Tree* (2016). He coedited *Comparatively*

Queer: Interrogating Identities across Time and Cultures (2010). His current project, "Reading across the Color Line: Racialization in the French Americas," seeks to foster dissonance between Anglo American readers' expectations and French representations of race.

JOLENE HUBBS is associate professor of American Studies at the University of Alabama, where she teaches and writes about the literature and culture of the US South. She is at work on a book exploring the formative role that representations of poor white southerners play in shaping both middle-class American identity and major American literary genres.

MONICA CAROL MILLER is assistant professor of English at Middle Georgia State University. She is the author of *Being Ugly: Southern Women Writers and Social Rebellion* (2017). She is the president of the Flannery O'Connor Society and the secretary-treasurer of the Society for the Study of Southern Literature. She is the editor of the forthcoming *Dear Regina: Flannery O'Connor's Letters from Iowa*.

TRAVIS A. ROUNTREE is assistant professor of English at Western Carolina University. His research interests include queer archival research and pedagogy, country music scholarship, Appalachian rhetorics, place-based pedagogy, and public memory studies. He has been published in *The North Carolina Folklore Journal; Journal of Southern History;* and *Appalachian Journal*.

GARTH SABO is assistant professor in the Center for Integrative Studies in the Arts and Humanities at Michigan State University, where he teaches classes in climate fiction, graffiti, regional American literature, and the medical humanities. His research focusing on scatological literature, waste studies, and material ecocriticism has appeared in *Arizona Quarterly, Midwestern Miscellany,* and *CR: The New Centennial Review*.

JIMMY DEAN SMITH is professor of English at Union College in Barbourville, Kentucky. His recent work has appeared in *North Carolina Literary Review; Summoning the Dead: Critical Essays on Ron Rash; Western American Literature; Flannery O'Connor Review; Small Screen Souths; Critical Insights on Flannery O'Connor; Representing Rural Women;* and *Ecocriticism and the Future of Southern Studies*.

CATHERINE EGLEY WAGGONER is professor of communication at Wittenberg University in Springfield, Ohio. She is the coauthor of *Making Camp: Rhetorics of Transgression in U.S. Popular Culture* (2008), which won two book awards within the National Communication Association. Her coauthored book, *Realizing Our Place: Real Southern Women in a Mythologized Land* (2018), was nominated for a Mississippi Institute of Arts and Letters Award.

CHARLES REAGAN WILSON was the Kelly Gene Cook Sr. Chair of History and professor of southern studies at the University of Mississippi (1981–2014), director of the southern studies program (1991–1998), and director of the Center for the Study of Southern Culture (1998–2007). He is the author of *Baptized in Blood* (1980); *Judgment and Grace in Dixie* (1995); and *Flashes of Southern Spirit* (2011). He also edited the *Encyclopedia of Southern Culture* (1989) and the *New Encyclopedia of Southern Culture* (2006–2013).

SUSANNAH YOUNG is a self-employed communications strategist, writer, and creative director living in Chicago. Over the course of her career, she has worked with political candidates, in movement politics, for hundreds of nonprofits across the United States, and with a number of Fortune 500 companies. Since 2009, she has also worked as a music critic, with her criticism appearing in *Vinyl Me, Please: 100 Albums You Need in Your Collection* (2017), on *Vinyl Me, Please*'s editorial site, and *Pitchfork*, *KCRW*, among other publications and outlets.

Index

153–55; whiteness, 11, 41, 73–74, 82, 106–110, 116, 138, 150, 152, 171–72, 199; whitewashing, 78, 83, 109, 113. *See also* Creole; critical whiteness studies; hierarchy: race; plaçage; poor white; quadroon; slavery; taste: race; white trash

racial identity. *See* identity

racial politics, 84

racism, xii, xv, 8, 11, 23, 108, 110, 115–17, 140, 156, 266; white supremacy, 200

Rafferty, Milton, 180, 186

Randolph, Vance, 176; *Pissing in the Snow*, 176

Rash, Ron, 57, 61; *Saints at the River*, 57

Rawson, K. J., 208

reality television, 14, 119–132; *Big Brother*, 125; exploitation, 120, 122–23, 126, 132; *The Hills*, 121; *Jackass*, 125; *Laguna Beach*, 121; *The Osbournes*, 123; *The Real World*, 124–25; *Slednecks*, 126; "trash TV," 120. *See also Buckwild; Duck Dynasty; Here Comes Honey Boo Boo; Swamp People*

Reconstruction, 56, 195

Red Hat Society, 9, 136, 139, 143n4

red velvet cake, 12, 15, 189–97, 200–201; mythology, 190–91, 200

redneck, x, 121–27, 129, 131, 170, 186, 265, 273, 276; stereotype, 127

redneck fulfillment, ix

regionalism, 16, 87, 112

Reid, Jan, 206

reification, 41, 47, 68, 71, 254, 257–59

religion: African American, xiii, Bible Belt, 81, 130, 272; Christian, ix, 93, 127–30, 207, 238, 243; Genesis, Book of, 258–60; missionaries, 92; Yoruba, 82

reparative, 251, 255, 261–62

representation, 16

rhetoric: aesthetic, 78, 86, 89, 134–35; Appalachian, 92–93

Robinson, Lori, 55–56

Rogers, Roy, 251, 253, 256

Rolling Stone, 250

romanticism, 53, 80, 82, 85, 108, 112, 181, 251

Rombauer, Irma, 196

Romine, Scott, xvii, 12; *The Real South*, 12

Rountree, Travis, 7

RuPaul's Drag Race, 240–42

rural, xi, 8–9, 13, 32, 119–32, 186, 237, 240, 246, 257, 259; African Americans, xiii; brier, 58–60; nostalgia, 82; white, 9, 119–132. *See also* identity

Sabo, Garth, 14

Saenger, Gerhart, 179

Salter, Edward, 39

scatological, 176

Scott, Cynthia, xvii

Sedgwick, Eve Kosofsky, 255, 262

Sekula, Allan, 31

semiology of fashion, 156–57

semiotics, 81, 83, 87, 261

sense of place, 81, 244

sentimentality, 86–87, 92, 99, 171, 205, 247n2, 259

sexual exploitation, predation, 91–92, 94–103, 123; assault, violence, 108, 117n1, 182, 257

sexuality, 96, 98, 106, 108, 113–14, 130, 208–209, 227n7, 243, 272; availability, 259; boundaries, 256; compulsory heterosexuality, 259–60, 262; conformity, 260–61, 272; norms, 217; transgressive, 72, 102; stereotype, 93–95, 102, 176–83, 234–35. *See also* Parton, Dolly: sexuality

Shack Up Inn, 77–89

Shapiro, Henry D., 92; *Appalachia on Our Mind*, 92, 99–100

sharecropping, 77, 80–86

shipbuilding, 37–39, 41–43, 47

Silence of the Lambs, The, 149

Simms, William Gilmore, x, 198; *Partisan, The*, x

Simpson, Jessica, 87

sincerity, 9–10, 85, 165–67, 169, 171–72, 219, 253–54; putative, 91. *See also* authenticity; Parton, Dolly: sincerity

Skeggs, Beverly, 29

slavery, ix, xv, 11, 38–44, 47–48, 79, 88, 106, 115–16, 158–59, 170, 198–99; effective, 252; free people of color, 150; slave culture, 88; slave trade, 39, 42

Small-Screen Souths, 107

Smith, Jimmy Dean, 14

Smith, John, x

CPSIA information can be obtained
at www.ICGtesting.com
Printed in the USA
LVHW030839020822
724972LV00003B/125

9 780807 177891